"Value migrates in all industries, including ours. Tomorrow's value creators will combine great content with even greater relationships. *Relationships That Enable Enterprise Change* tells the truth about what it really takes to create effective relationships between insiders and outsiders, and how much success those relationships can create. It will make both executives and advisers rethink their approach (and change their behavior) when going about the serious business of creating real partnerships to create real value."

—Adrian Slywotzky, author of *Value Migration,*
The Profit Zone, and *Profit Patterns*

"Business leaders rely more than ever on trusted relationships with a few key professionals who can bring insight, wisdom, and inter-personal agility to important strategic and organizational issues. Ron Carucci and Bill Pasmore have produced a masterful, battle-tested roadmap that will enable consultants and other outside advisors to break into this inner circle and have a truly lasting impact on client success."

—Andrew Sobel, author of *Clients for Life*

"A great resource for anyone who consults to senior managers. Full of wonderful insights, useful tools and instructive case examples."

—Edward E. Lawler III, most recently author of *Corporate Boards: New Strategies for Adding Value at the Top;* Director, Center for Effective Organizations; Marshall School of Business; University of Southern California

"As a CEO and a consumer of consulting services, Carucci and Pasmore don't just tell it like it is—they tell it like it should be. The book is a pragmatic how-to-help-your-client guide that I'm sure will be highly valuable to those who are guiding managers to manage change."

—Charlie Strauss, CEO, Unilever HPC North America

Practicing Organization Development

**The Change Agent Series
for Groups and Organizations**

MISSION STATEMENT

The books in this series are intended to be cutting-edge, state-of-the-art, innovative approaches to organization change and development. They are written for and by practitioners interested in new approaches to facilitating effective organization change. They are geared to providing both theory and advice on practical applications.

Other Practicing Organization Development Titles

Relationships
That Enable
Enterprise
Change

Relationships That Enable Enterprise Change

Leveraging the Client-Consultant Connection

Ron A. Carucci, William A. Pasmore, and the Colleagues of Mercer Delta

Forewords by Richard Beckhard and David A. Nadler

JOSSEY-BASS/PFEIFFER
A Wiley Company
www.pfeiffer.com

Practicing Organization Development

Published by

JOSSEY-BASS/PFEIFFER
A Wiley Company
989 Market Street
San Francisco, CA 94103-1741
415.433.1740; Fax 415.433.0499
800.274.4434; Fax 800.569.0443

www.pfeiffer.com

Jossey-Bass/Pfeiffer is a registered trademark of Jossey-Bass Inc., A Wiley Company.

ISBN: 0-7879-6080-2

Library of Congress Cataloging-in-Publication Data

Carucci, Ron A.
  Relationships that enable enterprise change : leveraging the
client-consultant connection / Ron A. Carucci, William A. Pasmore, and
the colleagues of Mercer Delta.
      p. cm. —(The practicing organization development
series)
Includes bibliographical references and index.
  ISBN 0-7879-6080-2 (alk. paper)
  1. Business consultants. 2. Interpersonal relations. I.
Pasmore, William A. II. Title. III. Series.
  HD69.C6 C268 2002
  658.4'06—dc21

2001006124

We at Jossey-Bass strive to use the most environmentally sensitive paper stocks available to us. Our publications are printed on acid-free recycled stock whenever possible, and our paper always meets or exceeds minimum GPO and EPA requirements.

Acquiring Editor: Josh Blatter   Senior Production Editor: Dawn Kilgore
Director of Development: Kathleen Dolan Davies   Manufacturing Supervisor: Becky Carreño
Developmental Editor: Susan Rachmeler   Interior and Cover Design: Bruce Lundquist
Editor: Rebecca Taff   Illustrations: Richard Sheppard

Contents

List of Figures, Tables, and Exhibits

Foreword
to the Series

ON 1967, Warren Bennis, Ed Schein, and I were faculty members of the Sloan School of Management at MIT. We decided to produce a series of paperback books that collectively would describe the state of the field of organization development (OD). Organization development as a field had been named by myself and several others from our pioneer change effort at General Mills in Minneapolis, Minnesota, some ten years earlier.

Today I define OD as "a systemic and systematic change effort, using behavioral science knowledge and skill, to transform the organization to a new state."

In any case, several books and many articles had been written, but there was no consensus on whether OD was a field of practice, an area of study, or a profession. We had not even established OD as a theory or even as a practice.

We decided that there was a need for something that would describe the state of OD. Our intention was to each write a book and also to recruit three other authors. After some searching, we found a young editor who had just joined the small publishing house of Addison-Wesley. We made contact, and the series was born. Our audience was to be human resource professionals who spent their time consulting with managers in their development through various small-group activities, such as team building. More than thirty books have been published in that series, and the series has had a life of its own. We just celebrated its thirtieth anniversary.

At last year's National OD Network Conference, I said that it was time for the OD profession to change and transform itself. Is that not what we change agents tell our clients to do? This new Jossey-Bass/Pfeiffer series will do just that. It can be seen as:

- A documentation of the re-invention of OD;

- An effort that will take us to the next level; and

- A practical effort to transfer to the world the theory and practice of leading-edge practitioners and theorists.

The books in this new series will thus prove to be valuable resources for change agents to keep current with the new and leading-edge ideas and practices.

May this very exciting change agent series be most creative and innovative. May it give our field a renewed burst of energy and awareness.

Richard Beckhard
Written on Labor Day weekend 1999 from my summer cabin near Bethel, Maine

Introduction
to the Series

THERE ARE WATERSHED MOMENTS—moments in history that change everything after them. The attack on Pearl Harbor was one of those. The bombing of Hiroshima was another. The terrorist attack on the World Trade Center in New York City was our most recent. All resulted in significant change that transformed many lives and organizations.

Practicing Organization Development: The Change Agent Series for Groups and Organizations is a series of books that was launched to help those who must cope with or create change. The series is designed for the authors to share what is working or not working, to provoke critical thinking about change, and to offer creative ways to deal with change, rather than the destructive ones noted above.

The Current State of Change Management and Organization Development

Almost as soon as the ink was dry on the first wave of books published in this series, we heard that its focus was too narrow. We heard that the need for theory and practice extended beyond OD into change management. More than one respected authority urged us to reconsider our focus, moving beyond OD to include books on change management generally.

Organization development is not the only way that change can be engineered or coped with in organizational settings. We always knew that, of course. And we remain grounded in the view that change management, however it is carried out, should be based on such values as respect for the individual, participation and involvement in change by those affected by it, and interest in the improvement of organizational settings on many levels—including productivity improvement, but also improvement in achieving work/life balance and in a values-based approach to management and to change.

A Brief History of the Genesis of the Series

A few years ago, and as a direct result of the success of *Practicing Organization Development: A Guide for Practitioners* by Rothwell, Sullivan, and McLean, the publisher—feeling that OD was experiencing a rebirth of interest in the United States and in other nations—wanted to launch a new OD series. The goal of this new series was not to replace, or even to compete directly with, the well-established Addison-Wesley OD Series (edited by Edgar Schein). Instead, as the editors saw it, the series would provide a means by which the most promising authors in OD whose voices had not previously been heard could share their ideas. The publisher enlisted the support of Bill Rothwell, Roland Sullivan, and Kristine Quade to turn the dream of a series into a reality.

This series was long in the making and has been steadily evolving since its inception. The original vision was an ambitious one—and involved no less than reinventing OD and re-energizing interest in the research and practice surrounding it. Sponsoring books was one means to that end.

There were to be others. Indeed, after nearly a year of planning, the editors are pleased to note that the series is hosting a website (www.pfeiffer.com/go/od). Far more than just a place to advertise the series, the site serves as a real-time learning community for OD practitioners. Additionally, the series is hosting a conference, entitled "Practicing Cutting-Edge OD," which is to be held at The Pennsylvania State University in University Park in April 2002 (see www.outreach.psu.edu/C&I/CuttingEdgeOD).

What Distinguishes the Books in this Series

The books in this series are meant to be challenging, cutting-edge, and state-of-the-art in their approach to OD and change management. The goal of the series is to provide an outlet for proven authorities in OD and change management who have not put their ideas into print or for up-and-coming writers in OD and change management who have new, sometimes unorthodox, approaches that are stimulating and exciting. Some books in this series describe inspirational concepts that can lead to actionable change and purvey ideas so new that they are not fully developed.

Unique to this series is the cutting-edge emphasis, the immediate applicability, and the ease of transferability of the concepts. The aim of this series is nothing less than to reinvent, re-energize, and reinvigorate OD and change management. In each book, we have also recommended that the author(s) provide:

- A research base of some kind, meaning new information derived from practice and/or systematic investigation and

- Practical tools, worksheets, case studies, and other ready-to-go approaches that help the authors drag "theory" to "practice" to make these new, cutting-edge approaches more concrete.

Subject Matter That Will (and Will Not) Be Covered

The books in this series are varied in their approach, but they are united by their focus. All share an emphasis on organization development (OD) and change management (CM). Hence, books in this series are about participative change efforts. They are not about such other popular topics as leadership, management development, consulting, or group dynamics—unless those topics are treated in new, cutting-edge ways and are geared to OD and change management practitioners.

This Book

Successful consultation in enterprise change hinges on the ability to develop client intimacy. Access to a leader's thoughts, feelings, and needs is the differentiating factor between consultants who are true catalysts for change and the far greater number who routinely fail in their engagements because of poorly managed relationships.

Featuring personal interviews with some of today's most prominent CEOs and senior leaders, and drawing on the experiences of a dozen veteran consultants, the authors explore these interactions through the lens of "relationship intelligence"—six elements defining the type of consultant/client relationship essential to bring about sustainable change. *Relationships That Enable Enterprise Change* uses client examples to illustrate how consultants can build leaders' trust, enable them to confront tough issues, build their endurance for long-term change, and accelerate their ability to adopt new ways of thinking. In a world that now recognizes that leaders need to seek help in confronting globalization, new technologies, and new business models, only those consultants with well-developed relationship intelligence will be indispensable agents of change.

William J. Rothwell
University Park, PA

Roland Sullivan
Deephaven, MN

Kristine Quade
Minnetonka, MN

Statement
of the Board

IT IS OUR PLEASURE TO PARTICIPATE in and influence the start up of *Practicing Organization Development: The Change Agent Series for Groups and Organizations.* The purpose of the series is to stimulate the profession and influence how organization change is defined and practiced. This statement is intended to set the context for the series by addressing three important questions: (1) What are the key issues facing organization change and development in the 21st Century? (2) Where does—and should—OD fit in the field of organization change and development? and (3) What is the purpose of this series?

What Are the Key Issues Facing Organization Change and Development in the 21st Century?

One of the questions is the extent to which leaders can control forces or can only be reactive. Will globalization and external forces be so powerful that they will prevent organizations from being able to "stay ahead of the change curve"? And what will be the role of technology, especially information technology, in the change process? To what extent can it be a carrier of change (as well as a source of change)?

What will the relationship be between imposed change and collaborative change? Will the increased education of the workforce demand the latter, or will the requirement of having to make fundamental changes demand leadership that sets goals that participants would not willingly set on their own? And what is the relationship between these two forms of change?

Who will be the change agent? Is this a separate profession, or will that increasingly be the responsibility of the organization's leaders? If the latter, how does that change the role of the change professional?

What will be the role of values for change in the 21st Century? Will the key values be performance—efficiency and effectiveness? And what role will the humanistic values of more traditional OD play? Or will the growth of knowledge (and human competence) as an organization's core competence make this a moot point in that performance can only occur if one takes account of humanistic values?

What is the relationship between other fields and the area of change? Can any change process that is not closely linked with strategy be truly effective? Can change agents focus only on process, or do they need to be knowledgeable and actively involved in the organization's products/services and understand the market niche in which the organization operates?

Where Does—or Should—OD Fit in the Field of Organization Change and Development?

We offer the following definition of OD to stimulate debate:

> Organization development is a system-wide and values-based collaborative process of applying behavioral science knowledge to the adaptive development, improvement, and reinforcement of such organizational features as the strategies, structures, processes, people, and cultures that lead to organization effectiveness.

The definition suggests that OD can be understood in terms of its several foci:

First, *OD is a system-wide process.* It works with whole systems. In the past, the bias has been toward working at the individual and group levels. More recently, the focus has shifted to organizations and multi-organization systems. We support that trend in general but honor and acknowledge the fact that the traditional focus on smaller systems is both legitimate and necessary.

Second, *OD is values-based.* Traditionally, OD has attempted to distinguish itself from other forms of planned change and applied behavioral science by promoting a set of humanistic values and by emphasizing the importance of personal growth as a key to its practice. Today, that focus is blurred and there is much debate about the value base underlying the practice of OD. We support a more formal and direct conversation about what these values are and how the field is related to them.

Third, *OD is collaborative.* Our first value commitment as OD practitioners is to bring about an inclusive, diverse workforce with a focus of integrating differences into a world-wide culture mentality.

Fourth, *OD is based on behavioral science knowledge.* Organization development should incorporate and apply knowledge from sociology, psychology, anthropology, technology, and economics toward the end of making systems more effective. We support the continued emphasis in OD on behavioral science knowledge and believe that OD practitioners should be widely read and comfortable with several of the disciplines.

Fifth, *OD is concerned with the adaptive development, improvement, and reinforcement of strategies, structures, processes, people, culture, and other features of organizational life.* This statement describes not only the organizational elements that are the target of change, but also describes the process by which effectiveness is increased. That is, OD works in a variety of areas, and it is focused on improving these areas. We believe that such a statement of process and content strongly implies that a key feature of OD is the transference of knowledge and skill to the system so that it is more able to handle and manage change in the future.

Sixth and finally, *OD is about improving organization effectiveness.* It is not just about making people happy; it is also concerned with meeting financial goals, improving productivity, and addressing stakeholder satisfaction. We believe that OD's future is closely tied to the incorporation of this value in its purpose and the demonstration of this objective in its practice.

This definition raises a host of questions:

- Are OD and organization change and development one and the same, or are these different?

- Has OD become just a collection of tools, methods, and techniques? Has it lost its values?

- Does it talk "systems," but ignore them in practice?

- Are consultants facilitators of change or activists of change?

- To what extent should consulting be driven by consultant value versus holding the value only of increasing the client's effectiveness?

- How can OD practitioners help formulate strategy, shape the strategy development process, contribute to the content of strategy, and drive how strategy will be implemented?

- How can OD focus on the drivers of change external to individuals, such as the external environment, business strategy, organization change, and culture change, as well as on the drivers of change internal to individuals, such as individual interpretations of culture, behavior, style, and mindset?

- How much should OD be part of the competencies of all leaders? How much should it be the sole domain of professionally trained, career-oriented OD practitioners?

What Is the Purpose of this Series?

This series is intended to provide current thinking about organization change and development as a field and to provide practical approaches based on sound theory and research. It is targeted for full-time external or internal change practitioners; top executives in charge of enterprise-wide change; and managers, HR practitioners, training and development professionals, and others who have responsibility for change in organizational and trans-organizational settings. At the same time, these books will be directed toward cutting-edge thinking and state-of-the-art approaches. In some cases, the ideas, approaches, or techniques described are still evolving, so the books are intended to open up dialogue.

We know that the books in this series will provide a leading forum for thought-provoking dialogue within the field.

About the Board Members

David Bradford is senior lecturer in organizational behavior at the Graduate School of Business, Stanford University, Palo Alto, California. He is co-author (with Allan R. Cohen) of *Managing for Excellence, Influence Without Authority,* and *POWER UP: Transforming Organizations Through Shared Leadership.*

W. Warner Burke is professor of psychology and education in the department of organization and leadership at Teachers College at Columbia University in New York. He also serves as a senior advisor to PricewaterhouseCoopers. His most recent publication is *Business Profiles of Climate Shifts: Profiles of Change Makers,* with William Trahant and Richard Koonce.

Edith Whitfield Seashore is an organization consultant and co-founder (with Morley Segal) of AUNTL Masters Program in Organization Development. She is co-author of *What Did You Say?* and *The Art of Giving and Receiving Feedback* and co-editor of *The Promise of Diversity.*

Robert Tannenbaum is emeritus professor of development of human systems, Graduate School of Management, University of California, Los Angeles, and recipient of the Lifetime Achievement Award by the National OD Network. He has published numerous books, including *Human Systems Development* (with Newton Margulies and Fred Massarik).

Christopher G. Worley is director, MSOD Program, Pepperdine University, Malibu, California. He is co-author of *Organization Development and Change* (7th ed.), with Tom Cummings, and of *Integrated Strategic Change,* with David Hitchin and Walter Ross.

Shaolin Zhang is senior manager of organization development for Motorola (China) Electronics Ltd. He received his master's degree in American Studies from Beijing Foreign Studies University, Beijing, China, and holds a Ph.D. in sociology from York University, Toronto, Ontario.

Foreword

ALMOST A QUARTER CENTURY AGO, in the late 1970s, I had the opportunity to begin thinking about a different approach to consulting. The world, it seemed, was bifurcated between two types of consultants.

The first type focused exclusively on *content*—on the delivery of value through study and recommendation. They were smart people who worked hard and occasionally brought some new tools to their engagements. They collected data, analyzed the problem, and developed a recommended solution. This approach characterized virtually the whole management consulting world at the time.

The second type of consultant focused on *process*—on the interpersonal and behavioral dynamics of organizations. Their approach was much less prescriptive, and their work involved a lot of interaction in teams and one-on-one settings. This approach was generally labeled "organization development." In the extreme, the chief practitioners of this approach argued against the consultant ever giving advice or recommending to clients what they should do. Instead, they argued that clients should be helped, in a type of clinical model, to understand their problems and develop their own solutions.

So at that point the world was divided between the content consultants, who approached the client with the stance of "I have studied your problem and I will tell you what you need to do," and the process consultants, who walked in and asked, "What do you want to do?"

As I began to work with clients, first from an academic base and then as we created Delta Consulting Group (now Mercer Delta Organizational Consulting), I felt that there had to be a better way. It seemed to me that clients could be helped in new and unique ways if one could bring about a synthesis of content and process. Perhaps this reflected my own training, which at the time was seen as nontraditional, and by some, strange. My interest in the field of organizations and organization change began with the process side. I thought of myself in the organization development camp, and my earliest training was at National Training Labs with a strong interpersonal relations group and group process orientation. On the other hand, I had a Harvard MBA, which gave me a set of skills and an appreciation for the "hard" side of the enterprise. I then spent three years earning a Ph.D. in organizational psychology, which reinforced the fact that there is indeed a body of content knowledge and that there is value to rigorous and scientific methodology.

I thought that there could be a better way. I believed that we could combine content—especially content about organizational effectiveness, leadership, and change—with process. I believed that we could combine the concepts of engagement, collaboration, and client ownership of the problem with scientific method and knowledge about possible solutions to organizational problems.

Over the next twenty years, my colleagues at the firm and I had the opportunity to test and further develop this point of view. We tried this new approach at the level of the total enterprise, working with some exceptional leaders who were open to our concepts. These clients (and in many ways collaborators) included David Kearns and Paul Allaire at Xerox, Jamie Houghton at Corning, and Henry Schacht at Lucent. We learned from them. We learned how to help them and how to help different types of leaders deal with different types of problems through the creation of different kinds of consulting relationships. In addition to my own consulting work, my colleagues at Mercer Delta also became partners in the development of this approach. We ultimately worked with more than 150 companies in the United States, Europe, and Asia.

At the core of all of this work, however, were relationships that were built one at a time, usually between one client and one consultant working together and creating something that was unique and special. In each case, for the relationship to work, we found that it had to embody elements of both content and process. This came into stark focus for me one day in 1983. I had been working with David Kearns, who at that time was the chairman and CEO of Xerox. We had begun work the previous year, focusing on how to design and implement total quality management in a way that would have a positive impact on the business through changes in the behavior of 100,000 Xerox employees. Having successfully worked together to design and launch the quality effort, Kearns then asked me to work with him on other issues, including management succession and organizational structure.

One day, as I walked into his office for our regular monthly meeting, he said, "David, I'm glad to see you." He then went on to say, "And that's more than a polite greeting. I find that when I look at my calendar for the day and I see that you and I have time together, I feel good because I look forward to our sessions. I enjoy the time we spend together." Then he added, "And that's important, because you could be the smartest guy in the world with a lot to offer us, but if I didn't enjoy spending the time with you, we probably wouldn't be working together." In retrospect, the "enjoyment" was not because we had interests in common or had become friends—it was a reflection of the nature of the relationship we had built. Without that relationship, and without our special process of working together, all the content in the world would have been of little value.

Client by client, we began to better understand the consulting relationship. Along the way, we worked on developing what we call "the theory of the case," or the basic logic for how we work with clients, why we do it that way, and how we apply this approach, especially with senior executives. However, to be truthful, much of the theory of the case remained unwritten. It was tacit knowledge, which we passed on through training and mentoring to group after group of new consultants who came to Mercer Delta.

There's an old quip about the economist who looks at a successful new approach and comments, "It works in practice, but will it work in theory?" In a sense, that was our challenge. Could we clearly articulate what we had learned and what we had been doing in a way that makes sense and can be generalized? That's the task that Ron Carucci and Bill Pasmore undertook as they began to write this book.

Ron and Bill made the investment to help us make the implicit become explicit. They built on their own very rich experiences and years of consulting, but they also drew heavily on the experiences of our colleagues at Mercer Delta. You will read about these experiences throughout the book. They've done the necessary reflection and have constructed a very useful way of thinking about the consulting relationship.

They have focused more on the process or relationship side of consulting, because that's where we think we have something unique to add. Having synthesized process and content, they now have new ways of thinking about process, particularly the process of the relationship between the consultant and the client. Those who are interested in the content side of consulting can find extensive material about organizational architecture, change, leadership teams, organizational climate, and so on, in the other books that we have published during the past ten years.

So why write a book about this? Why not just capture these insights for ourselves and our immediate colleagues?

The answer to this question lies in an understanding of how we see our mission at Mercer Delta. We have always aspired to have a major positive impact on the effectiveness of human enterprises. That impact happens, in part, through our direct work with our clients. But we also achieve impact indirectly, through our writing, our teaching, and our contributions to the state of the art.

This book is in that second tradition—the tradition of indirect impact. This book is primarily for other consultants. We want to help them understand the elements of the special relationship that can be created with clients. It also is for executives, who increasingly find themselves in need of consulting assistance, but frequently are frustrated determining how they can obtain the greatest value from their relationships with consultants.

Finally, I want to recognize and thank some individuals who helped us (and me specifically) over the years to develop the approach that will be described in this book. Ed Lawler and Paul Lawrence were critical in helping to understand the value of content in organizational consulting. Ed Schein and Harry Levinson were fundamental in providing ways of thinking about the process, although each did so from a dramatically different perspective. Finally, all of us owe a great debt to the late Dick Beckhard, who was a role model and an inspiration to us. Dick was one of the pioneers in bringing together content and process in a no-nonsense, practical, and down-to-earth fashion that provided real, significant help to clients for more than half a century.

I hope I've made clear what we're trying to do. Read and enjoy this book.

David A. Nadler
Chairman, Mercer Delta Organizational Consulting

Preface

❶F YOU HAVE PICKED UP THIS BOOK, chances are you have a vested interest in a relationship, either *as* a consultant looking to do better work with your clients or *with* a consultant looking for ways to enhance the value you receive. Regardless of your situation, this book will provide you with a new set of perspectives on how these complex relationships work and on how they can function better. Whether you provide or receive the advice of a trusted confidant, whether you provide it from inside or outside a client organization, whether you receive it from the top or the middle of that organization, there is a universality of how these relationships can operate effectively—with mutual gratification and gain.

For the purpose of writing with a consistent voice, we will assume you are the *provider* of the advice and consulting. Although we've included the voices of a number of *recipients* of that advice on the pages ahead, the predominant voice you will hear is that of the consultant. We'd like you to think of your time with this book as if you were watching a television series. In each episode, we will act as your hosts, inviting into each scene a set of guest speakers drawn from our colleagues and clients. Our guests will help us obtain a closeup look at the deep relationships formed between consultants and clients. We will study, dissect, and analyze these relationships, culling from them a set of principles and approaches that we believe make these relationships engines of change throughout the organization. We will offer our own insights and experiences along the way, sometimes jointly, sometimes as either Bill or Ron. We hope that, by the end of our time together, you will have had the opportunity to reflect on and rethink one or two of your most important client relationships.

You will be able to put some of the things we'll discuss into practice very quickly. We've provided some tools and frameworks to guide you in that application. Other issues we'll come across, by their nature, will require a great investment of time on your part. So be sure to approach your reading with a perspective of openness, patience, and the view of learning as a lifelong process. Some of what you will discover about yourself and your clients may reveal issues you have wrestled with for as long as you can remember. We'd like to think that, in some cases, you may find a novel insight tucked away on one of these pages that could help you find a new direction. In other cases, some of what you read may open up entirely new ways of thinking about your practice, your clients, and how you create value in the context of the relationships you form with those you advise.

Since everyone experiences relationships, business or personal, in unique and individual ways, you ought to "customize" your trip through this book to fit your stage of life and career, your comfort level in dealing with often intangible and complex issues, and how you best learn. We've designed this book to be highly interactive so you can use it in your own way to guide your own reflection and capability building.

How This Book Is Organized

In the first chapter, Why Change and Relationships Go Hand in Hand, we set a broad and comprehensive context for the book and lay out how it is designed. We talk more about the stories you will hear and how they are told, and give some rationale behind the book's unique design. This will provide additional guidance in deciding how best to use the book for your development.

Each of the next chapters in the book explores one of six dynamic elements of client-consultant relationships. Like this section, these chapters are flagged with an rQ logo. This is intended to help you, the reader, navigate through the book more easily. Case material appears in a different font to help with transitions between content and illustrations. A summary listing of elements, practices, and assessments is at the end of each chapter.

In Chapter 2, we introduce the first of our "live cases" in which you, the reader, get to "ride along" with a consultant who describes his or her approach to building trust with a client. In this chapter, the case focuses on the element of trust, which is key to all that follows. As the consultant describes his approach to building rapport and trust, we step back and look at what trust building requires and the actions that can be taken to accelerate and deepen the development of trust in relationships with clients. It takes some effort for clients to overcome initial misgivings, leftover feelings from previous relationships, or concerns about the integrity of people in the consulting profession. The key to building trust, as the case illustrates, is to behave in a trustworthy manner—to tell the truth as you see it, whether the news is good or bad.

Chapter 3 examines the personal investment that is required on the part of both parties to build a relationship that enables significant change. It's remarkable to us, and we're sure to many of you, how much money is spent on consultation to which no one is deeply committed. The cases in Chapter 3 illustrate how personal investment is manifested by consultants who are truly committed to their craft and their clients.

Chapter 4 is one of our favorites because it tackles the topic of courage. Change-focused consulting relationships demand more courage than casual friendships. They also demand more courage than expert consulting, in which the consultant performs a dispassionate analysis, drops the findings on the client's desk, and then walks away. Change consulting involves almost daily tests of courage as the status quo is challenged and the new order is tested. The stories in Chapter 4 revolve around things such as giving clients feedback, testing commitment, and calling out non-productive behaviors in groups. As the stories in Chapter 4 demonstrate clearly, this business isn't for the faint of heart.

Chapter 5 examines the consultant's role as an advocate for the client, at both a personal and an organizational level. We think readers will find this one of our more interesting and controversial chapters, as advocacy clearly involves taking sides. In a sense, the cases in Chapter 5 argue that there is no such thing as change consulting without consultant advocacy; the only question is how far one goes and how one demonstrates his or her beliefs to others.

Chapter 6 provides an in-depth look at collaboration, an element involved to some degree in all relationships. Our point of view is that change consulting requires a deeper and more synergistic form of collaboration than we often see being practiced. We need to pay more attention to discovering how to share the load, developing ideas together, and taking mutual responsibility for outcomes.

Chapter 7 probes the importance of interpersonal agility in forming solid and productive change-oriented relationships. Consultants who only know how to behave in one way will find the success of their work with different clients limited by their own inflexibility. By developing a wider repertoire of styles, consultants can meet their clients where they are, instead of forcing the client to adapt to them.

Finally, in Chapter 8 we pull it all together and look ahead to what factors will likely influence the future of client-consultant relationships. Relationships will always be important in this work, but learning to build deep relationships faster will become even more important as time goes on.

In the Appendix, you will find a questionnaire to help you further assess your relationship-building strengths and areas for development.

Preparing to Learn

We'd like to offer you some "starter" questions you can use to determine where best to begin your learning. Take the time to answer the questions below as a way of assessing your current views and proficiency in the area of relationships. Look for patterns across your responses, and see what these patterns tell you. This up-front inventory will help you determine how you can best prioritize your time with this book. You may even want to grab a notebook and begin a journal to capture your learning and action plans as you travel through the book.

1. In attempts to build closer relationships with others (not just clients):

   - What have been your greatest challenges?

   - When have you been most successful?

   - Do you experience more difficulty or facility with:

     - Certain types of relationships (hierarchical, collaborative, social, work, etc.)?

- Certain kinds of situations (in large groups, one on one, in trying to influence someone, in being influenced, during conflict, etc.)?

- Certain kinds of emotions (anger, feeling hurt, affection, feeling manipulated, excitement, dependency, etc.)?

- Different phases of the relationship-building process (new relationships, maintaining relationships, ending relationships)?

- Different kinds of people (men/women, competitive, autocratic, tough, tender, distant, demanding, passive, intellectual, energetic, judgmental, etc.)?

- What patterns do you draw from your observations?

2. If someone were to ask your clients what the most *valuable* aspect of their relationship with you was, what would you imagine your clients saying? If someone were to ask your clients what the most *difficult* aspect of their relationship with you was, what would you imagine them saying?
   - How confident are you in your speculation?

   - If you had difficulty inferring how your clients might respond, what does that suggest to you?

3. Fast forward the tape six months into the future. Assuming you have worked on gaining greater capability, what aspects of your relationships would you hope to be significantly different?

Continue to revisit these responses as you learn more so you can plan how you want to apply what you are learning. As with any good learning process, attempt to stretch without being too ambitious. Focus on finding ways to better leverage your unique gifts while shoring up areas where you lack the desired level of capability. Solicit the insights and ideas of a trusted colleague whom you can use as an ongoing sounding board for testing new ideas and the application of new concepts. Most importantly, have fun with this. See it almost like anthropology—the beginning of a great expedition. Search for new levels of wisdom, and be prepared to discover opportunities and talents in yourself you'd never considered or imagined. If, at the end of the book, your conclusion is, "I feel I have more to learn about relationships than I'd ever thought," then the time you spent here will have been very profitable. In reality, you're *never done* learning how to make relationships richly rewarding, mutually gratifying, and optimally productive. And you'll find that, as you learn more and achieve a greater level of mastery, a vast terrain waiting to be discovered and explored will open up before you. Don't recoil from this truth. Accept it, and celebrate it. It's the only way to take on the great challenges and thrills of the fine art of client-consultant relationships.

Contributors

We'd like to introduce you to our colleagues whose stories you will be hearing and whose thoughts and ideas helped shape the framework of this book.

Marc Bassin works primarily in the areas of large-scale organization and cultural change, senior team development, executive leadership and coaching, leadership development, and strategic human resources management. He has worked in the financial, consumer goods, and healthcare industries. Marc holds a B.A. from City College of the City University of New York, an M.S.W. from New York University, and a Ph.D. in educational administration from Columbia University Teacher's College.

Michel A. Buffet specializes in applied research activities. He works in the areas of organizational diagnosis and change and action research, with an emphasis on survey methodology and feedback. His research has primarily been on the global aspects of organizational architecture and change. Michel received his DESS degree in clinical social psychology from the Universite Paris VII—Denis Diderot and his Ph.D. in organizational psychology from Columbia University.

Laura Christenson combines a multi-disciplined and multi-industry global background with her consulting work in strategic alignment, large-scale organization change, executive team development, organizational architecture, and the intersection of organizational and process design. Laura holds a B.S. in business administration/economics from Seton Hall University and an M.S. in human resources and organization development from the American University under the American University/National Training Laboratories (AU/NTL) Program.

Caryn Kaftal works primarily in the areas of change management, senior team development, executive leadership, and global management. She has been involved in the global expansion of the firm, including opening an office in Paris, France. Caryn received her undergraduate degree in international relations and European history from the University of Pennsylvania, an M.A. in liberal studies and communications from Wesleyan University, and an M.B.A. from the Harvard Business School.

Mindy Millward focuses her work with CEOs and senior levels of management on planned organizational changes in the retail, financial services, healthcare, manufacturing, and nonprofit sectors. She has helped clients plan for and navigate through large-scale change related to mergers and acquisitions, organizational redesigns, and transition of senior leaders. Mindy holds a B.S. in finance from Georgetown University and completed doctoral work (ABD) in organizational theory and behavior at the University of Southern California.

Kathy Morris provides consulting services to major corporations and other institutions in the areas of strategic level organizational design and change, culture change, senior team development, transition management, and strategic human resources management. She co-led a team expanding the capabilities of the firm into leadership alignment and development. Kathy holds a B.S. in behavior sciences from Drexel University and an M.S. in organizational behavior from Goddard College. She has authored several articles on the subject of organizational change.

David A. Nadler is chairman of Mercer Delta Organizational Consulting. He consults at the CEO level, specializing in the areas of design and leadership of large-scale organization change, executive leadership, and senior team development. He is well-known for his research and writing on organization change, feedback, group performance, management, quality improvement, and organizational design. He has written numerous articles and book chapters and has authored and/or edited fourteen books. David holds a B.A. in international affairs from The George Washington University, an M.B.A. from the Harvard Business School, and an M.A. and Ph.D. in psychology from the University of Michigan. He is a member of the Academy of Management, was elected a Fellow of the American Psychological Association, and is a member of the board of Mercer Consulting Group.

Richard Rosen focuses on helping executives develop strategy, building senior team effectiveness, designing organizational architecture, and implementing, managing, and leading large-scale organization change initiatives. He has worked internationally, providing development and change consultation to USAID and the Peace Corps. Richard holds a B.S. in biological science and an M.A. in psychology and was trained in organizational effectiveness and intervention in the doctoral program in organizational behavior at Case Western Reserve University.

Janet Spencer heads the international consulting arm of the firm and has worked with executives and their teams worldwide in many industries, including consumer goods, financial services, information technology, pharmaceutical, airline, retail, and manufacturing. Her work focuses on issues related to strategy formulation, executive team development, and the strategic implementation of large-scale organization change. She co-leads our intellectual capital development efforts. Janet has published several book chapters and articles on the subject of managing change and is co-editor of *Executive Teams* (Jossey-Bass, 1997). Janet holds a B.A. in psychology from Clark University and an M.A. and a Ph.D. in organizational psychology from Columbia University.

Peter Thies specializes in the areas of organizational architecture, organizational diagnosis, large-scale organization change, and information technology strategy. Peter holds a B.A. in psychology from SUNY Albany, an M.S. in educational psychology from the University of Pennsylvania, and an M.B.A. and Ph.D. in organizational behavior from Rensselaer Polytechnic Institute (RPI). He also was an adjunct professor of organizational behavior at RPI's School of Management.

Dennis Tirman works primarily in the areas of organizational architecture, corporate governance, senior team development, change management operating environment, and executive leadership and development. He has led or collaborated on large-scale organization change efforts in the United States, Central and South America, Europe, and Japan. Dennis holds a B.A. in clinical social work from the University of Cincinnati and holds an M.S. in human resource development from the American University and the NTL Institute for Applied Behavioral Science.

Roselinde Torres heads the organization change consulting group for the firm and consults to CEOs and senior executives of major corporations on the design and leadership of large-scale change. She works primarily in the areas of cultural change, organizational diagnosis, organizational architecture, executive leadership, and executive team development. She led a team that developed practices and methods for successful mergers, acquisitions, and other strategic combinations. Roselinde is a contributing author to *Executive Teams* (Jossey-Bass, 1997). She has an A.B. double major degree in English and Spanish from Middlebury College and an M.S. in human resource development from the American University and NTL Institute for Applied Behavioral Science.

David Wagner specializes in the areas of organizational assessment, organizational architecture and design, change leadership, and executive teams. He also created and developed the firm's organizational research group. David has been a contributing author to a number of books and articles. David holds a B.A. in psychology from Concordia College and M.A. and Ph.D. degrees in industrial and organizational psychology from New York University.

Acknowledgments

NO BOOK EVER COMES TO LIFE without the efforts of many people over countless hours. This book redefines that truth. We are grateful to the many talented people whose literal heroics made it possible for us to complete this project in an audacious amount of time. Specifically, our heartfelt gratitude goes out to:

Laura Christenson, for your vision to bring this opportunity to our firm in the first place, and for your masterful project management to keep all of the many moving parts (a) moving and (b) not crashing into each other. Your corralling of the many consultant and client stories and your "stitching" together of all the mechanics made this possible!

Michel Buffet, for your relentless search for supporting information and research, for your passion on our team to make our message clear and different, for your pushing us to always keep our focus on how this book *is* different, and for your brilliant insights that added a fine touch to our message. You have been a great asset to the team, and a lot of fun to work with—even if your inner child is younger than ours!

Michael Russell, Lynn Roberts, and Kim Braxton, for your impeccable editorial talents which helped to sharpen our message and make our language and imagery crisp and compelling. It must have been during the wee hours of many mornings that you worked your magic, but whenever you did it, it certainly was magical. Thank you for the time and sacrifice you made to help us pull this off!

Jessica Thomas and Stacey Wright, for tackling the administrative nightmare this must have been to collapse countless versions of edited manuscripts into one, keeping them updated, making sure all the "color coding" was clear, and making sure everything kept moving. Thank you very much!!!

To our colleagues who shared their stories with us, thank you for the time and investment you made to this, for believing along with us that talking about the quality of our client relationships is a good and noble thing to do, and for being vulnerable enough to allow us to peek into your sacred relationship experiences. It's an honor for us to work alongside you in the great cause of enterprise change.

And finally, to our clients. You have our deepest thanks for allowing us to partner with you in the pursuit of ever greater achievements in your organizations. For your courage, for your trust in us, for allowing us to fidget and tinker around your organizations, and for thinking the big thoughts with us—without you, there would be no reason to have written this. From all of us, thank you.

Best regards
Bill & Ron

Relationships
That Enable
Enterprise
Change

① Why Change and Relationships Go Hand in Hand

It is 7:30 A.M. The division president of a major telecommunications firm is sitting behind his desk staring out the window. In just half an hour, he will go into the company's board meeting to discuss the potential acquisition of a large European wireless supplier. The numerous conversations with his top leaders, deal makers, analysts, and external experts about the possible risks and rewards have done little more than cost him sleep. He has weighed the pros and cons of the options a dozen times. The ramifications are significant; his reputation is on the line. In fact, this could be the deal that either defines his leadership or pushes him into an early retirement. He knows that his company's track record in past acquisitions is lackluster, but the pressure from the Board and the Street for faster and more significant growth is relentless. To pass on this particular deal would allow a major competitor to snatch the opportunity away. Still, he has misgivings about the economics of the deal, especially about a successful integration of such an acquisition. There is no more time to debate. The financial experts have given him their best analysis. His senior team members have each weighed in on the effects on their departments. People are looking to him for an answer and for instructions about what to do now.

You know all of this because you are in the room. You didn't suggest the deal or help with the economic analysis, but you're as responsible as anyone for the CEO's feelings this morning. You helped him sort out the expectations of the Street, the Board, and other constituencies. You worked with him to engage his senior team in formulating a strategy for growth. You coached him on ways he could demonstrate leadership. In a very real sense, he would not be doing what he is doing this morning if you had not been his consultant. After a few minutes he looks you square in the eye, and says, "So, what do *you* think I oughta do?"

These are the "moments of truth" that define client-consultant relationships. After more than twenty years of partnering with senior leaders on the complex organizational decisions necessary to bring about dramatic change, we have come to believe that fundamental enterprise-wide change begins in the context of challenging issues like the one we have just portrayed. The consultants who develop close relationships with these leaders understand their role to be trusted advisor, confidant, and provider of counsel. It is not to give the leader *the right answer*—it is to help guide the leader in discovering the answer that is *as right as it can be* for that organization at that time.

Think about it. Consider the times in your career, and in your life, when you embarked on significant change. Think about what led to your decisions. It's likely that, somewhere along the way, you've relied on the advice, counsel, and expertise of someone trusted to both understand your situation and keep your confidence. It's also likely that you made an informed decision as a result of the advice and expertise of others, in addition to your own perspective and ideas. We're not suggesting that it's best to rely soley on others or that trusting your instincts is a bad thing. We're simply pointing out that leaders faced with profoundly challenging choices can be well-served by having a trusted source of advice and expertise with whom they can test their options. Several types of consulting resources may be present during complex change—technical experts, process re-engineering consultants, training consultants, and financial or legal advisors. They will each bring specific value to the organization. But in this book, we will specifically be looking at those consultants who, as change management experts, provide advice and counsel to leaders in the organization in the context of close, change-enabling relationships. From this vantage point, the questions become: What constitutes such a close relationship? How do you know how your clients experience their relationships with you? What is the leader's role in making change happen? and What is your role in this situation?

Leaders Drive Organization Change

The most significant changes that happen in organizations come about when the leaders personally embark on a course of action. Sometimes, their efforts are successful, resulting in improved organizational performance and added value. Other times, their efforts fail, and momentum or value is limited or even destroyed. In all our years of consulting, we have never run into a leader who intended to lead a failed change effort or a consultant who intended to be of no value. But these things do happen.

After studying a substantial number of consulting engagements and the relationships between the consultants and their clients, we believe that the expertise, independent viewpoint, and guidance of a trusted change expert is a critical element in the successful leader's effort to bring about beneficial and sustainable change. In successful consulting relationships and the resulting change processes, our clients seem to value the role of a trusted advisor as well. Here's why.

1. Leaders Often Begin the Process of Change with Faulty Assumptions and Data.

Most leaders arrive at their positions of seniority because of certain personal skills and behaviors that have achieved the desirable results that advanced their careers. Over time, success reinforces the leaders' trust in these skills and behaviors to such an extent that decision making becomes almost mechanized. They believe what worked well in the past will continue to work well in the present. Schwenk (1984) described this phenomenon as "problem set," the repeated use of a strategy, which is likely to impede the development of alternative strategies.

In addition, like the rest of us, the majority of leaders are notoriously bad observers of their own reality. This creates two problems. First, the leader's belief about how the organization experiences his or her leadership is based, in large part, on the career success he or she has achieved up to this point. As such, leaders can develop a distorted picture of their shortcomings, and whether they really matter.

Second, a leader's view of how things really are is usually a perspective seen through the lens of his or her track record, that is, the behaviors that have been successful in the past. New problems are redefined to fit the mold of previous challenges, and in the process can be minimized in their severity. It is hard to resist the temptation to think, "Oh, this is just like the time we faced the problem in Asia four years ago. All we have to do is. . . ."

By reflexively seeking a familiar solution, the leader gives up the opportunity to explore new alternatives. Bourgeois and Eisenhardt (1988) have shown what a mixed blessing prior success can be if it encourages CEOs and executive teams to pursue obsolete strategies. Also, the leaders' conclusions that the assumptions on which they are making decisions are well-founded may lead them to believe that there is no need for additional data. The existing data will support the cases they have made. The problem is that such data sets are often incomplete and frequently contain inaccuracy and exaggeration.

2. These Faulty Assumptions and Data Narrow the Leader's Belief in What Is Possible and Limit the Menu of Available Choices. A leader's view of the options available to her when strategic decisions are required is often limited to the repertoire of historically tried and true approaches she's used successfully before. Unfortunately for change leaders, limiting options in this way is an almost certain recipe for failure. When organizations reach critical crossroads, it's usually because external forces are requiring something more or different from the organization than has been required before. New technologies, global competition moving into local markets, industry consolidations, economic trends, and social forces may act separately or in concert to create a profoundly new context for competing operations. Old business models, outdated organizational structures, restrictive contracts with employees or suppliers, or a shortage of a critical talent to deal with new challenges or take advantage of opportunities all require change from the familiar to the unfamiliar.

Using only *precedent* to navigate *unprecedented* circumstances can lead to disaster. New challenges present leaders with the opportunity to build broader capabilities, increase value, and open markets. But fear of the unknown and discomfort with ambiguity can provoke leaders to opt for the pre-set boundaries of what they believe to be possible and for the well-worn list of choices they believe have worked well before. The leader's reliance on what is "safe" can result in lost opportunities and an inability to react to change that is quite dangerous for the organization.

3. A Narrow View of What Is Possible and a Limited Menu of Choices Inevitably Limit the Success of Interventions. It's not hard to see how a leader's faulty assumptions about how she is perceived and "what is so" about current circumstances can lead to an overly narrow understanding of what is possible and a dangerously limited set of choices from which to select a direction for change. Trapped by her own assumptions, the leader will select interventions that, although well-designed and properly executed, fail to deliver results. Although many consultants have more experience with this scenario than they'd like to admit—and some have even been blamed for the failure—the reality is that applying any intervention, even with excellence, to a strategic problem that isn't fully understood or defined can never be successful. It's often easy to recognize this in hindsight. But the seeds for the disaster are sown the moment the leader faces a challenge that he misjudges and repeats formerly successful but currently inappropriate solutions because they are familiar. If there is no corrective influence in that moment, the intervention usually heads toward an organizational dead end that at best wastes energy and at worst harms both the organization and its leaders' reputations. Figure 1.1 illustrates how the leader's views impact organization change.

Figure 1.1. A Leader's Views Shape Organization Change

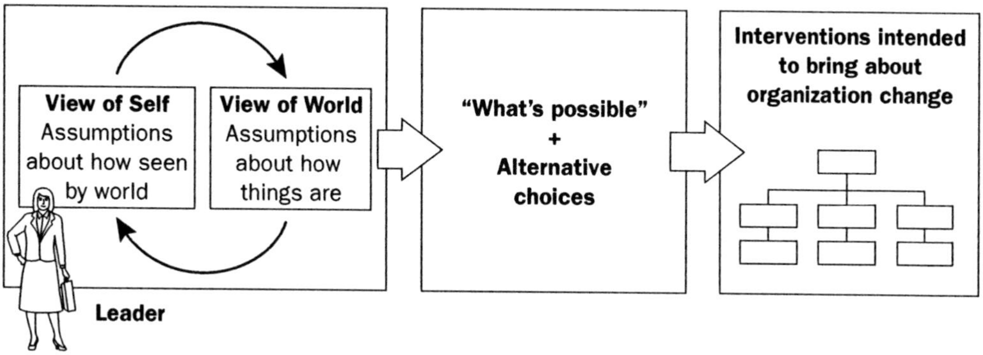

Again, the important thing to note is that we are not the only ones who are aware of these dynamics. *Leaders are too.* When they engage us, they do so with a healthy dose of self-awareness and a *desire to do things right,* even if it requires introspection, learning, and experimentation with new behaviors. Often, this awareness comes at the price of previous failed interventions. Once burned, leaders are more likely to reflect on the causes for their difficulties and may be more open to seeking assistance. The best clients, in our view, don't wait for disaster to strike before reaching out for help. They recognize that change is a complex undertaking requiring careful thought and expert management planning. They also have the self-awareness and confidence to recognize that their views may be limited and that seeking organizational expertise to expand their list of possible actions is appropriate, responsible behavior.

Table 1.1 summarizes these points.

Table 1.1. Limitations of Leader-Driven Change

- Leaders often begin the process of change with faulty assumptions and data.
- These faulty assumptions and data narrow the leader's belief in "what is possible" and limit the menu of available choices.
- A narrow view of what is possible and a limited menu of choices inevitably set up the execution of failed interventions.

We aren't claiming that leaders can change organizations successfully only with the assistance of consultants. We do think that involving a consultant in guiding organization change efforts is often helpful. We also know many clients who would say that their changes would have been less successful or would have failed completely without trusted, experienced advisors to turn to (Buchen, 2001).

Consultants as Catalysts for Sustainable Change

Organizational history is replete with examples of failed interventions that drained huge volumes of resources, time, and effort without yielding any positive outcomes. In the aftermath of failure, reflective consultants will review and analyze what they could have done differently. Those wanting to escape blame and disown the failure will claim, "Well, if he'd just listened to me from the beginning, this never would have happened." While lessons can be helpful, what's really needed is the right kind of relationship with the leader from the outset. For the consultant to be a critical part of successful fundamental change, he or she must start and continuously guide the client on the right course. Let's continue the tape on the example from the chapter opening and see how it might play out when the leader turns to you as his trusted advisor from the start.

"So, what do *you* think I oughta do?"

"Bob, I know you're feeling pressure to reach a decision, but my guess is that you'll feel better if you are certain you've done everything you can to make sure this is the right deal for the company. Am I right?"

"Yeah, I guess so. I've been over the deal a hundred times. I just can't get comfortable with the risks involved. I feel like I'm betting the company's future and all of our careers on this one decision. I haven't come this far to end up being blamed for taking unreasonable risks."

"That's natural. Let's think about how to deal with that. You're concerned that, if the deal doesn't work, others will blame you for taking the risk. Do you know how other people feel about this? Are there others you trust who can give you their reactions or help you think about the best way to handle this?"

"I guess I could discuss this some more with the Board or with our Chairman, John. I'd feel more comfortable if they understood the amount of thought I've put into this."

"That seems like a good idea. I'm sure that John and the Board would be happy to spend some more time on this. It's a big decision. What else do you need to do to feel comfortable?"

"The economics of the deal are one thing. I've got to make sure they're right. But I know from what I've read and what you've told me that the outcome will depend as much on how we implement this as on the logic behind the deal. I'm not sure my team is ready to do what it will take to make this work. We can sign the deal tomorrow, but what if we fumble this thing afterwards?"

"What do you think needs to happen?"

"It would be helpful if we could lay out each of the steps in as much detail as we can and take the team through them, just to make sure they're prepared for what's to come. I need to feel confident that when the starting gun goes off, my team is ready to run the race. Then, I need to take a hard look at some of the members of the team. It may be that they were the right people to run a smaller company, but that they don't have what it's going to take to run a much larger one."

"It's good that you're thinking about these things. Based on what I've seen in other companies that have gone through this, I think getting the right leadership team in place and preparing them to lead this change will be critical. I can prepare an overview of the steps involved in implementation and review them with you and the team right away. Then, we should get together again to talk about your views of each member of the team. Based on that, we can put together a plan of action to deal with the situation."

Figure 1.2 illustrates how productive change can occur with the inclusion of a trusted advisor's input from the moment a leader begins to contemplate change.

Figure 1.2. Practitioners Help Broaden a Leader's Views and Implement Sustainable Change

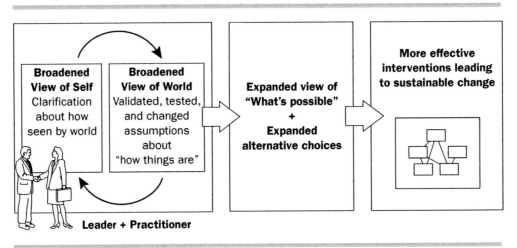

Building Relationship Intelligence (rQ)
Six Elements of a Change-Enabling Relationship

This case illustrates many of the dynamics we think are important in leader-consultant relationships. In our exploration of successful relationships in which leaders and consultants worked together to achieve sustainable change, we have identified six attributes that are pervasive. Not all of these elements are applicable to the same degree, nor are they all required for every part or phase of a relationship. But by and large, if consultants gain mastery in these six elements, it will radically increase the impact of their consulting. We refer to the collection of these elements as a consultant's "rQ" or his or her degree of "relationship intelligence." Let's explore these six elements using the case example above.

 ### rQ Element 1: Enable the Leader's Acknowledgment of Personal and Organizational Shortfalls by Getting Close to Build Trust

In every consulting engagement that adds value, the consultant brings something that doesn't exist inside the organization. Helping the client understand the value the consultant brings is the first task. The second task is building an emotional link between the consultant and client. Again, think about whom you turn to for advice on your own personal problems. Usually, it's not a stranger on the street; it's someone you know and trust. In the case example, the long-term relationship between the CEO and the consultant enabled them to have a deeply personal and profound conversation that could not have taken place on the first day of the consultant's work with the organization.

Martin (2001) reports that, in times of vanishing company loyalty, CEOs will continue to rely on the same trusted counselors. For example, Martin presents manufacturer Manville's experience during its asbestos liability crisis during the 1980s. Then-CEO Tom Stephens was faced with the tough job of wrestling with lawyers and insurance companies under the scrutiny of media and shareholders. He also faced the unpleasant prospect of implementing massive layoffs and contending with crippling morale problems. Deeply frustrated, Stephens turned to Bob Chapman, a consultant with a strong background in psychology. Stephens appreciated Chapman's objectivity and his willingness to challenge Stephens to be a better leader. Under Stephens' watch, Manville successfully reorganized and ultimately emerged from Chapter 11. After he took the top job at MacMillan Bloedel, a forest products company, Stephens continued to consult Chapman. Stephens credits the Manville experience for solidifying his relationship with Chapman, noting that working through a difficult time with someone can greatly increase the level of trust.

In addition to trust, Stephens' comments speak to another critical issue regarding confidantes. Relationships don't happen overnight. Trust is usually built up over time. People become confidants when they share some strong history.

Many consultants ignore the emotional side of the client-consultant relationship. This may happen because they see it as unprofessional, because they need to maintain distance in their relationships with their clients or because they are uncomfortable dealing with the emotional facets of consulting work. But a significant change in an organization produces emotions of all kinds, whether we want to acknowledge them or not. The most effective change management consultants assist their clients in dealing with both the emotional and the content issues they are facing.

 rQ Element 2: Build the Leader's Sense of Significance and Confidence Through Personal Investment

Some consultants think the client is the one making the primary investment in the client-consultant relationship. The client takes the risks, pays the bills, and lives with the outcomes of the interventions. But good consultants make an investment too. In the case example above, the consultant could simply have said, "That's your call, not mine" and washed his hands of the matter. By accepting shared responsibility for the outcomes of the intervention, the consultant was able to reassure the client that he would receive continued support, even when things got tough. We all have heard that change consultants shouldn't make decisions for their clients because doing so reduces the client's commitment to the intervention. As a result, some of us have become hesitant to declare our views and opinions. However, there is a difference between making a decision and having a point of view. We contend that clients want to know that the people they hire as consultants care about the issues, know about the risks, and are personally committed to helping resolve them.

 rQ Element 3: Accelerate Receptivity to, and Acceptance of, Tough News and Messages by Having the Courage to "Confront the Moose"

In the case above, the consultant confronted the client about his fear of showing leadership during the acquisition. It was the consultant's challenge to say, in so many words, "Either step up and do your job or step aside and let someone else do it." Clients value consultants who will tell them things about themselves that other people are thinking but not saying. This is what we call "confronting the moose." The expression comes from the behavior we have observed whenever people are faced with issues that are too hot to handle. It is as if these issues are a big hairy moose standing right there on the conference table. Everyone sees it, but they talk as if the moose isn't there (Perkins, 1988). Confronting the moose means appropriately but honestly naming the behaviors or issues blocking progress and helping people deal with them productively, as uncomfortable as it may be to do so at first. As long as this is done in a spirit of helpfulness, caring, and support, few clients will become angry with their consultants. If you are unfortunate enough to encounter a client who becomes angry when you confront the moose, it's critical to the change effort that you find effective ways to educate the client regarding the effect his or her behavior is having on the process. If there's still no acknowledgement by the client and dysfunctional behavior continues, it may be time to end the relationship. Unless you can be honest, confront the moose, and guide people toward new behaviors, there's little hope that the organization will achieve significant, sustainable change.

 ### rQ Element 4: Build the Leader's Endurance for Long-Term Change by Showing Advocacy

Clients need our advice, but also need our support. As clients interact with their teams and units of their companies, they frequently face individuals who disagree with the direction they are proposing or the methods they advocate for accomplishing certain results. While it is the client's primary responsibility to win over those who disagree, we as consultants can and should help to educate people about what our clients are trying to accomplish. No significant change can be undertaken without some resistance and misunderstanding. Clients know this at an intellectual level, but sometimes grow weary in the face of continued push-back or lack of action. When we find ourselves with people who "don't get it," we can act as an advocate for our clients by helping to explain the reasons for change, the thinking behind the approach, or the logic of decisions that were made. Many resistors simply want to understand why things are being done as they are before they commit to action. Our clients can't talk to every individual or group personally. Memos to the entire workforce and large-group communication sessions only go so far in answering specific questions that individuals pose. When we help enlist the support of key individuals or groups, we are playing the advocate role.

 ### rQ Element 5: Enable the Leader's Deep Ownership of and Commitment to Change by Working Collaboratively to Combine Expertise and Knowledge

The consultant in the case above could have said, "Let me go away and put together a plan for managing this deal." Instead, he said he wanted to work with Bob and his team to put together a plan that would provide a roadmap for success. When consultants take over the work, clients no longer feel engaged, responsible, or committed. The consultant becomes just another project manager, rather than a peer who can assess the situation and provide expertise, support, and guidance. When the client turns over responsibility to the consultant, it's the consultant who is committed to success, not the client. As most of us know from experience, that is often a recipe for disaster.

 ### rQ Element 6: Accelerate the Leader's Ability to Adopt New Ways of Thinking and Acting with the Interpersonal Agility to Vary Your Means of Influence

Depending on the circumstances, good consultants can vary the ways in which they influence their clients. Direct appeals, like the one exemplified by the case above, are certainly the most common means of influence. But effective consultants have a palette of influencing options to help their clients deal with the many challenges that accompany change leadership. Benchmarking other companies, putting their client in touch with peers, collecting diagnostic data, and working with the senior team to shape decisions are just a few of the options that are available. In addition to these different methods are the behaviors the consultant can employ: agreeable friend one moment, challenging adversary the next; wise advisor in one situation, fellow inquirer in another—in each instance doing what is required to help the client through the issues he or she is facing at the moment. One wise veteran of many consulting relationships advocates the "180-degree rule": Whatever your client is feeling, you should feel the opposite. If the client is overly confident, you should express doubt; if the client is uncertain, it's time for your reassurance; and so forth. Whether or not you accept the 180-degree rule, the important thing is that you are thinking about what styles of influence are available to you and that you are comfortable using them to help your clients succeed.

Table 1.2 summarizes the six elements of relationship intelligence (rQ).

Table 1.2. The Six Elements of Relationship Intelligence (rQ)

Trust	Enable the leader's acknowledgment of personal and organizational shortfalls by getting close to build trust
Personal Investment	Build the leader's sense of significance and confidence through personal investment

Table 1.2. The Six Elements of Relationship Intelligence (rQ), Cont'd

Courage	Accelerate receptivity to, and acceptance of, tough news and messages by having the courage to "confront the moose"
Advocacy	Build the leader's endurance for long-term change by showing advocacy
Collaboration	Enable the leader's deep ownership of and commitment to change by working collaboratively to combine expertise and knowledge
Interpersonal Agility	Accelerate the leader's ability to adopt new ways of thinking and acting with the interpersonal agility to vary your means of influence

Prerequisites to rQ

There are two sides to effectively building relationships that enable change. There is a *process* side of the relationship, which is to say *how* one goes about it. There is also the *content* side, that is, the *what* around which the consultant builds the relationship. Many of the books in this Practicing Organization Development series pay deep respect to aspects of the *what*, important content issues for which we should all continue to expand our knowledge and skill. We believe there is a set of foundational content pieces *all* change consultants must come equipped with, and we'll discuss those below. But our focus in this book is aimed at just one side of the relationship coin, the process side, or the *how*. We've focused on this issue for a specific reason. There are few books that really provide depth on the process issue, which we believe is becoming increasingly important to our profession. Many consultant failures can be traced back to relationship issues, the *how* of consulting. It is less common for consultants to fail because they lacked sufficient expertise in their respective fields.

We decided to make the attempt to identify a set of attributes essential to successful client-consultant relationships. By codifying these dimensions, we realize we may risk either trivializing them or making them sound somewhat clichéd by suggesting that mastery of them comes by working one's way through a checklist.

Nothing could be further from the truth. Mastering the subtlety of these behaviors requires years of trial and error and continual, intense self-reflection.

Before we begin our discussion of these dimensions, we should take a quick look at the basic content, or the *what's,* of change consulting we believe must be in every change consultant's repertoire. While we won't spend much of our time in this book exploring these "prerequisites," we believe it is essential to acknowledge their importance as a foundation. Having mastery in the dimensions of relationship intelligence without these basics in place is just as much a road to disaster as having mastery in many of the basics, but being relationally "tone deaf." As we said earlier, the latter is a far more common dilemma in the consulting field. But ultimately, we believe that it is a consultant's rQ *in concert* with his or her mastery of these basics (see Table 1.3) that distinguishes truly gifted consultants from the hired guns and extra pairs of hands.

Table 1.3. Prerequisites to rQ

1. An understanding of organizations as dynamic systems

2. Knowledge of leadership theory and leadership effectiveness

3. Knowledge of groups and teams

4. An underlying base of theory and knowledge of change

5. Technical expertise in consultants' respective fields

6. A working model of the consulting process

7. Business knowledge—how to talk in the client's language

8. Relevant experience from which to draw insights about the client's challenges

An Understanding of Organizations as Dynamic Systems. In order to understand the dynamics and dimensions of change, it's helpful to have a conceptual understanding of how organizations work (Burke, 1993; Katz & Kahn, 1978; Morgan, 1986). Nadler and Tushman's (1977) congruence model of organizational behavior (see Figure 1.3) is an approach that many organizations have found useful. The model shows any organization as a system; at its heart is a transformation process in which the enterprise, in accordance with its strategy, performs work that converts input to output. This core element of the organization consists of four components: the work or the series of tasks required to perform each function in the value chain; the people who carry out those tasks; the formal organization of structures, processes, and practices that specify how work is assigned and performed; and the informal organization, the patterns of behavior that shape the daily interactions between people and their supervisors, employees, co-workers, and customers. At any given time, each of the four components exists in some relative degree of fit, or congruence, with the other three. The tighter the fit, the smaller the gap between strategic objectives and actual performance. Total congruence is the ideal goal, but in reality, organizational systems are in a constant state of flux. In most organizations, the job of managers is to make decisions constantly that will realign the fit between work, people, formal structures, and the informal operating environment.

Figure 1.3. Nadler and Tushman's Congruence Model of Organizational Behavior

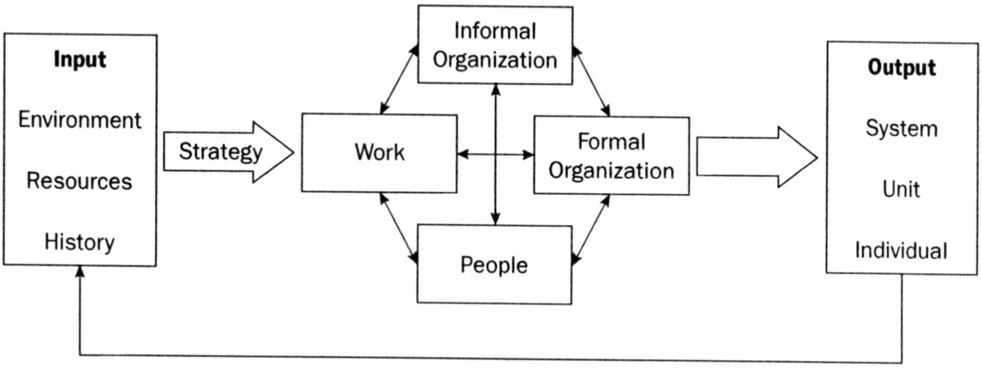

From David A. Nadler, Marc S. Gerstein, Robert B. Shaw, and Associates, *Organizational Architecture*. San Francisco, CA: Jossey-Bass, 1992.

This model involves several important implications for leaders of change. The first is that major change nearly always originates in the external environment. The nature of that change will, in turn, influence the scope, intensity, and sequence of changes involving the internal components. Second, the congruence model suggests that changes in any of the internal components will have a ripple effect, altering the pattern of relationships among multiple components. Finally, it serves as a reminder that change does not occur in a vacuum; it requires that top executives demonstrate ambidextrous leadership in that they must simultaneously implement change while continuing to meet the ongoing demands of the business.

Knowledge of Leadership Theory and Leadership Effectiveness. When you think about organizations as systems and roles, it's critical to consider the special demands and characteristics of the roles filled by the organization's top leaders. Simply put, a leader is someone who sets direction for efforts and influences people to follow that direction. How a leader sets that direction and influences people depends on a variety of factors. To really get your bearings in the territory of leadership, you should have some knowledge of the major leadership theories, have some experiential knowledge of the various styles of leadership, and have developed some point of view on the traits, characteristics, or behaviors that leaders should demonstrate to be effective. Notable authors in leadership theory include Bass (1990), Bennis (1992), Goleman (1998a), Kotter (1999), Kouzes and Posner (1997), and Tichy (1990), to name a few.

Knowledge of Groups and Teams. Leadership is a team sport (Nadler & Spencer, 1997). This implies that consultants working at the top of their client organization have to engage not just the leader but her immediate collaborators in the change effort. Consultants are brought in to facilitate the development of teams and to work with these teams on issues of strategy, organizational design, culture, change management, and leadership development. For this reason, it is critical that consultants have a good understanding of the theory, research, and conceptual aspects of group behavior, as well as personal insight into the factors that influence executive team effectiveness. Specific skills might include the following abilities:

- To apply models for team leadership, team facilitation, and group dynamics in order to assist the team in its work;
- To describe what makes an effective team and an effective team leader and how to diagnose and improve team performance;
- To apply team leadership and facilitation principles in decision-making and problem-solving situations to generate beneficial results for the organization; and

- To observe group processes and give structured, meaningful feedback that can help team members improve their skills and enhance working relationships.

An Underlying Base of Theory and Knowledge of Change. Consultants have been managing change efforts for years and have collectively accumulated a pool of theory and knowledge that is quite valuable. You can draw on this knowledge pool for models to guide you—there is no need to reinvent the wheel or feel alone in your endeavors. Like any field that consists of applying skills and implementing a particular practice, experience accompanied by related feedback is the best teacher. The second best way to become a good change consultant is by some combination of academic and nonacademic training. Courses that will provide a good background include group dynamics, adult learning, counseling and interviewing, organization development, action research and consultation, and process consultation, including interpersonal and intergroup conflict. Nonacademic programs or avenues include basic laboratory training, personal growth seminars, consultation skills, and supervised experience.

In the field of change management, the following authors can provide a useful perspective: William Bridges, Daryl Conner, William Fulmer, Art Kleiner, John Kotter, Rob Leboe, David Nadler, David Noer, Robert Quinn, Peter Scott-Morgan, and Robert Tomasko.

Technical Expertise in Consultants' Respective Fields. Technical expertise is needed in a specific field (for example, technology, HR, finance, strategy, and so forth) to understand what the client is talking about. Either in college or in our first jobs, we were trained in specific fields or functions. This might be engineering, sales, accounting, counseling, or any other area of technical expertise. The foundation for consulting skills is some expertise—whether it be very scientific, such as molecular biology, or very nonscientific, such as management or organization development.

Working Models of the Consulting Process. According to Block (2000), each consulting project, no matter how long, goes through five phases. The steps in each phase are sequential, so if you skip one or assume it has been taken care of, you could be in trouble. Skillful consulting is being competent in the execution of each of the consulting phases listed in Table 1.4. Examples of steps are included.

Table 1.4. Phases in a Consulting Project

Phase 1 Entry and Contracting	Phase 2 Discovery and Dialogue	Phase 3 Feedback and the Decision to Act	Phase 4 Engagement and Implementation	Phase 5 Extension, Recycle, or Termination
Setting up the first meeting	Helping the client and yourself develop a sense of the problem	Reducing a large amount of data to a manageable number of issues	Getting different parts of the organization together to address a problem	Evaluating what went on during engagement and implementation
Exploring what the problem is	Determining who will be involved in defining the problem	Handling resistance to the data	Starting implementation with an educational event (e.g., series of meetings, training session)	Deciding whether to extend the process to a larger segment of the organization
Determining the fit, client, and consultant expectations	Identifying what data should be collected	Deciding how to proceed	Becoming involved in design work	Assessing whether the real problem was addressed
Describing how to start	Identifying what methods will be used Determining a timeframe	Selecting ultimate goals for the project Selecting the best action steps or changes	Running meetings or training sessions	Terminating involvement with the project

Adapted from *Flawless Consulting* (2nd ed.) by Peter Block. Copyright © 2000 by Peter Block and Jossey-Bass/Pfeiffer. Reprinted by permission of John Wiley & Sons, Inc.

There is much more to the client-consultant relationship than the simple substance of the problem or project the consultant is working on. There are several elements to the affective side of the interaction that are always operating:

- *Responsibility.* To have a good contract with your client, responsibility for what is planned and what takes place has to be shared and balanced.

- *Feelings.* You need to be aware of how much the client is owning feelings versus playing an observer role. You also must be aware of your own feelings about the client. For example, perceiving defensiveness or controlling behavior in yourself is just as important as perceiving feelings in the client.

- *Trust.* It is useful to find out whether clients trust your confidentiality, whether they trust you not to discredit them or to take over. Putting the real or potential distrust into words actually helps to build trust.

- *Your Own Needs.* Consultants have a right to acknowledge their own needs. You may have the need to show your worth by having a client. You will probably have needs for acceptance and inclusion by the client, and you undoubtedly require some confirmation that what you do is valuable.

Skill in consulting is not only about providing a program or processes; it's also skill in being able to identify and put into words these issues about trust, feelings, responsibility, and your own needs.

Business Knowledge—How to Talk in the Client's Language. In addition to being familiar with organizational science theories and techniques, you need to know the basics about how businesses operate and function in order to be an effective organization consultant. This entails knowing the product, industry, or process "language" your client speaks and being comfortable discussing issues of strategy, finance, accounting, budgeting, operations, marketing, and management in his or her terms. If you have formal training in these areas, so much the better. If you do not, you need to develop a plan to become more knowledgeable.

Relevant Experience from Which to Draw Insights About the Client's Challenges. No one knows better than the newly minted graduate student in organizational psychology/behavior that formal education is only a small part of becoming a good consultant. The ability to tell war stories and draw analogies to current issues can be extremely valuable in supporting change efforts. Having industry experience is not only useful for relating, but also invaluable in helping clients through major change interventions. Unfortunately, relevant experience only comes from actually doing this work over time, so you might consider borrowing war stories and doing some shadow consulting.

A Unique Format for a Unique Topic

The next six chapters of this book are focused on each of the six elements of rQ. We will provide rich case examples told in the first person by the leaders and consultants who experienced them. We've chosen to allow these consultants and clients to give their views in their own voice for a very important reason—relationships are personal. Professional relationships are no exception to this rule. How we approach them, develop them, and sustain them is a reflection of our participation in them. Therefore, we feel it is important to let people tell their stories. Since relationships are dynamic and complex, we felt it was important to choose a writing style and format that acknowledges the fact that there is no one-size-fits-all approach to building strong, sustainable, trusting relationships between clients and consultants. But it's not a deep mystery either. We believe that mastery of the art and science of relationships that enable change can be learned and developed. What's more, for people to be successful consultants in the 21st Century, they will *have* to learn and develop what it takes. We, and our colleagues whose stories appear on the pages ahead, have taken the time to share our views on how we believe we all can improve our capability because we believe that these relationships are an invaluable component of future success.

As we relate our experiences in developing relationships with our clients, we will stop at the end of each chapter to look at two important things. First, we will examine what we call change enablement—what effect each dimension should have on a client's behavior in order to move change forward successfully. Second, we will look at the tools consultants can use to help clients develop the behaviors and capacities they need to make change possible. These tools will also help you gauge your current level of capability and will give you some thoughts on how to build and increase your mastery in each—the sum total of which we believe defines your degree of rQ.

It's also important that we say a few words about the nature of the stories you will read. Our own consulting work focuses on CEOs and senior leaders of large organizations. Accordingly, the majority of these cases focus on relationships with leaders who preside over the enterprise or large portions of the enterprise. We realize that not all of you reading this book practice your consulting with such leaders. Many of you are doing great work at other levels of organizations, as well as in education systems, nonprofit sectors, and small businesses. We believe that the fundamentals of building lasting, sustainable, and trusting relationships apply regardless of who your client is. The context of your consulting may be different, and the sphere of influence your client has may differ. But *how* you establish, nurture, sustain, and mature your relationships with those who receive your advice and expertise should not differ.

②

The Heart of It All: Getting Close to Build Trust

IT MAY SEEM SELF-EVIDENT that you need to get close to your client in order to serve as his or her confidant. Many consultants probably feel that their interactions with clients in the normal course of business build a level of familiarity that is perfectly adequate for the work they are doing. When we picture the first element of rQ, however, we're talking about a closeness with our clients that entails building a level of trust that is deeper and more substantial than anything likely to arise through simply working on presenting problems.

Our colleague, Rich Rosen, has the ability to form a close relationship with his CEO clients quickly. He uses that emotional connection to help them see how their behavior influences their ability to lead change in their organizations. Let's take a look at how this played out in one of his actual engagements. Rich tells the story in his own voice, but we'll interrupt the story from time to time to analyze the situation and point out some things that Rich did to help him build emotional closeness with his clients.

"My partner and I had a close relationship with both the CEO and COO of a company going through IPO, succession, and critical product issues. We knew we needed to be able to have open and intimate private sessions with them individually and together on critical business concerns. The organization was facing hard global and social issues on its biotech products. They had to completely change the way they had been operating from an arrogant 'we know the answer' point of view to really opening their relationships, making their process transparent, and really listening to multiple stakeholders, including governments, nongovernmental organizations, activist groups, media, and the public end-consumer. They were also facing intense scrutiny from Wall Street, as they had already implemented a partial IPO and were planning for a complete spinoff.

"The CEO and COO had to come to grips with role clarity. This included defining the role of the chief technical officer (CTO), who acted like a COO, as well as succession issues. The organization was not up-front with who its executive team was and really needed to sanction its top leadership as a team to be more decisive and clear about strategy.

"One critical event in our ability to build trust while helping them change their organization and the way its leadership interacted with each other came as we were sharing the feedback we had collected. The intention was for each individual leader to receive personal feedback independently while the whole team received the organizational feedback. An unplanned design emerged when we discovered that the COO and CTO shared their individual feedback documents with each other. They told us that sharing these results, although difficult, had been extremely worthwhile. They suggested that all feedback be shared with everybody. The rest of the leadership team agreed. At the offsite they each shared what they had learned about themselves both as individuals and as a team working together. This created an emotional connection between team members and us that exceeded our greatest expectations."

There were several challenges in Rich's engagement: helping the client deal with an IPO, succession planning, and critical product issues. Many consultants would approach these as strictly technical challenges, void of emotional content. A technical expert, for instance, might tackle each issue with a list of steps in hand, intending to lead the client through them one by one. It happens all the time.

What's wrong with this approach? On the surface, nothing. The technical expert would satisfy the client's need for guidance through a difficult and unfamiliar process. In most cases, the client would be satisfied with the technical guidance they received and view their decision to engage a consultant as a good one. The error would not be one of commission, but rather one of omission. *Neither the client nor the consultant would be aware that, from a change management standpoint, something important was missing.*

What was left out? In the first paragraph of Rich's story, we heard that the client needed "to be able to have open and intimate private sessions"; and in the last few paragraphs of the story, we begin to hear hints of some of the underlying emotional issues among members of the senior team. The technically oriented consultant would gloss over these issues; consciously or subconsciously, he would in effect say to himself, "These issues are not directly related to the IPO or to the absence of a succession planning process or the problems this company is having with new products. What's more, they're probably none of my business."

This attitude highlights one of the key differences between technical consulting and change management consulting. Significant changes in organizations evoke powerful emotions. If these emotions are not explored and managed productively, they can lead to individual and interpersonal behaviors that block progress toward goals. In the case above, Rich and his partner were attuned to the emotions of the executives and viewed it *as their business* to develop emotional proximity with their clients so that they could help them manage their emotions effectively. Let's look at how Rich and his partner went about developing trust as they got close to the client and as they worked on the IPO and succession challenges.

"First and foremost we listened to where people on the team were at the outset. We let them know that we heard them by sharing what we understood and having empathy for the world they lived in and the challenges they faced. We learned how to talk with the CEO and the COO by paying attention to their respective styles.

"The CEO was a run-on talker who tended to like ambiguity and confusion around him so he could sort out the answers when he wanted to. In my direct discussions with him, I brought this to his attention. I even confronted him on how much he liked this pattern. He admitted he was aware of it and knew he needed to change. I had to learn how to interrupt his run-on ramblings and get him to focus. I also used humor to have some fun with helping him to develop awareness—and assured him that all of us were human and struggling to deal with our own adult behavior patterns.

"I had to challenge myself to interrupt the CEO when we was going on and on and let him know that—while I respected his process—I was there to engage him as well as listen to him. I spoke the truth and didn't do overt things to please him. I maintained confidentiality and let him know that I had no other agenda than to be of service.

"My partner and I called the CEO and the executive team on their propensity to go off on tangents and give everything importance. Effectively, they were used to 'taking deep dives in shallow ponds'—they indiscriminately examined all issues deeply rather than focusing on the important few. We challenged them to become aware of this behavior as it was happening and then work to get focused on what was most important. The saying became part of their lexicon.

"My partner and I confronted some very sensitive issues on succession. The CTO and COO were vying to be the heir apparent. We put the issue on the table in our data collection—and we brought it up in private conversations with the CEO and then the COO. We never collected data that we didn't first run by the CEO in private conversation. He learned that he could trust us to go to him first and help him determine how to bring things to the others in his group.

"As a result, we were brought into more private conversations, and we talked about specific people and trust issues that hadn't been explicit before. We also received direct acknowledgement about the critical role we played in the succession issue: The client told us that the way we got them to address this issue by tackling it head on without overplaying it was 'a real art form.' We used conversations on role clarification for the whole team to get the message across about succession without being too overt. The CEO would say things like 'I need you [the COO] to focus externally and to lead negotiations because it is a strength and it is the role the organization will need you to play as you develop and expand your responsibilities.' The CEO also supported the importance of the CTO's role and focused the CTO's responsibilities. The group got the message that the COO was the successor in a way that enabled them to thank us for the sensitivity and adroit way we enabled them to communicate.

"In retrospect, one of the success factors was our approach in having a team of two work with the client. My partner and I developed a very close relationship and truly partnered in our work. Having two people who both saw the connections and emotional content enabled us to read the situation, both at the moment with the client and also as we debriefed. Another strength was our ability to get close to two of the executive team members. We were able to use these two as internal allies to help bring about and reinforce the changes."

Rich called attention to things the CEO already knew about himself and his team, such as his tendency to ramble and let his team skate over the surface of deep issues; his covert endorsement of the rivalry between his COO and CTO; and the lack of trust between him and some members of his team. These issues didn't directly block progress toward the IPO, but they clouded the team's thinking and had the potential to affect the ability of the CEO and his team to manage the organization effectively in the future. Rich and his partner helped the CEO and his team work their way through the IPO and succession issues, but they also did something more: They strengthened the capacity of the leadership team to tackle difficult issues associated with change. By developing trust through building the needed emotional proximity, Rich and his partner were able to "raise the level of the senior team's game," enabling them to deal more effectively with the transitions taking place in the organization and preparing them to manage future changes more effectively as well. Rich and his partner left more behind than a laundry list of steps to follow in completing an IPO—they left a strengthened CEO and senior team. Due to their ability to establish emotional proximity with the CEO and his senior team, their work had several important consequences that would not have occurred otherwise. Rich continues:

> "The COO understood he was the successor and needed to change his job responsibilities in line with his larger public profile and in preparation for his moving up in two or three years. The CTO understood he was essential but not in line.
>
> "We designed a true executive team with appropriate membership for governing the company. We established clear charters with the top two leadership teams for how they worked together. We clarified all the senior executive roles and communicated them to the organization.
>
> "Decisiveness and speed increased exponentially. Large teams were recommissioned to do real value-added work in line with their charters and membership. The senior team members were more direct with each other and took much more responsibility for calling issues and making the process work."

In reflecting on his work with the client, Rich concludes:

"Add value. Internalize the fact that you are already in a valued relationship—always there to care and add value—without trying to win them over and *prove* value. Act as if you have always been in a long-term relationship as a trusted member of their team and confidant of the leader—be real without looking for affirmation. Step up and—while it is always essential to listen first—step forward and show you are there to engage and provide additional points of view to their critical issues.

"Use humanness to share in their struggles and bring humor to serious situations so the process is not overbearing—but always maintain that the content is important. I share my own humanity and get to know leaders personally so I can talk about their lives—both professional and personal. I'm careful to not go too far in assuming intimacy—but I show that who they are is important to me and that who I am is something I share as part of a real relationship with them."

A consultant must be skilled and committed in order to get close enough to develop trust. There are several avenues to building trust, but sincerity is the unifying factor. Clients quickly pick up on insincere attempts by consultants to gain their trust. Many consultants, like glib salespeople, begin their relationship-building efforts with superficial small talk about personal interests. Rich did not begin his relationship building that way. Instead, he took a risk by calling attention to the CEO's rambling in discussions—a behavior that was interfering with the progress the CEO said he wanted to make toward the IPO. Rich was sincere in his feedback, which was intended to be helpful to the CEO. He also chose his words and tone carefully so his client would really hear what Rich was saying. By being both sincere and mindful of his tone, Rich began to create a relationship with the CEO of a more personal nature—one that was characterized by emotional closeness.

As we'll see in later chapters, you can sometimes discover common interests or experiences in conversation that will resonate with your client and help deepen your relationship. Again, we emphasize that there has to be a genuine connection for this commonality to serve as the bridge to a relationship. You should not expect generic small talk to build the trust that is ultimately required to help a person change his or her behavior, however. Since a leader's behavior is highly visible to others, it's important that leaders realize the effect it has on those around them. Rich pointed out that the CEO's desire to ramble on in discussions and never delve into important issues gave others the impression that the CEO didn't want them to deal with issues directly and efficiently. The CEO was able to see how superficial discussions led to poor decisions that could negatively affect the implementation of organizational strategies. In this case, Rich's work with the CEO at a personal level helped him lead his team more effectively through the many issues surrounding the IPO. Rich's work with the COO and CTO helped prevent a potentially explosive and damaging conflict from paralyzing both players and the senior team.

The Importance of Getting Close to Build Trust

Given a choice, we would prefer that our clients trust us instead of not trusting us. Why then are clients so frequently mistrustful of their consultants? Is trust between consultants and clients a requirement for successful change consultation?

Some consultants seem to treat assignments like business transactions: a simple and straightforward exchange of money for services. Perhaps some of these consultants would justify this approach by saying that they are remaining objective by avoiding emotional bonding with their clients. They might go on to say that when they need to push their clients hard to do things that they don't want their relationship with the client getting in the way.

While we suppose there are clients who would prefer to maintain a distant, objective relationship with their change consultants, we haven't met many of them. Change tends to involve a great deal of emotion, some of which washes back over the person leading the way. CEOs who are insensitive to how people are feeling about a change are less likely to make good choices about how to lead the change. Being empathetic requires the capacity to feel, and with that capacity comes vulnerability to the same emotions being felt by others. Effective leaders of change are therefore emotional, as are effective consultants.

When CEOs detect signs that their consultants are not invested in their work emotionally, they suspect that they are being treated as sources of revenue rather than as important clients. Consultants who are unavailable for meetings, slow to return calls, quick to leave at the end of the day, or who demonstrate little enthusiasm for their work will generally be mistrusted. Some CEOs want their consultants to argue with them at length, just to make certain that the consultant is heavily vested in their point of view. Other CEOs may expect support on weekends or evenings, travel to distant destinations on short notice, or a report turned around in an impossibly short time. Most clients will watch carefully how their consultants treat confidential information. CEOs are surrounded by people who say they want to help but who cannot be trusted. CEOs need to be certain about who they are dealing with before they open themselves to support on issues that are highly personal or organizationally significant.

Trust can't be built by using simple techniques. Trust is something that a person earns by virtue of his or her integrity and personal investment. Consultants can't gain their clients' trust by faking trustworthiness; they have to be trustworthy people, through and through. There are many outward signs of trustworthiness:

- Being reliable;
- Being available, physically and emotionally;
- Treating confidential information with care;
- Taking responsibility, even when things don't work as planned;
- Sharing reactions openly;
- Taking risks and being transparent;
- Holding oneself to the same standards expected from others;
- Accepting criticism without defensiveness;
- Stating beliefs openly and then standing by them;
- Demonstrating commitment to one's work; and
- Caring about how things turn out, every day.

When the relationship between a consultant and the client is built on trust, no one needs to put effort into figuring out whether advice is being offered in earnest. It's still perfectly reasonable for clients and consultants to disagree about the best way to approach change, but the argument will center on the approach itself and not on the intelligence, experience, or intentions of the parties involved.

When trust is present, unexpected obstacles that are encountered will not be taken as reasons to end the relationship. Instead, they will be met with additional effort to learn what is happening and to develop a new and more effective approach. Leaders can continue to press forward with confidence, knowing that they have received the best counsel they can obtain.

When trust is present, leaders aren't quick to jettison their consultants at the first opportunity in order to save a few dollars. In fact, when trust is present, dollars are rarely an issue. Clients and consultants who trust one another will know that they cannot let negotiations over money become the focal point of the relationship, and both work hard to make certain the other is comfortable with the arrangements that have been made.

In the long run, when trust is present, the relationship will last through many cycles of change. The work may ebb and flow as the situation demands, but the relationship will remain one of importance for both parties. The client will know that a trusted advisor is always ready to respond when needed, and the consultant will know that when he or she is needed, the client will call.

Ultimately, when trust is present, changes in the organization will be more profound, because both the consultant and client learn to work together effectively in pursuit of the goal of improvement. Change will be deeper and continuous, because it is undertaken with an openness to the data and to the possibilities. Change won't proceed jerkily in a series of unconnected programs led by different consultants—rather it will proceed in an integrated, focused manner, with each step building on the foundation laid by the last. Even as unanticipated jolts are experienced, they are dealt with in the context of a deep understanding of the organization's history, strengths, and aspirations. This level of closeness perfectly illustrates what we mean when we talk about the trust element of rQ.

The trust element of rQ enables consultants to help their clients manage issues that could thwart their efforts at organization change. To establish the necessary bond, it is important to understand the skills and commitment required to establish it:

- Self-Awareness;
- Modeling;
- Emotional Intelligence; and
- Ability to Set and Keep Boundaries.

Let's explore this element of rQ further by examining each of these skills.

Self-Awareness

It's difficult to develop trust without feeling emotion. Some consultants, in the name of professionalism, work to block out any emotions they might feel in the course of doing their work. Like surgeons who don't allow the sight of blood to sicken them, these consultants pride themselves on their ability to stay emotionally detached from their clients.

Clinical detachment may work for technical consultants dealing with issues confined to their areas of expertise. Effective change management consultants, however, focus on the whole orientation; clinical detachment will actually isolate change consultants from the things they have to know in order to be effective. Change consultants need to have empathy (Hass, 1984; Wispé, 1986); they must be able to experience what their clients are experiencing in order to know how the clients' emotions might be affecting their attitudes toward change. Failure to pick up on clues indicating emotional discomfort with a decision can lead the consultant to believe that the decision has been accepted when in fact it has not. Far too often, people involved in change say they are committed to doing the right thing but fail to back their words with behavior (Ickes, 1993). We'll talk more about empathy in the section on emotional intelligence below.

Most seasoned consultants have learned that their own emotions are a good barometer for what their clients are feeling. When we feel angry with our clients, there's a good chance that they are also angry with us. When we're bored with the discussion or uninspired by the thinking we're observing in the room, chances are that others are tuned out or not engaged as well. When we're excited, emotionally charged up, and feeling like we're the best consultants the world has ever known, our clients probably feel that things are going well too. By being aware of our own emotions and making them available to our clients by verbalizing them, we can check on the emotional health of our clients and deal with whatever issues they are experiencing. Even if our emotions are out of tune, just the act of checking them out will open up communication channels with our clients that were not available before. Once we know how our clients are feeling, we can redirect our energy to make certain that our work together addresses issues that might otherwise be barriers to progress.

In order to be self-aware, we need to define clearly what self-awareness is. At its most basic level, self-awareness involves recognizing one's emotions and their effects on a situation. People with this cognitive competence know which emotions they are feeling and why they are feeling them. They realize there are links between their feelings and what they think, do, and say. They also recognize how their feelings affect their attitudes or behaviors. Accurate self-awareness leads individuals to be aware of their strengths and weaknesses, to be reflective, and to learn from their experiences. It also leads to more openness to candid feedback, new perspectives, and self-development opportunities. It makes individuals more likely to show a sense of humor and to gain perspective about themselves.

By the way, it's just as important to discuss what is happening when emotions are positive as to discuss them when there is a problem. Positive emotions provide the fuel for continued efforts to change. It's important for us to understand why a client feels positively about the work we are doing together so that we can improve our batting average in selecting interventions that fit our client's needs and style.

Consider the following suggestions when trying to raise your level of self-awareness.

Calibrate by Asking. Build routine checkpoints into your agreements with clients to ask them how things are going. Ask questions such as:

- Is there anything else I could do that would be helpful to you?

- Are there things you'd like me to do more of/less of?

- My intent in our relationship has been to build our trust through making sure my team delivers the basics in a high-quality way. Do you feel that's working?

When you let your clients know that their opinion of your value is important, it can have an exponential impact. First, it models an important behavior of being open to the candid thoughts of others. Second, it forces them to own their side of the relationship and step up to opportunities to make it better. It also allows an opportunity to air concerns that your client may have written off as "minor" in order to avoid raising them with you. Stockpiled minor issues often add up to significant derailers of relationships.

Use the Johari Window. The Johari Window (Figure 2.1) is a conceptual model for describing, evaluating, and predicting aspects of interpersonal communication that can be a useful tool in your quest to build trust. As individuals exchange feedback, the size/shape of the panes expand or contract (as shown by the arrows). This model helps reveal the movement of information from one pane to another as trust ebbs and flows. Joseph Luft and Harry Ingham (1955) created this model to demonstrate that, for public knowledge to increase in a relationship, blind spots and secrets must decrease. This can only happen if you reveal some of your secrets and others let you know about your blind spots. This process is essentially achieved by giving and receiving feedback. The more feedback received, the smaller the blind spot. The more self-awareness, the smaller the hidden self.

Figure 2.1. The Johari Window

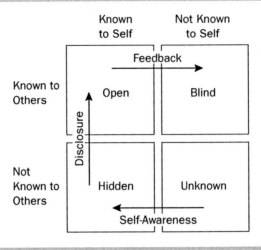

From J. Luft and H. Ingham, *The Johari Window: A Graphic Model of Interpersonal Awareness.* Proceedings of Western Training Laboratory in Group Development, Los Angeles, 1955.

Keep a Journal. It's a myth that people learn from experience. People learn from the *analysis of the experience.* Without sufficient analysis, seemingly intelligent individuals (both consultants and clients) will repeat unintelligent experiences. If you don't build into your personal development time deliberate opportunities to reflect on how you are practicing your craft, it simply won't happen. Keeping a journal of your client relationships that documents the ebbs and flows, highs and lows, challenges and successes will enable you to detect patterns in relationships that might not otherwise be visible when just looking at discrete interactions. Consider regularly jotting down your thoughts to capture reflections such as the following:

- Things I'm glad I said that made an impact
- Things I wish I'd said or I'd said differently
- Things my client said that felt helpful
- Things my client said, or didn't say, that felt awkward or uncomfortable
- Disagreements or conflicts that were challenging to resolve
- Characteristics about my client I found helpful or energizing
- Characteristics about my client I found unhelpful or troublesome

The idea of keeping a journal might sound cumbersome, but we repeatedly hear consultants talk about how powerful it is to look back on the history of their client relationships and uncover insights embedded in patterns and trends that would otherwise have gone unnoticed and, therefore, unleveraged. Keep a small notebook in your briefcase and use plane time, train time, small pockets of in between meetings time to jot down some reflections and thoughts. Once it becomes a habit, this simple practice can be a powerful tool. The following grid (see Exhibit 2.1) can also be used to organize your perceptions and look for patterns (for example, agreement, blind spots, and so on).

Exhibit 2.1. Sample Perceptual Grid

	Self	Client
Actions Taken		
Positive impact		
Negative impact		
Things Said		
Positive impact		
Negative impact		

Be a Fly on Your Own Wall. Often, the intensity of our client interactions forces us to focus so sharply in the moment that we miss the moments as they pass by. This is frequently compounded by the complexity of our own lives. While we are focusing on the client, we are trying to force out distractions like the overdue expense report, the kid's little league game to get to this afternoon, the memo you promised your other client by 2:00, the need to get the oil changed on the car, and so on. Consequently we find we have little mental capacity left to observe the moments while being in them.

Build your mind's capability to "watch the movie" while being in it by asking yourself, "If I were a fly on the wall watching this interaction happening, what would I be noticing and concluding?" What you'll find is that your mind is in fact noticing a lot more than you might think. Listen to that little voice in your head as it whispers: "He's furrowing his eyebrows; he obviously isn't getting what I'm telling him." Or, "I'm taking this a little fast; he's still looking back a few pages in the document to figure out what I meant." Or, "She's smiling at that point; it really hit home." Making such observations to yourself is what it takes to start being a good fly on your own wall. The next step is to determine whether your interpretations are accurate.

To determine that, you should ask questions such as:

- Is the conversation unfolding as I would have hoped?

- Is the client hearing and understanding my thoughts as I express myself?

- What questions or concerns does the client have at this point that he or she may not be voicing?

- How is the client reacting to me? Am I engaging her enough? Is she becoming defensive or getting lost? Does she seem to be connecting to my ideas? How do I know?

- What are my words and countenance signaling to the client? Does she seem at ease? Anxious? Alert? What impact did I intend to have?

- What is the client saying that tells me to what degree I am having the effect I intend? What surprises me about what the client is, or is not, saying?

As you master the ability to collect, interpret, and act on data *about the movie* while at the same time *being in the movie,* your ability to gain emotional access to your clients will rise significantly. The insight you can bring to bear about yourself, your clients, and your relationships will draw them to you because they will conclude that it is safe to be vulnerable with you. Clients are more likely to risk disclosing their thoughts, feelings, and shortfalls with someone who has demonstrated an insightful understanding of them and how they interact, as well as with someone who pays attention to the impact he or she has on others.

Keep Your Own Emotional Needs in Check. As we discussed earlier, relationships are emotional experiences. The closeness we experience with our clients can often be very gratifying, and that is as it should be. Problems appear when we move from being gratified in that closeness *with* our clients to being gratified in that closeness *at the expense of* our clients. Imposing our emotional needs onto a client relationship is a dangerously alluring trap that must be avoided. Specifically, there are three emotional needs that consultants must keep in check to maintain a healthy balance in client relationships.

- *The need for approval.* Desiring the approval of others and enjoying attention are natural human motives, but as consultants they can get pushed to an extreme. A consultant's success resides largely in her ideas and opinions. This can create an inextricable connection in her mind between those ideas and opinions and her sense of self. Given that a consultant's every word or action is judged and evaluated and that her ideas are always assailable, her ego is continually open to potential assault. Differences of opinion or opposition to her ideas can become a threat to her sense of self. When this happens, the consultant reacts to protect herself. Suddenly her contained need for respect and approval can run amuck, and she can begin to seek her client's approval to excess. Looking for reinforcement and recognition, she may inappropriately draw attention to her work, subtly remind her client of which ideas she's offered that have worked well, or directly ask her client for "feedback" when she is really looking for reinforcement.

- *The need for power.* Being influential—and seeing the fruit of that influence— is one of the most satisfying parts of consulting. Knowing that you have helped shape the direction of an organization, influencing the work and lives of potentially thousands, even tens of thousands of people, can be exhilarating. But when our need to be influential, to be the one to make things happen, is over-indulged, we may start looking for opportunities to be movers and shakers in ways that can cripple our clients' organizations.

  While the ultimate goal should always be to conclude the consulting relationship once the client is able to solve problems on his own, it can be a source of comfort to both the client and consultant to prolong the relationship indefinitely. The consultant's contribution to perpetuating this relationship is frequently rooted in the need for continued power and influence. When his or her natural desire for influence swells to a need to be indispensable to others, a consultant has forfeited the opportunity to help create fundamental change because he or she has obstructed the client's opportunity to become self-sufficient. This consultant operates under the assumption that, the stronger and more capable the client becomes, the less useful and important he or she becomes. To avoid such a state, the consultant indulges his or her need for power by prolonging the relationship beyond what is really useful.

- *The need for inclusion.* As outsiders to a client organization (whether as an internal or external consultant, we still need to remain outsiders), keeping a healthy distance enables us to offer objective perspectives that true insiders often cannot. But one of the down sides to this role is sometimes a sense of isolation, of not being one of the gang. True, the goal is to become close with our clients, but not so close that we can't be distinguished as an outsider playing a unique role. Being included by others, often a signal of their acceptance, is something each of us naturally desires. And it's natural to conclude that the most logical way to gain such inclusion is to ensure we never do anything that angers, hurts, or disappoints those from whom we are seeking it—in this case our clients. This belief is only a step away from thinking that doing or saying anything that would anger, hurt, or disappoint a client forever risks our inclusion, that is, their acceptance. Although this is a false belief, many consultants are ensnared by it. The need to gain inclusion by keeping peace, harmony, and agreement drives many consultants to avoid the very conversations and actions their clients need to achieve lasting change. These consultants deceive themselves into thinking that "keeping a positive attitude" will help things work out for the best, and that it is better than adding distress and discomfort to an already troubled organization. These consultants are chameleons, adapting their opinions and perspectives to the situation at hand and gratifying an overextended need for inclusion. Their unmet needs have clouded their judgment and eliminated the possibility of helping drive change by doing what they were hired for—to offer a point of view that *did not* already exist.

By effectively monitoring these important needs, for approval, power, and inclusion, we can ensure that our relationships remain mutually gratifying for both ourselves and our clients. The key, of course, is being aware enough to know when and how these needs arise. We each experience these needs differently. Accordingly, we have to pay attention to our own emotional patterns in order to know when these needs are in check, and to recognize when we are feeling tempted to impose them on our clients in an unhealthy way.

Modeling

The ability to model behaviors you expect your client to demonstrate is an important part of any change consultant's repertoire (Bryant, 1995; Fox, 1988; Hultman, 1986; Mayer, 1987; Pescuric, 1996; Werner, 1994). Change often requires that people engage in new behaviors. However, expecting them to do this without a model is like expecting someone to locate a city in a foreign country without a map. Yes, there's a chance that, by stumbling around long enough, a person might have success; but it's not an efficient or fun way to learn.

The most important behavior for consultants to model as they build emotional closeness with clients is *openness.* For example, Rich modeled openness by sharing his reactions to the CEO's behavior. He told the CEO how his behavior made him feel and shared the impact he felt it was having on the senior team. By modeling openness, an implicit contract was created between Rich and the CEO that called for reciprocal behavior on the part of the client. In this case, the CEO admitted that he was aware of his tendency to ramble on in meetings and sometimes even enjoyed doing so. Once the foundation for openness is laid, it becomes easier to discuss difficult emotional issues associated with change.

As in this example, the consultant usually leads the way toward greater emotional closeness through modeling. In many corporations, there is a macho climate among senior leaders, who are hesitant to form close relationships with one another or with outsiders. Modeling on the part of the consultant demonstrates the consultant's willingness to take the first step. By taking a risk to be honest, the consultant challenges an existing norm, which is to leave emotions outside the boardroom. History is rich with examples of emotional needs compelling decisions that bring unfortunate consequences. President Kennedy's abortive attempt to invade Cuba was motivated more by a deep psychological need to stand up to the Communists than by a real likelihood of success. NASA's decision to launch the space shuttle Challenger despite warnings of a possible explosion was likewise influenced by the space agency's emotional desire to demonstrate how regular and routine shuttle flights were—delay was not an option.

Although corporations usually do not make life-and-death decisions, emotions certainly play a prominent role in everything from acquisitions to product launches to succession. Denying that such emotions exist is seldom the most productive way to manage them, especially when major changes are underway.

Self-aware consultants who can model behaviors such as openness help decision makers recognize the full impact of the decisions they are contemplating.

Here are some ways to consider modeling:

Self-Disclose. By deliberately disclosing to your client how you feel at any moment in the engagement, in the simplest sense, you give the person permission to do the same. As we discussed earlier, talking about one's feelings in the business community has been rendered taboo. While the goal isn't to hold a group therapy session with your client, the fact is that emotions play a key role in the context of any important relationship. Move beyond the stigma of being soft to help your client see the strength in disclosing how you are feeling and see how influential this disclosure can be. As the client learns to disclose, he will learn to do so in the context of his leadership role as well. Be vulnerable and let your client know when:

- An option she is considering for a major decision makes you feel uneasy;
- A recurring behavior frustrates you;
- Reaching a major milestone on a project makes you feel proud; or
- You are anxious about his lack of attention to a specific issue.

By openly displaying your feelings, you demonstrate to your clients the importance of building trust through genuineness and risk taking. You then help pave the way for them to do the same.

Ask Clients to Share Their Insights About You. The client relationship is predicated on the notion that the consultant is the one to influence the client. One of the most dignifying and trust-building experiences you can introduce to your client relationships is letting *the client* influence *you.* Demonstrate your willingness to subject yourself to the insights of your client by asking her to share her thoughts, observations, and feelings about working with you. This is more than just asking for feedback about the caliber of your work, as we discussed earlier; this is asking the person to talk about what his experience has been in the context of the relationship with you. As you let clients' insights and observations shape your behavior, clients' sense of dignity in the relationship is enhanced. You are conveying to them that they are important enough to you for you to want to know what they think and feel. As a result, the level of influence you bring to bear can shift from a transaction for which they pay you to an esteemed and mutual component of your relationship. The respect you show in opening yourself constructively to clients' comments and criticism is likely to return to you in the form of greater willingness on their part to be influenced by you. Ask your clients questions such as:

- In our relationship, what do you find most helpful? Most enjoyable?
- Are there aspects of our relationship you wish were different?
- Are there things about the ways I attempt to influence you that you find unhelpful?
- Do you feel good about how we spend our time together?
- I'm struggling with a particular problem in one of my engagements, and I'd really value your perspective on it. [Keep the specific context anonymous.] What suggestions do you have about. . . ?

In the context of these types of conversations, your client will learn more about your character, your values, and your humanness than he would otherwise. You will model the type of humility necessary for fundamental change to take place and demonstrate the inherent potential for greater credibility and influence in such behavior.

Mirror Required Behavior for Your Clients. There will inevitably be times throughout the engagement that will demand new behavior from your client in the service of change. At first, such new behavior will be difficult for your clients to produce, and they will likely revert to tried and true behaviors that might be unproductive for the circumstances. At this point, it can be helpful for the consultant to model the behavior the client needs to show, but for some reason, cannot display. Here are some examples:

- When your client is avoiding a tough issue, model *assertiveness* and *productive confrontation* to ensure that important problems are surfaced and owned by the right people.
- When your client is reacting to setbacks with harsh judgments and ranting, model *dialogue* and *open-ended questions* to learn more about the issue at hand. The key is to draw out information the client will need to help get things back on track.
- When your client is being indecisive, model *thoughtful consideration of options and consequences* to help get momentum going and to engage the client in the process of taking action.

Emotional Intelligence

Emotional intelligence, a concept made popular by Daniel Goleman (1995) in his book of the same title, includes two sets of competencies. On one hand, there are competencies that determine *how we manage ourselves.* These include self-awareness, as we described earlier in this chapter, as well as self-regulation: being able to manage our thoughts and feelings, keeping disruptive emotions and impulses in check; maintaining standards of honesty and integrity; taking responsibility for personal performance; showing flexibility in handling change; and being comfortable with novel ideas, approaches, and new information. A strong motivation helps guide and facilitate reaching our goals. Individuals with strong motivation strive to improve or meet their standards of excellence; align with the goals of the group or organization; and show readiness to act on opportunities and be persistent in pursuing goals in the face of adversity.

On the other hand, we have competencies that determine *how we handle relationships.* These include our ability to experience *empathy*—our awareness of others' feelings, needs, and concerns. Empathy naturally builds on self-awareness and self-regulation. Understanding our own emotions is essential to understanding the feelings of others. The lack of empathy has been identified as a serious threat to achieving high performance, and it is often the culprit in mishaps and problems in consulting relationships. To make matters worse, empathy as a skill is often poorly understood by those who need it the most. For example, there is a common belief that empathy is like a talent: You either have it or you don't. In consequence, many are left blind to opportunities for developing their empathy. These individuals use only their reasoning skills to make sense out of the world, and they wonder why everyone can't see things their way.

"Empathy" is defined as "the identification with and understanding of another's situation, feelings, and motives." It is also often described as the ability to see things from the other person's point of view. Goleman (1997) defines it as the "ability to read other people." All these definitions imply more than a cognitive understanding. Empathy implies that you can connect the feelings you are witnessing to your own experiences. You share and identify with emotional states. Empathic skills are those that involve paying attention to people: listening and attending to needs and wants of others in the context of building relationships. Far from being marginalized as "touchy-feely," it's a critical skill for consultants to have and nurture in order to interact well with their clients and deliver on their value propositions. The need for empathy is strongly felt in situations in which the message to be delivered is sensitive and likely to trigger a heavy load of emotions from a client. Such situations include offering criticism to a CEO, who predictably will become defensive, or forcing the conflict-avoidant executive team to deal with one of its member's disruptive behavior. The first step in dealing with any negativity is to empathize. The next step is to focus back on the goals and the tasks at hand. Empathy naturally involves genuine curiosity and a desire to know and understand others. There is a sincere interest in what the person is saying and feeling. Empathy starts with comments such as the following:

- "Can you say more about that?"

- "I wasn't aware of that. Tell me more."

- "Let me see whether I understand you correctly. Here is what I hear you saying. . . ."

- "How do you feel about that? What are some of your concerns?"

Several benefits are associated with empathy. A review of the literature indicates that these benefits include conflict resolution (Tjosvold & Johnson, 1977), facilitated communication (Flavell, 1974), increased problem solving (Falk & Johnson, 1977), and cooperation (Johnson, 1975a, 1975b). In his examination of empathy in a managerial context, Ken Fracaro (2001) proposes the following list of benefits[*]:

- Win people's trust
- Increase knowledge
- Reduce friction between people
- Increase productivity
- Enhance quality
- Increase positive work relations
- Inspire commitment
- Broaden understanding
- Develop insight
- Resolve problems

---

[*]Reprinted by permission of © National Research Bureau, P.O. Box 1, Burlington, Iowa 52601-0001.

It can be argued that these benefits can all be linked to a common cognitive process of seeking to understand others' perspectives, which increases the likelihood for one to make accurate inferences about others' perspectives (Dymond, 1949, 1950; Ickes, 1997). In return, one's empathy toward others—through seeking to understand their perspectives—enhances one's ability to evaluate one's own performance accurately (Matsui, 2000). Other research on empathy (Vetlesen, 1994) suggests that the emotional intensity and proximity of the relationship between two people will be related negatively to the likelihood of unethical behavior—a critical issue for consultants who, through their work with top leadership, have access to extremely sensitive and competitive information about their clients' organizations. Vetlesen (1994) argues that, as a "deeply rooted human faculty," empathy offers a "trigger" into the field of ethics, establishing whether a person perceives that he or she is facing an ethical situation—a situation in which the other person might be harmed.

How we handle relationships also depends on a set of social skills aimed at causing the responses we desire from others. Such social skills include persuasion; communication skills; negotiation skills; inspiring and guiding individuals and groups into new activities; collaborating; and nurturing relationships. Recent studies by various practitioners and theorists, including Boyatzis, Goleman, and Rhee (2000), indicate that emotional intelligence does indeed exist and, like other managerial competencies, can be developed. This is good news; people who feel that they are "emotionally challenged" can take heart in knowing that becoming more sensitive to others' emotions is a skill that can be learned.

Change consultants need to have well-developed emotional intelligence to be able to tune in to issues that are potential threats to success. While it's true that some people seem to have more emotional intelligence than others, we've noticed that most good change consultants have been able to develop emotional intelligence. A lack of emotional intelligence is often apparent among new consultants. Overwhelmed by their own anxieties, less experienced consultants tend to fall back on tools, techniques, and gimmicks, expecting them to cause a breakthrough in the level of their clients' awareness or effectiveness.

More experienced consultants learn to trust their gut—to tune in to their inner feelings and use them to sense what is happening. They also learn to read the subtle verbal and nonverbal cues that indicate clients' emotional state. Some consultants refer to the competency of emotional intelligence as their truth meter, meaning that they can detect when clients express one emotion verbally but are actually feeling another. When asked how they feel about the decision to communicate a significant change to their employees, a client might say, "I feel fine," while nervously twisting a pencil. An emotionally intelligent consultant knows how to probe the client to get at the source of the anxiety. The consultant might say, in this instance, "Perhaps we should explore this a bit more. What could go wrong if we communicate this message now?" This would allow the client to express concerns without it appearing that he didn't support the need to communicate.

A consultant's inability to apply emotional intelligence renders him or her relationally challenged. *Using* emotional intelligence as a means of building gratifying relationships is where its fundamental value lies. It is an important part of a consultant's overall rQ.

Ability to Set and Keep Boundaries

We have examined how self-awareness, modeling, and emotional intelligence contribute to the trust element of rQ. At the same time, it is important to note that change consultants should not try to be their clients' personal therapists. It's easy to cross the line from helping clients deal with the emotions they feel as they go through major organizational changes to helping them deal with personal problems. Often, because they do not experience a great deal of emotional support from others, clients find the support offered by their consultants satisfying. Once consultants have established emotional closeness with their clients, it's not uncommon for clients to seek support on personal issues that are related to their careers—or even their families.

Many change consultants fall into the trap of responding to such requests in the hope of expanding the scope of the relationship. This changes the focus of the relationship from helping the organization to helping the person—a subtle but important distinction.

When we work with leaders on style issues, as Rich did with the CEO, we do so because we believe they are detracting from a client's ability to lead others through the change process. While improving the skills that will help the organization might also improve relationships in other parts of clients' lives, that is not our primary concern. If we become therapists instead of change agents, two things happen: First, we take our eyes off the change process we are there to facilitate, and, second, we step into potentially dangerous territory that we are not qualified to handle. Even if we are qualified through education and/or past experiences, it is not part of our current engagement and role with the client.

If we attempt to help clients with their personal problems, the nature of our relationships with them change. While we may feel closer to them and even enjoy the dependency we are creating, providing personal therapy is not what we are there to do. It's important that we, as change agents, set and maintain boundaries with our clients regarding our roles. When it comes to helping our clients work through the emotions they are experiencing in connection with organization change, we have all the time in the world. But when it comes to their personal lives, it's time to recommend that they speak to another professional. Caryn Kaftal, one of our colleagues, puts it this way: "There is a fine line between a relationship that is helpful and one that is too close. When the client is so comfortable that he shares overly intimate information, it is essential to decide thoughtfully what information to reciprocate with, without revealing things that 'upset the balance' of the relationship or risk compromising your influence, and therefore your effectiveness in your relationship with the client."

It is also important that we set limits on the way our clients use our services. Some clients want to avoid the emotional discomfort of taking risks, communicating unpopular news, or resolving conflict with a colleague. These clients may ask us to do their dirty work for them. Instead of owning the change process, the client may refer to it as "Rich's program." Clients may ask the consultant to communicate the need for change to employees on the grounds that the consultant understands the initiative that is going to be implemented. Or they may ask the consultant to have a conversation with a colleague who just doesn't seem to see things in the right way.

All of these requests should be rejected, because they transfer emotional ownership of the change from the client to the consultant. Inexperienced consultants fear that, if they deny these requests, the client will fire them. More experienced consultants recognize these requests as opportunities to educate their clients about their role in leading change at both a personal and organizational level. If the consultant accepts emotional responsibility for the change, the change will last only as long as the consultant is present. Permanent change requires emotional ownership by the client.

Some important aspects of boundary setting include the following:

Build Clear Boundary Settings into Your Agreement. It can be helpful in planning your work with the client to establish certain boundaries from the beginning. Talk openly with your client about where you are flexible in the relationship and in the context of the work and where you set limits, what the limits of your services and capabilities are, and any requirements or preferences you have in terms of work style, decision making, information sharing, and so forth. Of course, it's equally important for clients to share their views on the same issues and to build mutual agreement and understanding on specific boundaries. You should also agree that, as the relationship unfolds, you will continue to do "border patrol" tours of the agreed-on boundaries to ensure they are being respected.

Nip Boundary Violations in the Bud. Don't give in to the temptation to ignore early warning signals of boundary infringements. While you certainly shouldn't come across as an inflexible fanatic looking to play gotcha at every possible turn, it is important to ensure that agreements are kept. Boundaries should have some degree of elasticity to them, or they will become rigid rules and you will become a rule monitor and erode trust. But when your internal barometer suggests discomfort with emerging boundary conditions, you can actually enhance trust by caring enough about the relationship to raise the concern and, if necessary, renegotiate the agreement.

We'd like to conclude our discussion of getting close to build trust by looking at how these capabilities can enable our clients to make change happen and the tools we need to help facilitate this.

▶ Change Enablement
How Getting Close Builds the Necessary Trust for Clients to Explore Personal and Organizational Shortcomings

Let's see how getting close to a client can build the necessary trust for that client to explore personal and organizational shortcomings. As we discussed earlier, change happens in organizations when leaders decide to make it happen. Starting programs, launching campaigns, reorganizing departments, or swapping one manager for another are not methods that will necessarily work. Remember, we said that for change to stick, it must be approached systemically. So it is vital that leaders come to grips with issues, both within their organizations and in their leadership. Without the acknowledgement of the fundamental need for change, it's likely that efforts to make things better will fall short, and even robust initiatives will have little staying power.

Once leaders have established trust with their consultants, they are more willing to shine the spotlight on the personal and organizational issues they have worked long and hard to obscure. Most leaders avoid taking such risks. In environments often characterized by self-protection and dog-eat-dog competition for coveted spots on the career ladder, openly exploring shortcomings may seem like career suicide. But as leaders come to realize the power in facing organizational and personal issues head on and they note the visible improvements to performance that ensue, their ability to trust more, and face more, also increases. For some, such trust takes a great deal of time and patience to build. For others, it may come relatively quickly. It is imperative that consultants stay the course in building such trust. They must establish the necessary degree of emotional closeness required for each client to step up to the challenge of taking on organizational and personal shortcomings that hinder the progress of change. ◄

A summary of how to build trust by getting close is shown in Table 2.1.

Table 2.1. Summary of How to Build Trust by Getting Close

Practices	Behaviors	Self-Assessment
Self-Awareness	Calibrate by asking	I can detect in others the signs of emotional discomfort
	Keep a journal	
	Be a fly on your own wall	I have confidence in my own work capabilities
	Keep your own emotional needs in check	I verbalize my emotions to my clients
Modeling	Self-disclose	I am able to model the behaviors I expect my clients to demonstrate
	Ask clients to share their insights about you	I keep my emotions and behavior in check
	Mirror required behavior for your clients	I take responsibility for shortcomings in my performance
		I demonstrate flexibility in handling change
		I welcome new ideas and methods that can move the work forward

Table 2.1. Summary of How to Build Trust by Getting Close, Cont'd

Practices	Behaviors	Self-Assessment
Emotional Intelligence	Know and manage yourself to facilitate reaching your goals	My inner feelings help me to sense what my clients are experiencing
	Demonstrate empathy by being aware of others' feelings, needs, and concerns	I read my clients' emotions through their verbal and nonverbal cues
		I am able to detect discrepancies between my clients' felt and expressed emotions
	Demonstrate social skills to induce desirable responses in others	I look for the causes of my clients' anxieties
Ability to Set and Keep Boundaries	Build clear boundary setting into your agreement	I remind my clients of their responsibilities when they make out-of-role requests of me
	Nip boundary violations in the bud	

③

Skin in the Game: Personal Investment

THE FACT THAT CLIENTS ARE WILLING to pay for our services is a sure sign that they are, in some way, invested in the work we are doing. It's important that we make an investment too. Change consulting is more than a simple business transaction. While true that, at its very core, consulting is an exchange of expertise for money, it does matter *how* the expertise is delivered. If clients were only after our expertise and if saving money were all they cared about, they would read a few books on change and go it alone. Most clients want more than that. They want to work with a consultant who will take the time to get to know their situation, help them develop an approach that fits their unique needs, and be there when the going gets tough. Clients are looking for a consultant who makes their success a matter of priority and personal concern. In the simplest terms, clients are looking for a consultant who cares.

Change consulting requires a different level of personal investment than technical consulting. Clients may not need to know that a consultant on economic trends cares about them or their organization; they just need the economic knowledge the consultant brings. The same might apply to patent attorneys, auditors, and a host of other experts organizations engage from time to time. Expert consultants are almost like encyclopedias; clients consult them for information, close the cover, and walk away. There is very little emotional attachment between the client and the consultant.

Change consulting is different because there are no answers to look up in a book and then apply. Organizational changes are crafted one by one and evolve over time. They are custom-made; they can't be bought off the rack, and one size definitely does not fit all. Moreover, major change evokes strong emotional reactions in most clients. During a significant change effort, it's not uncommon for clients to be criticized by others, develop self-doubt, or become angry with a consultant as difficulties emerge. Change involves personal transitions, as William Bridges (1991) points out. Emotionally, these transitions are not unlike those accompanying experiences of personal loss; feelings of denial, anger, and mourning frequently appear before the client is ready to implement change. Change consultants need to understand these emotions and make the personal investment required to support their clients through the emotional aspects of change.

They need to make sure that they have "skin in the game"—that they put themselves at some personal risk as a way to demonstrate their commitment. Beyond mere words of assurance that you care about what you are doing, putting skin in the game means that you have something to lose if things don't go well. This is the key to the personal investment element of rQ.

Consultants who excel in change work take the time to get to know their clients and the organization. Change consultants don't apply cookbook methods without diagnosing the client's needs and readiness for change. They don't recommend interventions that exceed the capacity of people in the organization to implement, and they don't wash their hands of problems at the first sign of trouble. Good change consultants inspire their clients to undertake the demanding and sometimes risky journey toward improvement by demonstrating their own faith and commitment. The most successful change consultants clearly project that they have confidence in the client's ability to succeed and that they are personally committed to the client's success.

Let's explore how some successful consultants demonstrate their personal investment to their clients.

Listen to Mindy Millward as she describes her approach to working with one of her clients:

"The client was a VP and general manager charged with integrating the after-market businesses of four business units. Effectively, this meant creating a 1,300-person organization where none had previously existed. The business unit heads perceived this change as a reduction in their power and span of control and did not support it. The business units were trying to keep the good profitable pieces and smart capable workers in their respective spheres while 'dumping' the pieces they didn't want into the client's unit.

"The client was extremely smart and experienced. Although he could probably figure out the organizational design issues by himself, he knew he needed buy-in across the four business units. His personal style was often challenging and confrontational. Given the resistance to the change, this could have been a big problem.

"I started out by taking time to gain knowledge of the business. This included doing diagnostic work up-front to speak knowledgeably about the core processes and the market. I understood where he was coming from—I learned his career aspirations and continued to use that to advise/counsel him. We spent a lot of time together in large design sessions, in smaller 'kitchen cabinet meetings' with his direct reports, and one-on-one. In those sessions I often pushed him to rethink how he was approaching powerful individuals in the organization. I leveraged my knowledge of his personal career goals and referenced his strengths as a way of getting him to appreciate a different point of view and take the time to consider the implications for his actions.

"As our relationship continued, I called him on inappropriate behavior, behavior that had actually gotten him to a senior leadership position in the organization but was no longer working in a scenario in which he had to influence rather than mandate. He needed to trust me enough to hear feedback on his style, which had to be changed in order for him to be effective. He also had to know I was a peer to him in terms of being able to understand the business model and whether the organization design would work.

"I pushed him hard on several issues in our one-on-one sessions but also facilitated many discussions between him and the business unit presidents. I tried to keep the conversations focused on the process and put things on the table, even when he yelled in frustration at me or others. I showed him that the way he handled this would directly influence his ability to move into his next role. He knew how to get to an end result, but relied on me to bring change management expertise—particularly in terms of developing the buy-in he needed from the business unit presidents.

"Working so closely with a smart, tough, demanding leader like that is exhausting. There was a period of two months where I was with him almost every day. He expected me to commit myself fully—at the expense of other priorities. I had to get better at not personalizing things and finding a way to bring up tough issues repeatedly. At times we agreed to disagree until outcomes supported one of our views. I had to work to understand that the business unit presidents initially saw me as someone working for him, not working for the best solution. I had to push him in the room for them to see I was unbiased.

"I stood my ground instead of telling him what he wanted to hear. He trusted me enough to share data with me that he hadn't shared with others, and I maintained his trust by sharing it with no one. He came to rely on my opinion for things other than the organizational design work. He would send me e-mails and memos before he sent them to others so I could review the tone and message and provide feedback.

"In the end, the organizational design work was accepted, and a 1,300-person business was created. Profit margins and sales grew dramatically during his tenure. He ran the business for twelve months and then was promoted to business unit president. He built a leadership team of people from the various businesses who didn't trust him at the onset into a team of high potential leaders who would work for him anywhere."

What dimensions of the personal investment element of rQ did Mindy demonstrate? First, she proved she had skin in the game, that is, that she would invest time and energy and take personal risks to help her client succeed. She worked hard, stepped into tough situations without hesitation, and made herself available for advice whenever it was needed.

Mindy showed real passion for her work and for her client's success. She got to know the organization and her client. She was able to learn things about her client that she could use to help him succeed. When things got rough, Mindy was able to remind him of his career aspirations and point out that how he handled the challenges would have a lot to do with how he was perceived by others. She helped him understand that his style was effective for some things but not effective for others. In short, she helped her client develop and grow.

Mindy remained committed even when the client's anger became directed at her. At one point, she recalls persevering "even when he yelled in frustration at me or others." Good change consultants don't quit at the first sign of displaced anger. They remain personally invested because they recognize that change is frustrating and that strong emotions often are misdirected.

Clients can't afford to alienate powerful people they are angry with, so instead they take out their feelings on people near them and those whom they trust. While never pleasant, this part of the work is an important test of commitment. By remaining engaged, Mindy demonstrated to her client that he could be open about what he was feeling and even behave inappropriately without losing her support. She gave him constructive feedback that no one else dared give, indicating that she was willing to take the risk of offending him in order to help him succeed.

Clients like to know that, if they are taking risks, their consultants are too. The trust that develops from mutual investment in a relationship enables work to continue when it would actually be easier to quit and walk away. Consultants who fail to make personal investments in their work find that their clients fail to invest as well. The result can be aborted efforts, short-term engagements, or a shift in focus from the most important changes to ones that involve less risk. Consultants who lament that their clients have no appetite for making real changes in how their organizations work need to ask themselves whether they have made the personal investment required to prepare their clients for change.

In the example above, Mindy had to spend almost every day with her client for a period of months. The investment required to move clients from a place where they fear change—or see no way to get through it—to a place where they can confidently lead change is often underestimated. New change consultants mistakenly assume that their clients should automatically respect their expertise. Even the most experienced consultants find that clients are wary of accepting advice at first. Being experienced or having content expertise is only a part of what clients are looking for in a change consultant. Clients also want someone who will take the time to get to know them personally, understand the dynamics of their situation, and demonstrate a real understanding of everything the client is facing before recommending a course of action. Consultants who quickly size up the situation, or who reflexively compare it to one that was similar and recommend the same course of action without real analysis, may *think* they are demonstrating their expertise. In fact, by using a cookie-cutter approach, they are demonstrating a low level of personal investment. True, being able to spot patterns from past experiences that are relevant to a current situation is critical. However, it must be done in a way that pays respect to the uniqueness of every challenge. Even if the consultant's advice is correct, clients will resist being treated like a cash register. The fact that Client A lived through the experience of change does little to dispel the personal doubts of Client B.

Clients need to know that their consultants understand their strengths and weaknesses, the politics of the situation, the history of the clients' relationships with peers, the dynamics of the market, what happened to the last person who tried to change things, and much more. They need to know that their consultants accept them, warts and all, and are committed to helping them succeed. Clients want to see signs that whether they succeed or fail matters to their consultants at a personal level. In short, clients want to feel that they and their consultants are in the thing together.

Good consultants make personal investments in helping their clients succeed, but they also know not to do their clients' work for them. At the end of the day, clients want to feel that *they* have succeeded, not that they needed someone else to do their jobs for them. Part of the personal investment good change consultants make is to help their clients learn about themselves and to teach them how to lead changes successfully.

In the example above, Mindy didn't go to meetings *for* her client; she went *with* her client. While she may have been able to avoid some of the yelling and screaming between her client and his peers by acting as his emissary, she knew that he wouldn't learn how to influence his peers unless he was forced to do it himself.

Consultants who do their clients' work for them believe they are helping their clients when, in fact, they are undermining the clients' development and long-term success. Clients may appreciate and even become dependent on consultants who do the difficult work for them. In the short run, consultants who form dependent relationships with their clients may benefit psychologically by feeling needed. In the long run, however, both lose. Clients don't grow in their own abilities to manage change, and consultants become viewed by clients as subordinates rather than as strategic partners. In this case, the consultant may be busy but not recognize that he is missing one of the key dimensions of a successful relationship. There is a level of personal investment the consultant must make, not only to the outcome of the engagement but also to the success of the client. It takes a level of personal commitment and caring to want to have the client succeed.

Our colleague Kathy Morris has a perspective on this level of commitment, seen from the vantage point of twenty-seven years of both internal and external consulting. Kathy has developed the ability to demonstrate the personal investment she makes to her clients. Listen to how Kathy's personal investment in the success of her client allowed him to become more confident, thereby substantially changing the outcome of a tricky situation.

"What my clients have in common is that, in the context of doing the work together, they come to view me as someone who is on their side and open to talking about things beyond the work itself. Typically, the issues have to do with their ability to influence their organization directly as an executive or a life/career issue that surfaces in the context of doing the work.

"In one case, a chief staff officer (CSO) with whom I had built a solid, close relationship over ten years viewed a change in the decision-making structure of the organization as a signal that he should take a lesser position and/or leave the company. His view developed as a result of a few unfortunate events before a change in leadership. These events led his newly appointed boss to feel that he wasn't well-served by the CSO's actions and couldn't trust his judgment.

"At issue was that my client, the CSO, felt he was acting ethically by being in conformance with what the new boss, former boss, and he had agreed to. His role, as he understood it, was not to go directly to the new boss with information but to let the old leader carry the message. The new boss felt betrayed, since he and the CSO had worked very closely together over the years. In his mind, the CSO should have come to him directly. My challenge was to help the CSO work through his own feelings about what had happened, the impact of his non-action, the outcome of distrust that was created, and how best to respond to the situation. To me, his taking a demotion or his leaving the company was not the right outcome.

"I got the CSO to describe the whole sequence of events without judging or offering my views. I empathized with the dilemma as he described it and his rock-solid belief that he had done what he needed to do. He had both followed what he thought was the agreed-to plan of action and then—when it became clear that the new leader didn't trust him—was willing to serve in a lesser role or leave the company.

"I then counseled him on what to say to the new boss to begin the rapprochement process. For a few tense weeks, it wasn't clear whether the new boss would forgive him. My client expressed his sincere apologies and hopes that they could rebuild their relationship, but the CSO also told the new boss that he would understand if the new boss concluded that it wasn't possible. The CSO was prepared to live with the consequences. I also listened a great deal because I could see that this situation had triggered very deeply held values in him. He couldn't be told to see it differently; if things were to change, he would have to make the shift inside himself, by himself. So I waited and looked for the moment when I could intervene.

"The hardest part for me is to determine when to support and when to confront. I typically do more of the former and less of the latter. Part of what helped build the relationship was that he knew he could count on me. In fact, he sent numerous personal notes to me over the years about the uniqueness of our relationship and how valuable a colleague I had been. It's not that I wouldn't push him on things, but I hadn't actually taken him on about something he personally felt so very strong about. I did feel strongly myself that the worst thing he could do in terms of the interests of the company was to leave. Equally bad would be to stay and take a lesser role. I didn't know when or how I would tell him this, but I knew that I needed to.

"The moment did come, and instinctively I acted. I can still hear myself painting a vision of the role he needed to play, why he should stay put, what the organization had historically left on the table or outsourced to consultants in the realm of effective change management, and that the new leader would need this more than ever given the challenges the organization would be facing. The CSO was the only person in the organization sufficiently skilled in change management to fulfill this role. The message got through, and he asked me to write up a white paper that he could use to describe his role in this new decision-making structure.

"Eventually, he did stay and did actually take a lesser role for six months, but not because of this situation. Today he is the senior person and trusted advisor to the new boss.

"What did I do to warrant this influence? I was present and available, demonstrated competence, met every commitment, exceeded expectations, was client-focused, invited personal connection, exhibited warmth and high positive regard, and created a no-surprises environment in terms of client deliverables. I knew he trusted me because he let me know the blow-by-blow set of events as they were unfolding and let me see the pain he was experiencing."

In her account of this episode, Kathy hardly mentions the content of the change work happening in the company. To gain the kind of respect that she does with clients, it goes without saying that she manages the "content" side of her work with expertise and professionalism. The products and deliverables that some consultants view as their primary point of connection with their clients are important, but fade into the background when emotional issues becomes focal. Without creating this deeper connection, Kathy may not have been aware that her client was struggling with whether or not to stay in his job. Imagine the disconnect that would have occurred had Kathy tried to engage her client's attention at this point with a PowerPoint deck about the change effort taking place. The client might have nodded politely, endorsed the next steps in the change process, and then announced his resignation.

By working at multiple levels, Kathy was able to prevent her client from leaving and, at the same time, keep the change effort he was supporting moving ahead. She helped both her client and the company by doing so. Had she not made the personal investment to her client's success and developed a close relationship, the work would have ceased.

What lessons can we learn from Mindy, Kathy, and our own experiences about building personal investment in relationships with clients? What follows are three skills that are required for making a deep personal investment:

- Put Skin in the Game;
- Connect Personal Aspirations with the Work; and
- Create Capable Clients by Avoiding Dependency.

Put Skin in the Game

Clients take risks at several levels when they undertake organization change. The organization could suffer, meaning that money or jobs could be lost. Individuals could find that their jobs have been redesigned or eliminated. Unions could take offense and go on strike. Shareholders could disapprove and withdraw support. The client's personal reputation could be damaged, thereby delaying or ending the progress of his or her career in the company.

What does the consultant stand to lose? Fees will be lost if the engagement is terminated prematurely, and the consultant's reputation will be damaged if problems with the project are made public. These things, however, are generally not of concern to the client. To balance the sense of risk being assumed by both parties, clients need to understand that their consultants are committed to their success at a personal level and that failure would hit the consultant as hard as it does the client.

Consultants demonstrate that they have skin in the game when they fight for what they believe in, even when the client disagrees with them. They also put skin in the game when they risk giving threatening, but necessary, feedback to a client. Consultants who never take a stand, are always willing to do what clients ask, or are exceedingly complimentary *think* they are doing what it takes to build good relationships with their clients when in fact they are doing just the opposite. Consultants who never disagree with their clients bring little value to the table, and their clients soon find that out.

Another way to indicate that you have skin in the game is to be emotionally available—simply being there to care when your client is going through a tough time. The depth of Kathy's involvement with her client is an example of how this can work. Our colleague Janet Spencer shares another example. Janet was working with a Fortune 50 CEO to plan his succession. The transition would symbolize the movement of power to another generation of leaders in a highly visible, global organization. Listen to how Janet describes her relationship with her client:

"We developed a fairly close relationship that led to some very private discussions regarding his own role in the company and his pending retirement. At the time, no one anticipated him stepping down from the CEO position, as he had been there only a few years. But he felt very strongly that the person who was going to lead the new organization through a multi-year plan to success needed to take the reigns upon the announcement. We began discussions of this several weeks before he went to anyone else, as he wanted a sounding board to clarify his own thinking. I didn't know how to disentangle the genuine regard and even affection I had for him from the behaviors I exhibited. I didn't consciously try to do anything other than be there for him, listen to him, empathize with his struggle, point out potential flaws in his thinking/approach, et cetera—things I would do for a friend. He was carrying a huge weight, and I simply tried to lighten it with him—not for him, with him."

Notice Janet's genuine personal regard for her client's struggle and the immense complexity associated with supporting a leader through the lonely part of a major decision. There is also a parallel between the way Janet helped her client and the way Kathy described the role her client needed to play. Neither interaction followed any sort of preconception or script; both arose from the depth of commitment to the relationships Kathy and Janet had with their clients.

Here are some things to consider to ensure your client understands that you have skin in the game.

Be Sure Your Clients Know How Much You Do Care and Why. Every relationship in our lives is prone to assumptions. We all assume our spouses know we care. We assume our bosses know we are committed. We assume our children know we love them. We assume our direct reports know we value them. It is vital that we *actually tell people* these things, however. And it is even more critical that our actions *back up our words.* We often assume our mere presence conveys these things, and we expect the benefit of the doubt from others. We want them to assume that, unless we do something horrible, by and large, we care, are committed, and respect and value them.

"Recently, one of my [Ron's] clients was in the middle of leading a major transformational effort—the single most radical departure from the old way of doing things the organization had ever experienced. The client is an extremely gifted leader and a brilliant woman. But she was leading change in a culture that had never experienced her kind of leadership, pace, intensity, and candor. Although she held her course tenaciously, the organization's deep instincts toward safe, incremental change often discouraged and frustrated her. Moreover, people in the organization acted like spectators, ascribing unfounded motives to her behavior and standing in judgment of her work, despite the recognition that everything she was attempting to accomplish was exactly what the organization needed to compete effectively.

"I wanted very much for her to succeed. I cared deeply about what she had begun and wanted her to have the chance to see it through. I sat in my hotel room until about two in the morning writing her a personal memo on how I thought she could best succeed in the context of what she was doing. I titled the memo 'Successfully Being a Maverick in Your Own Organization.' I was pointed with her about what I thought she needed to do differently. I also expressed my deep respect for her brilliance, my commitment to supporting her, and my care for the emotional toll I knew this was taking on her, which was most likely invisible to others in her organization. When I sent it, I was unsure how she would react to it. She told me it was one of the most caring things anyone had ever done for her. I felt really fortunate hearing that. And I watched her work harder than ever to stay on course with the change in a way that didn't push the organization beyond what it could assimilate or accept."

Here is what the client had to say about the experience with Ron:

"In order to add the value that Ron did in the context of our partnership, he had to be strong and resolute in his ability to deal with a sometimes contentious senior executive and help me accept opinions and commentary that may not always have replicated my own perceptions. I think the three characteristics that have made this partnership so valuable to me are (1) trust—from Ron, I can accept criticism and embrace praise; (2) we are totally honest with each other; and (3) Ron's respect for my feelings and insights and my deep respect for his insights, analysis, and feedback. In the context of this relationship, Ron's deep care for me as a person and a leader have enabled latent leadership potential in me to flourish and to help drive change, and ultimately, add value to the company's bottom line. Moreover, I have gained greater professional agility and knowledge, as well as greater personal and managerial self-esteem."

Hang Out with Your Clients. We've long understood that, in the context of important relationships, time is the most valuable currency. How we spend it, or don't spend it, conveys a great deal to others about what's important to us. Be sure you build time into your client relationships that can be used to convey your commitment. If your client senses that you always have a plane to catch or a call to make, or that you are somehow distracted by other issues, it isn't likely that she will conclude that your concern about her success is all that deep. Some ways that you can use time might include the following:

- Plan meals together to just catch up, such as an early breakfast before a meeting or a dinner after an all-day workshop. These are very important relationship-enhancing social times that create glue in ways you may not expect or predict.

- Offer unexpected support wherever you can. For example, if you hear that your client is giving a presentation or speech, offer to let him rehearse with you and provide feedback and suggestions. Spending an extra thirty minutes with him and making a few simple comments that will make him even more successful helps reinforce that you care. When you hear your client say, "You didn't have to do that. Thank you," you know you are sending strong messages that your skin is in the game.

- Spend some time with others who are important to your client. You might offer to have lunch with one of her direct reports who needs a bit of coaching and support. You are not expanding the scope of the work or infringing on pre-set boundaries; you're simply spending an hour with someone your client feels would benefit from time with you. Your willingness to give your time in this way again signals deep commitment.

Create Rituals That Add Your Personal Touch to the Relationship. One of the many things that can endear us to clients is the humanness with which we do our work. Clients are tired of the schtick many consultants use to establish themselves in the relationship. Endless slide presentations with graphs and charts, data, and statistics can be cold and impersonal, and they also confine you to the role of expert or technical consultant. Find a way to let the client know who *you* are in the context of the relationship. Use personal hallmarks such as your sense of humor or your use of metaphors to explain complex issues. Use your unique style and energy, send personal notes, find a common interest to talk about, and so on. Any one of these can serve as a means to help you demonstrate your personal investment in the relationship and in the engagement.

As Matsui (2000) points out, this type of interaction has a direct influence on self-awareness and empathy. Sharing personal information tends to increase the level of acquaintance between you and your client naturally, and through its effect on your motivation to understand one another, it increases self-awareness in both of you. In other words, the more acquainted you and your client are, the more likely you are to pay attention to and seek understanding of your client's perspective, which, in turn, enhances your level of self-awareness.

A second benefit is that, as the degree of familiarity between you and your client increases, the easier it will be for you to understand your client's perspective. Research has shown that such increased acquaintance between people leads to the availability of more and better information with which to infer one another's thoughts and emotions (Funder, 1995; Kenny, 1994). Acquaintance between individuals increases willingness and opportunities to discuss each other's thoughts and feelings (Kenny, 1994; Smither, 1977; Stinson & Ickes, 1992). This dynamic is a key success factor in all the client examples we've seen in this chapter.

Clients inherently know that our concern is real when we are willing to be ourselves with them to the fullest degree. When they sense we are somewhat guarded or just putting our best foot forward, they may privately wonder whether the veneer they are seeing is entirely genuine or if there is more available than meets the eye. Never give your clients the need to speculate about this. Let them see unique aspects about you that add personal touches to the relationship and signal you care about them as important people.

David Nadler, the founder and CEO of our firm, says he consciously creates rituals that begin his interactions with clients by finding some common ground on which to build. For example, he is a big fan of sailing, as was one of his clients. They would always include discussions of sailing as part of their interactions, compare boat war stories, and talk about the idea of going sailing together one day. According to David, "I knew we'd likely never go sailing together, but the idea of talking about it, and laughing about it, made the conversations rich with a personal touch. Rituals make it possible to create the connective tissue you can't get other ways." Personal rituals make it possible to add a degree of predictability to the interactions we have with our clients. They can see our names on their calendars and think, "I really look forward to my time with him."

Make the Work Fun. Simply put, if we can't have fun with our clients and make hard work fun for them, the interactions become arduous. Introducing a playful aspect—with humor, with jestful sparring, or sometimes with recurring jokes— creates a sense of levity about the work, and about the relationship. Your clients need to know that, while you may take the *work* very seriously, you don't take *yourself* too seriously. It's easy to lose broad perspective during the intensity of organization change. Little issues can feel enormous and overwhelming. Helping clients regain perspective by lightening the moment when it's appropriate helps them take a breath, regroup, and look at the situation with greater balance.

Find out things about your clients that they enjoy talking about, that they find fun, and, as we discussed above, incorporate a ritual into your relationships that naturally brightens their outlook. If they are avid golfers, find a way to work that in. If they have kids close in age to yours, the joys and woes of parenting are always a great discussion topic. Anything to add levity and laughter in the discussion or in the activity will convey to your clients that you care as much about them as people as you do about them as organizational leaders.

Learn About Your Clients and Their Worlds. Quite simply, you can't fake being genuinely interested in the lives of others. Clients know if we've taken the time to deepen our relationships with them by bothering to do our homework about their organizations, industries, challenges, and so forth. It is important that we develop a natural curiosity to want to know more about them. When a client casually mentions her daughter's school event, do we speed through the invitation she has given us into her life, or do we say, "Oh, you have a daughter? How old is she?" As you enter the room when a client is finishing up a conversation with someone about a major competitor's move that is threatening the organization, are you already up on what's happening, prepared to say, "Yes, I read about XYZ's intention to move into your markets. What are some of the countermeasures you are considering?"

Think about the times you have felt that someone else deeply respected you and cared about your well-being. Was it not due, in large part, to the genuine interest the person took in your life? Nothing feels more shallow than feigned interest. Superficial chit-chat actually keeps relationships from deepening. But taking the time to prepare for our client interactions by learning about what's relevant to them, their organizations, and their businesses sends strong signals of how much we care. Take the time to learn about your client's chief business challenges, competitors, customers, aspirations, and so on.

Moreover, when opportunities arise, take the time to find out about what's important to him outside the context of your relationships. Learn about how he spends his time, his interests, about his family, and so forth. Being able to talk about these things creates an intangible form of glue that connects you with your clients in important ways. Walking into a meeting and beginning your interaction with, "How was your son's wedding? Do you have any pictures?" sets a very different tone than, "Did you get the e-mail I sent you last night with today's agenda?" Again, the key is to ensure that we are genuinely interested in knowing, not just that we can ask the question.

Enjoy Your Clients. Sounds kind of basic, doesn't it? But on a fundamental level, if we don't truly like our clients, it's going to be an enormous challenge to get close to them. Once you've learned about your clients in the way we discussed above, can you then revel in what you've learned? Is there an unspoken chemistry between you and your client clearly indicating that you actually look forward to being together? Is it evident to your client that you like spending time with him? That you like her as a person? Can your clients see that having them as clients is something you feel glad about?

It is important that you find ways to make your clients feel special. The client organization is not just another place where you hang your hat. Enjoying our clients means we actively look for the characteristics, talents, and idiosyncrasies that make them the unique people they are. Having discovered these special qualities, we convey to our clients, through our demeanor, our countenance of ease and familiarity, and an evident positive anticipation of our time with them, that they are important to us, people we genuinely like to be around.

Connect Personal Aspirations to the Work

Not only is it important that clients know that you are invested in their success, but it is also important that they know why. Consultants usually know why the work they are doing is important to their clients; but do most clients know why the work is important to the consultant? If the consultant never offers any personal information on this score, clients readily assume that the work is a source of income for the consultant and little more. The client may feel that the consultant treats every job the same and sees every client as a cash register.

Good consultants do the work because it is a calling. They find the work intriguing, challenging, and rewarding. They enjoy learning from their clients and being able to help clients succeed. They immerse themselves in the literature of the profession and perhaps even contribute to the body of knowledge. They attend conferences, invest in their personal development, and seek advice from fellow consultants in an effort to hone their skills. The work isn't just something good consultants do to make a living; it's something they love.

By sharing a love of their work with clients and letting clients know about their personal aspirations, good consultants open the window to a different kind of relationship. Clients become fellow learners, and both parties can aspire to greater success in the future. Clients are reassured when they know that their consultants are deeply invested in what they are doing and that what happens matters to the consultant's career as well.

Some ways to connect your personal aspirations to the work are described below.

Know What Your Personal Aspirations Are. As we said above, most people who do this work exceptionally well do so because they genuinely love it. And they know *why* they love it. If you have never given any deep thought to exactly what is attractive to you about this work, you risk slipping into the robotic delivery of consulting as though it were nothing more than a cold, transactional exchange of money for advice and expertise. Your personal passion for this work, what you bring to it, and who you hope to become through it are important assets in expressing your personal investment to a client.

Think about the times you've listened to people describe the work they are involved in with energy and deep personal devotion. The sense of purpose they convey is palpable and often inspiring. Imagine what it would be like to be on the receiving end of the work of someone who viewed what they did so reverently. Clearly, you would feel deeply respected.

The work of influencing leaders in the context of organization change is an audacious proposition. Through these leaders, we are potentially influencing the lives of hundreds, even thousands, of people. If we do not pause to consider the ramifications of what we are doing and why it is meaningful to us, we may undermine our effectiveness and impact.

Therefore, it is necessary to reflect in a routine way on who we are and on what we hope to accomplish through our work. This becomes especially important for times when the work is particularly draining, thankless, or tough. If there isn't some other source of "fuel" to energize us, the risk of eroding the quality of our work and settling for the acceptable minimum is high. Anchoring our work in a clearly defined set of aspirations can raise our perspective when we're being pulled down. In turn, our ability to influence, even inspire, clients through these aspirations is an important way of expressing our commitment to their success.

Align Your Personal Values with How You Practice. Knowing *how* we want to do the work we do is just as important as knowing *why*. We all believe we are people of high integrity, with strong moral character, caring and collaborative, service-oriented, and committed to the highest quality work. But if you took any random set of consultants into a room, asked them what these values meant, and how they practice them, you would definitely find some variance in their responses. You'd find even greater variance if you asked their clients!

As a way of differentiating ourselves and ensuring that our relationships with our clients reflect what we value, it is important to be clear—both with ourselves and with our clients—about what these values are supposed to look like in practice. For example, we must tell our clients, as an expression of our integrity, how we will handle certain types of information, and we must ask the same of them. We must let them know our views if the decision-making process or results cut against what we believe to be honest and ethical, especially if we foresee negative consequences looming.

There is clear risk in putting stakes in the ground regarding these values. First, we have to stand by them, which sometimes feels like it may put the relationship at risk if we challenge the client. Second, by letting our clients know we have strong values and beliefs about certain issues, we have built a source of accountability into the relationship. They will remember what we tell them, and they will watch to see whether our actions align with our beliefs. By aligning our values with how we practice our work, we bolster our credibility in our clients' eyes. As such, the degree of respect we show our clients becomes more meaningful to them as they come to respect us as credible practitioners.

Celebrate Success. Nothing energizes change efforts more than a set of high-fives signaling the achievement of some important milestone, the demonstration of a new capability, or the performance metrics clearly indicating an improvement in results. By choosing to acknowledge important wins in the process of change, you are letting clients know that *their* achievements are important to you. You will also be telling your clients a great deal about yourself by the things you notice as successes.

Often, with nose to the grindstone of change, important wins can go unnoticed. Pointing out accomplishments that the client would not have noticed, however minute they may seem, helps in several ways. First, it tells clients you are paying attention to a broad radar screen. Second, it tells them what's important to you, as we tend to celebrate what we value. Noticing that a team member changed historically problematic behavior, noticing the speed at which decisions are being made, and noticing greater efficiency in processes all serve as ways to energize clients and tell them you care about the outcomes. It also helps to reinforce behavior that the organization should value.

Create Capable Clients by Avoiding Dependency

As we discussed in the cases earlier, successful consultants pay attention to the line between offering help and creating dependency. When a consultant helps a client learn how to manage relationships and lead change, the client's sense of significance and self-confidence increases. If the consultant does all the hard work, the client may develop a dependency on the consultant that actually reduces the client's self-confidence and limits the risks he or she is willing to take in the future.

Experienced consultants realize that strong, self-confident leaders make better clients than do dependent ones. Leaders who feel that their consultants are helping them become better leaders are more likely to pick up the phone and ask for advice than are leaders who are not challenged by their consultants to step up to the challenges they should face.

We're not suggesting that consultants ignore requests by their clients for help or fail to lend a hand in helping to get the work done. Good consultants have a sense of when to pitch in and when to hold back. Generally speaking, consultants should avoid taking on personal conflicts for their clients, making visible, public speeches about the change effort, and collaring individuals who are not supportive of the leader's plans. Each of these instances offers an opportunity for clients to develop their skills and to increase their personal commitment to leading change.

Some ways to think about building capability in your clients by avoiding dependency follow.

Assess Clients' Learning Needs. The first step in building capability is to identify those areas that, if fortified, could yield a significant improvement in personal and organizational performance. The consultant should begin by forming a clear understanding of the organization's strategic intent and then identifying those capabilities that will be required to achieve that intent. He or she should then assess the client's abilities, skills, and knowledge base in relation to the strategy, discuss the deficiencies with the client, and prioritize the list of capabilities to be built.

Set Learning Objectives. Using the prioritized list of capabilities, the consultant should work with the client to establish objectives for how the engagement at hand can serve as a vehicle through which the client can increase personal capability in a given area. Together, they will set concrete objectives for using the engagement to build these capabilities.

Pause for Teachable Moments. In the course of the initiative, there will be occasions when successful actions or mistakes can provide an opportunity for learning, but the occasions might not always be obvious. It is the job of the consultant to watch for those critical moments, to stop action, and to point out the potential for the emergence of a new capability.

Additionally, there may be critical crossroads at which the application of a new skill or insight could produce great progress, but where the client prefers to rely on the tried-and-true approach—what is familiar and comfortable. Here, too, is an opportunity for the consultant to stop action long enough to point out the client's reluctance to try something novel and to push him or her to consider ideas and approaches that might be counterintuitive, but that could be enormously beneficial to the initiative and to his or her professional growth.

Create Time for Reflection. Large, complex initiatives can produce levels of intensity that serve to propel the work mindlessly on cruise control. Although such forward motion can create great momentum, it can also rush clients past the need to pause long enough to ask, "What have we learned so far?" For those with strong biases for action, pausing to reflect does not come easily. If the consultant also speeds past opportunities to reflect, he or she will limit the client's ability to learn to do so. A consultant should schedule time with clients exclusively for the purpose of forcing reflection, to ask questions such as, "What made this work well?" or "Why are we still struggling with this?" or "If we had to do this over, what would we do differently or the same?" True learning comes out of discussions such as this, setting the stage for acquiring a new capability.

Provide Collateral Materials. Having set specific objectives to build certain capabilities, clients can benefit from additional resources such as articles, books, tools, seminars, videos, networking with experts outside their organizations, visits with some of your other clients who may have the capability being pursued, and so forth. A consultant can add tremendous value for a client by offering such resources. Your client will appreciate you taking the time to support her in this way, living up to your commitment to her development above and beyond the call.

Monitor Progress. It is essential to watch for evidence suggesting that the sought-after capability is appearing. Positive reinforcement is important to ensure that the client can repeat demonstrations of new behavior. Conversely, if progress isn't being made as expected, it is important to discuss why. It may be because the objectives were overly ambitious, that sufficient resources or support haven't been provided, or that the client just isn't trying hard enough. Without identifying and addressing obstacles to progress, the acquisition of new capabilities will be nearly impossible.

It is vital to a client's success that the consultant walk the fine line between helping a client without encouraging dependency. Clients who are dependent will not be able to make change happen. Let's look at how having skin in the game with a capable client enables change.

▶ Change Enablement

How Personal Investment Builds a
Sense of Confidence and Significance

Make no mistake about it, even the most confident leader will feel some degree of anxiety and apprehension when faced with the challenge of leading significant organization change. Such leaders will think twice about the decisions that require setting precedents for themselves and for those they lead. The lure of the familiar, comfortable, tried-and-true approaches will ring loud in their heads when faced with the risks, real or imagined, of the change being contemplated. The leaders may mask their fears well, showing a staunch face of self-assurance to those around them. But inside, they may sense deep feelings of uneasiness, doubt their ability to be successful, and fear looking foolish or losing credibility in the eye of peers, bosses, external constituents, and those they lead.

One of the many places from which leaders can draw the strength to push against these thoughts and feelings is the sense of confidence and significance they gain from their relationships with their consultants. If you, the one seen to have expertise in organization change, have invested yourself in this leader, seem confident he can pull it off, and have affirmed the talents and insights he has displayed that make him credible to take on the change, you could well tip the scale and prompt the leader to go forward. Your faith in his ability can serve as an important source of fuel when he is facing tough decisions.

Think about the times when you have faced difficult circumstances requiring risky choices. Think about those who supported you in the process. Didn't you feel a greater sense of significance and confidence because they, as credible advisors in your eye, seemed to believe you could succeed? It's not much different in the case of your client relationships. The client, as a human being, needs the energy that comes from knowing that a credible confidant has shared in some of the risk and has put his or her bet on the table that the effort has a good chance of being successful. Your investment in your client could well bring about the necessary confidence needed to put change in motion. ◀

Table 3.1 illustrates some of the ways to show personal investment we have described in this chapter.

Table 3.1. Summary of How to Show Personal Investment

Practices	Behaviors	Self-Assessment
Put Skin in the Game	Be sure your clients know how much you do care and why	I let my client know that I am committed to our work together
	Hang out with your clients	I create opportunities to meet more informally with my client to just catch up
	Create rituals that add your personal touch to the relationship	I volunteer help on miscellaneous tasks such as writing communications or preparing for speeches
	Make the work fun	My clients and I have conversations about non-work-related topics
	Learn about your clients and their worlds	I find common areas of interest with all my clients
	Enjoy your clients	Interactions with my clients are energizing and fun
		I find ways to lighten up the situation when my clients feel overwhelmed
Connect Personal Aspirations to the Work	Know what your personal aspirations are	I reflect on how the work helps me reach my personal goals
	Align your personal values with how you practice	In the midst of a project, I do not lose track of my personal objectives
	Celebrate success	I tell my clients about my aspirations in working with them
		I tell my clients how I would typically behave in certain situations
		I personally feel excited when I notice that the work we are doing is moving in the intended direction
		I bring positive signs of change to my clients' attention
Create Capable Clients by Avoiding Dependency	Assess clients' learning needs	I work with my clients to identify and prioritize their developmental needs
	Set learning objectives	I use my client work as an opportunity to improve or acquire skills and capabilities
	Pause for teachable moments	

Table 3.1. Summary of How to Show Personal Investment, Cont'd

Practices	Behaviors	Self-Assessment
	Create time for reflection	I encourage my clients to apply new skills or knowledge that I think will lead to greater progress
	Provide collateral materials	
	Monitor progress	On most projects, I schedule time with my clients to pause and reflect on on-going work
		I meet with my client at the end of a project to review and assess the work that was done
		Unsolicited, I provide my clients with resources, such as books and contacts, that can help them
		I update my clients on their progress in developing new competencies

4

Confronting the Moose: Courage

AS WE WORK TO BUILD CLOSER RELATIONSHIPS with clients, one of the biggest problems we face is running into situations that the client and teams in their organization simply do not wish to discuss. We describe dealing with this sort of a situation as "confronting the moose." The expression "moose on the table" was coined by consultant and author Dennis Perkins (1988) and refers to situations where time is spent on inconsequential discussions and peripheral issues, while the causes of the organization's deadlock remains "indiscussable" (Argyris, 1990). Perkins compares this avoidance to having a "great, big, ugly, hairy, smelly moose" standing on the table with people sitting around performing all sorts of contortions to address each other between the moose's legs, while never daring to ever acknowledge the awkward presence of the animal.

A big part of developing close relationships with clients is manifesting the courage element of rQ by confronting the moose wherever you find it.

In this account by our colleague Marc Bassin, he exemplifies the courage that is required to create close relationships with clients as they tackle difficult issues.

"Tom is the new CEO of the asset management unit of an international bank. He is extremely bright, hard-working, and decisive. However, his peers and subordinates sometimes find him overbearing.

"Tom was brought in to clean up after a poor integration with another asset management fund. He addressed the post-integration issues successfully. When a third very large asset management fund was suddenly acquired by Tom's company, Fred and Joe, two heads of that fund, approached Tom and asked to integrate their part of the business with his because they believed it would be a better fit. The three of them agreed that Tom would be CEO, Fred would be president, and Joe would become CFO.

"We were asked to help with this sudden, new integration. The acquisition made great sense on paper because Fred's fund was strong in retail markets and Tom's was strong in institutional markets. Everything seemed fine until the relationship between Tom, Fred, and Joe completely blew up, right in front of the whole organization. This threatened to derail the integration completely.

"The integration could not proceed with the senior leadership not only 'not aligned,' but totally at war, publicly showing their contempt for each other. What made this worse was the addition of Sam, the CIO, into the mix. While he should have been a key leader for integrating the investment process, he chose to join Fred and Joe in showing distrust of Tom. Rumors and speculation ran rampant that Sam would align with Fred and Joe to force Tom out.

"On one hand, Tom was micromanaging. He was stepping on their areas of responsibility and 'violating the deal' regarding roles and autonomy. On the other hand, in Tom's view, Fred and Joe were 'protecting' their own people and couldn't be trusted to provide honest data and assessments for difficult decisions regarding people and positions. Sam was publicly expressing his distrust of Tom's character and leadership abilities, adding fuel to the burning fires.

"The situation became so desperate that Fred and Joe went to Tom with a formal proposal to 'buy out' a part of the business, and Tom confided in me that he was completely overwhelmed and for the first time in his life believed he could not succeed.

"I began to meet with each of the four guys separately to understand the world from their perspectives. I used these informal one-on-one meetings to build relationships with each. Most importantly, I told each exactly what I thought. I explained where I felt their positions were valid and where I felt they were being immature and irresponsible. These were some very difficult and frank conversations. I stressed throughout that my agenda was to bring them together and change the dynamic among them so the integration could proceed.

"I spent most of my time with Tom because there was a lot of consistency in the negative way he was being perceived by the others. I told him point-blank he needed to make a fundamental change in his behavior and leadership if he was to succeed here. He absolutely had to listen more to others, not only to hear what was said, but also to incorporate at least some of the views of others into his decisions. Equally important, he had to become more human, admit to not having all the answers all the time, and seek the help and input of others. More difficult still was that he needed to be more empathic, be less task focused, show some warmth, and make personal connections with people.

"It was especially hard to get close to Tom. I began to ask him more personal questions and increased my contact with him. It became very clear to me that I needed to do two things simultaneously. First, I had to help these leaders, especially Tom, see the behaviors they each needed to change. At the same time, I needed to give them the energy and a belief that they could change and that they all would benefit from this in the long run.

"As the situation worsened and the tension mounted, Tom and I had almost daily contact. Being able to immediately point out small successes to Tom was critical to gaining some positive momentum. These meetings with Tom enabled me to get to know him on a very personal level. Behind the arrogant know-it-all was a very sensitive guy in great pain, beginning to doubt his ability and losing his confidence. At these moments, my task was to point to the progress he was making and share his frustration with the political, self-serving behavior he was encountering from all sides.

"I convinced Fred, Joe, and Sam to have individual 'marriage counseling' sessions with Tom and myself to candidly discuss their relationships and begin a new dynamic.

"Each of the four made an honest attempt to change their dynamic, be mindful of the boundaries we set among their roles, let the past go, and begin with a new slate. This enabled them to at least stop the public feuding and focus on the task at hand—building the business. We had moved from crisis to coexistence. While significant progress had been made, we had one more huge hurdle to cross.

"Fred and Joe had built a very successful small entrepreneurial boutique. The vision now was to create a first-class global firm, using the leverage of products, delivery systems, and relationships globally. This required paying careful attention to the processes a large global organization required, which Fred and Joe considered a bureaucratic waste of time. As the four were able to get beyond the daily entanglement of clashing interpersonal relationships and styles, this very fundamental difference became very clear. Tom and Sam shared a deep commitment to this global vision, despite their personal issues. Fred and Joe did not. Given this reality, we needed to shift gears. Could we use this shared global vision to get Tom and Sam beyond neutral to build a true partnership to serve as the fundamental platform to grow the firm? Tom felt it was the only way to proceed and was willing to give it his best shot. Sam was highly skeptical and felt leaving the organization was probably a better option because of his lingering distrust of Tom and Tom's leadership abilities.

"I used my close relationship with Sam to try to show him he should stay. He knew me well and trusted me. I acknowledged that Tom had a number of leadership competencies to develop, but personally assured Sam that Tom could be trusted and was totally committed to making the change he needed to make to be more effective and trustworthy. I pushed Sam very hard. I told him it would be incredibly foolish to give up at this point after all the hard work he had done. He needed to give this one last shot. I asked him to give us three months to turn it around.

"The difference in the organization now that those three months have passed is amazing. Tom, Sam, and I did the groundwork over two days locked up in a room in London with the global CEOs, working out the fundamentals of a new growth plan. We also worked on the new interpersonal partnership between Tom and Sam. As we finally agreed, Fred and Joe left the organization in a very professional and nondisruptive way. Tom and Sam have now pulled in a number of other senior key players to construct a new growth plan. They are cohesive, aligned, and personally supportive. The new growth plan has been announced, and implementation is underway. The new partnership between Tom and Sam has become very visible in the organization. They are actually beginning to trust and enjoy each other, and we are now building a strong senior team around them to make the plan a reality. I keep meeting with Tom and Sam, individually and collectively, to continue to strengthen their partnership. Sam is now very positive and tells me, 'Tom has changed.' Well, I guess sometimes you just get lucky."

Let's listen in now as Marc's client Sam describes his perspective on this same relationship:

"The relationship really started during a period of panic. The existing organization was imploding at the same time it was absorbing the second organization. The second was absolutely furious about being sold. To say this place was a mess is an understatement. Part of our problems were merger-related, but we had much deeper, more pervasive problems as well. I knew Marc could help us. We have come a long, long way. At the moment, we are about 70 percent of the way to being one organization and are on the road to being 100 percent.

"Marc, as an individual, is a master at communications. That is what he is all about. He makes sure people talk to one another to get the organization to work better. Since I have had a personal coach before, I can say that Marc's skill set is not at the individual level; it is on the organizational level. He gains people's confidences; he shows us he is confident in the success of the organization and that each of us is critical to that success. We all know he is an important advisor to the CEO, but he is not the mole for the CEO. He is really out for each of our best interests and that of the organization.

"Marc definitely pushes back on us. I feel like he is saying what he feels he has to say. The most important point is that he says things because that's what is best for the organization, not just because he was told by the CEO to say things.

"We have had many an animated conversation. Marc is open to me and us pushing back on him. Some conversations were very difficult. The organization has definitely made progress. One senior individual was even fired. There have been times when Marc has told me I have gone too far, that I let my emotions get in the way. I made it through those conversations because I trust him. He has earned my trust. Marc knew when I was angry. We put it all out on the table. With his help, I have learned to be much better when I am in front of people in my organization, to make sure my emotions don't show, and that my positive hat is on.

"My recommendation to others looking to build solid relationships with their clients is to make sure their actions are consistent with keeping the organization's and the individuals' best interests at hand. It is about facilitating rather than debilitating. Be consistent and keep coming at your client. We all tend to go back to the way we used to work, where we are comfortable. It takes a lot of shepherding. It's also really important to create a personal relationship. You need to get along personally. It is easy to trust if you like the person, not so easy if you do not like the person—you won't listen. All of this is definitely an art, and Marc is good at it."

Clients come to us with real problems, some of which have the potential to be career-threatening. Clearly, that was the case with Marc's client, Tom. While it is quite easy to say that our job is to provide the help they need, actually *doing* it is something else again. External consultants take special pride in their objectivity, claiming that they are able to tell executives the truth, even if it ends the engagement. They are taught that it is better to end the engagement than to be ineffective because the moose is not being confronted and real issues are not being addressed. Internal consultants are taught this as well, and the best ones behave exactly as Marc did in working with Tom.

Internal consultants have an interesting dance to choreograph: They have to be completely impartial, yet they are also part of the system in which they work. Delivering tough messages to your own employers adds another dimension to the challenges all consultants face.

Listen to our colleague Laura Christenson's reflection on one of her experiences as an internal consultant where she needed to confront the moose and deliver tough messages:

"I joined a new organization as director of global organizational effectiveness, and within the first week, Jim, the senior VP of HR, was in my office asking for my help in an HR re-engineering effort that was already underway. Jim was my second-line manager and a member of the Executive Committee. The good news was that I was going to have high visibility really fast. The bad news was that the re-engineering effort had been underway for almost two years and had just gone live. I'll never forget Jim saying, 'We've gone live to a shared services concept, reduced our head count, and have people calling in for services. Now, we need your help in putting together the change management plan.'

"You can imagine my first reaction . . . 'NOW you want to look at a change management plan!' I knew right away that it was not going to be an easy assignment. Even so, I told Jim that it provided a wonderful opportunity for me to understand the business quickly and understand how HR was transforming. I shared that I would need to have access to a cross section of the organization, HR and line, to understand what was happening. I also told him that I would gather data and would need to share that data with him—both the good and the bad. He was pleased, although I suspected he did not expect to hear the level of the noise that subsequently came out of the data.

"One of the first things I did was to follow Peter Block's contracting process. While I did not do an extensive letter of agreement, I did put together a one-page outline. It detailed the presenting business issue, objectives, measures of success, roles—including his, the project team leader's, and the head of shared services—a timeline for the project, and frequency for reviews with Jim.

"As we reviewed this outline, I gained my first insight into how Jim preferred to view the world. While I had written 'Presenting Business Issue,' he asked that it be changed to 'Presenting Business Opportunity.' In that meeting, I knew I needed to lay it on the line. I told him that for us to be successful, I needed to call it like I saw it and that he needed to be willing to hear it—the good, the bad, and the ugly. I was honest and shared my experiences that sometimes you find things out that are not necessarily easy for a senior executive to hear and that I needed to have free license with him to be able to have those open dialogues. Jim was very supportive and even commented how refreshing that was as he knew people in the organization did not necessarily share their honest thoughts.

"After the initial interviews and focus groups, the themes began to take life. There was little change management focus as they implemented new processes and systems and removed head count. Another theme—the level of intensity—took me by surprise. I had only been there a few weeks, yet I had to confront data indicating that Jim had the tendency to yell, to be aggressive, and as one said, to 'chew people up and spit them out.' He was also seen as removed from the HR initiative.

"I thought, 'Oh great, I get to be the one to tell him all this stuff.' I knew I had to share the findings and to help Jim to understand how his behavior was not supportive of the organization and the efforts. I put together a presentation to highlight the emerging themes and used examples of direct quotes to support the themes.

"I also outlined a plan moving forward that included far more collaboration between Jim, the HR executives in the lines of business, the line managers at the executive level and closer to the employees, the project leader, and the head of shared services. The remaining efforts needed to be leadership-led, driven by business needs, and not seen as just an HR initiative. Those efforts already in place needed some damage control to regain HR credibility. Correcting them was going to be a joint effort with Jim in the lead. Jim heard the data, admitted his flaws, saw the missteps, could see a path forward, and right then asked me to help him work to improve his leadership, his team's leadership, and HR's credibility.

"Another key in building this relationship was learning prior to our meetings what his day had been like. In talking to his assistant, I could gain insight into what his mood was. I learned to know whether I could spend a lot of time on an issue, or do a 'drive by' and then come back to it at a later time. There were definitely times in our meetings when he wanted to just focus on the organizational issues or those of others versus looking at his own personal leadership. Effectively using the time and choosing what to focus on with Jim was essential.

"Over time, he and I had many honest conversations about how he was being perceived in the organization, how he showed his 'human side,' how he showed his commitment to the efforts and the struggles through the reengineering efforts, and how he communicated. We discussed his role and progress in coaching the project leader and the head of shared services and how to hold them accountable for results. We discussed my observations on his leadership of his team and of HR.

"I would often share with him my appreciation for his continued openness and for giving me the space to be honest with him. I acknowledged his own work around being open to alternative views, but also knew that he could quickly remove that space, given his positional power. I believe the acknowledgement of both helped strengthen the relationship. He frequently commented that he was genuinely interested in my observations, my viewpoint, and my recommendations. He said that he wished others in the organization would be as free to be as honest. We continued to work that perception, both on what he needed to do to create the space for others and also on supporting others to have the courage to take the space.

"While it is not easy to deliver tough messages to a superior as an internal consultant, I learned it was vital to my own credibility and success. I had made plenty of mistakes along the way, colluding with the dysfunctional norms of previous organizations, and I had learned from them. When I was not fully honest in the past, the leader did not take the ownership needed to make change happen.

In this case, contracting up-front was key to setting the stage for Jim and his team to be receptive and to take ownership. Balancing the good and the bad news and knowing when to address issues was also essential. To be successful, I learned you have to have the confidence and the courage to call the question and to acknowledge whatever moose you encounter—regardless of whether you are internal or external."

Many consultants, both internal and external, have difficulty finding the courage to engage their clients in frank and open discussions about the client's problematic behavior. Consultants who may be excellent in thinking through strategy issues or organizational design options trip over themselves when confronted with situations like the ones Marc and Laura describe. It's as if there is an unspoken agreement that prevents them from discussing what is obvious to everyone: "You will continue to employ me as your advisor as long as I don't mention your personal ineffectiveness in leading the organization." It takes courage to cross the line, call out the behavior in question, and risk inviting the wrath of the client.

We've known internal and external consultants who won't do this under any circumstance. They take Herb Shepard's (1975) injunction to "first, stay alive" to the extreme. What Shepard meant was that getting yourself fired makes it hard to continue to change the organization; but he would be the first to confront clients about their behaviors rather than pretend he didn't notice them. Consultants who avoid giving direct personal feedback to their clients fail to understand that there is a high probability they will be fired anyway, either in reality or symbolically.

If clients' behaviors damage their ability to lead, the chances of them succeeding in directing a significant change effort are slim. When clients fail, their consultant fails by association. Consultants who are afraid to confront their clients often see the train wreck coming but feel helpless to prevent it. It's as if they are watching the events unfold from a distance—rather than being aboard the locomotive—until the moment the crash occurs. Then, of course, it's too late.

Staying with the metaphor for a moment longer, you should also avoid being sent to the back of the train where you can no longer see what is happening in the front. Clients who find no use for their consultants but are too benevolent to fire them will relegate them to the back of the train, that is, to positions of no importance in the organization to work on projects or programs that have little chance of making a difference in charting the course of the train. These consultants are easy to spot; they are the ones who are always complaining about their clients and looking for another job or another engagement—one with a client who gets it. The hard truth is that it's not their clients who don't get it—they don't.

Let's go back to the situation that Marc describes. Tom didn't look like the kind of leader who got it at the time Marc arrived. He was having difficulty in his relationships, and these difficulties were beginning to threaten his ability to lead. Still, we can guess that Tom was slow to point the finger at himself and hadn't received much direct feedback about his behavior.

Marc faced a choice. He could have colluded with Tom and helped him strategize how to get out of the deal he made with Fred. He could have told Tom that the issues he was experiencing had nothing to do with Tom's behavior, that these kinds of difficulties arise in every acquisition or merger and should be expected. Or he could have acted as Tom's emissary, meeting with each member of Tom's team individually to find out what it would take to smooth the situation over—without really confronting the underlying problems. Or he could have thrown up his hands, said "This client will never get it," and walked away to look for another engagement.

What Marc chose to do took courage. By confronting Tom, Marc risked Tom's anger. Marc knew that no matter how skillfully he handled the situation, there was a chance that Tom would fire him rather than start to work on changing his own behavior. At the same time, Marc realized that he could not help Tom in any meaningful way unless he addressed the defects of Tom's leadership style. In this instance, the only way Marc could remain true to his values and his mission as a consultant was to confront Tom, regardless of the consequences.

Laura displayed the same type of courage when she confronted Jim with the data on his behavior. As an internal consultant, she addressed the criticism that Jim "chewed people up and spat them out." Her candor and conviction helped Jim address the issues. Had she not been a brave and independent voice, she would have added far less value and may have eventually been spat out herself.

In the situations Marc and Laura both found themselves in, courage was a powerful tool. Clients sensed from the start that Marc and Laura were serious about their work and would accept nothing less from the client than a full commitment to success. The clients appreciated the risks Marc and Laura took in giving these messages—and with this appreciation came a deepening of the relationship.

Marc and Laura both delivered these messages with skill, of course. Their observations were insightful and their comments direct and firm. They didn't back away after giving feedback or ask that the client take on the work of changing without their support. They provided examples of what they had seen the client do and suggested alternative behaviors that would be more effective. They gave positive reinforcements when they were deserved and accepted that, as long as the client was trying, there was room for imperfection.

In the example Marc described, Tom did not ask for help at a personal level. He contacted Marc because the organizational aspects of the merger were complicated and he needed someone with an expert, objective perspective to help think through the right process to use in integrating the companies. Even after he engaged Marc, Tom probably expected Marc to stay focused on the organizational issues, not on Tom's personal leadership style.

As soon as Marc recognized that Tom's behavior was a factor in the success of the merger, he brought it to Tom's attention. He didn't wait for Tom to ask, or for some kind of incident to take place that would make Tom's behavior an obvious issue to be discussed. He told Tom what he thought and why it was important. By doing this quickly and directly, he risked Tom becoming angry with him and dismissing the problem out of hand; but he also took advantage of the opportunity to gain Tom's trust.

Once Marc gained Tom's trust, Marc was able to intervene in a much more powerful way than he could have before. With the issues on the table, he was able to engage the other members of Tom's team in open and frank discussions that resolved the issues with minimal damage to the individuals or to the organization. If he had shied away from addressing Tom's issues, it is unlikely that Sam and Tom would be together today, working cohesively to make the merger a success.

What are some of the skills that are required to be an effective change management consultant? We believe they are:

- Have Confidence to Call the Tough Questions;
- Hold the Client Accountable; and
- Provide Nonjudgmental Feedback

Have Confidence to Call the Tough Questions

In almost any group meeting, particularly when the task at hand is uneasy, constrained, or involves debating and making decisions, there is a pervasive, yet unspoken reluctance to raise issues that may be distasteful, irritating, or anxiety-provoking. In organizations, sore topics run the gamut from succession issues to unsuccessful business initiatives to dysfunctional personalities and relationships. These issues, and more, are vitally important for the CEO and his or her team to tackle in order to protect the integrity of the organization and move it forward— yet these are the issues most likely to remain in the vault.

Marc confronted the moose on the table by raising the tough question with Tom concerning his behavior. Tom may have had others call the question with him before, but he hadn't heard the message. Part of calling the question effectively is to do so directly and insistently. Marc didn't mention to Tom in a passing conversation that he might consider reflecting on his behavior; he called the question loudly, directly, and with the intent that Tom listen to what was being said. Marc didn't allow Tom to slide out of the conversation by saying, "I've heard it all before. It's just how I am, so let's not worry about it," or "That's not what we're here to talk about. Let's stay focused on getting those other guys in line." Marc insisted that Tom understand the feedback and the impact that his behavior was having on the success of the merger. Once he knew that Tom had heard and understood the feedback, Marc worked with Tom to begin to change his behavior.

Laura was observant enough to spot a moose right off the bat. She heard Jim mention that people didn't share their views honestly with him. Then her data indicated that Jim was perceived as an aggressive person who yelled. No one in the organization was going to risk telling Jim things he didn't want to hear. Just as Marc had with Tom, Laura confronted Jim with this feedback and was able to help him improve.

Here are some important things to consider when *raising tough issues* with your client by confronting the moose.

Confront Personal Avoidance of Rejection and Conflict. Start with yourself. Each of us, to some degree, may be uncomfortable with the idea of calling tough questions because of the possible defensiveness or conflict it may incite. If your own uneasiness is preventing you from addressing important issues with your client, your ability to be a truth teller for your client will be limited. You must get to the bottom of your own avoidance to make sure that you can manage it, even in the heat of the moment. You can't recoil from circumstances requiring truth-telling.

Pick and Choose Your Battles Wisely. Sometimes opportunities for confronting the moose are a mixed blessing. While they certainly present the chance to help your client grow, learn, and correct problems that might otherwise go unaddressed, they can also, to some degree, be a reflection of your own issues. Consultants who feel the need to confront every issue that even remotely appears to have a covert side may be motivated to do so more out of the need to experience the surge of their own power than to be helpful to their clients. Part of confronting the moose is learning to monitor our own motives for doing so. While we do not want to collude in organizational situations that need to be dealt with directly, we need to be sure the client is ready to deal with the issue once it is raised and that he or she will see real and obvious benefit from doing so.

Rehearse the Messages. Good intentions count very little when raising tough issues. Even the best motives can lead consultants to botch the delivery of the message. The presence of discomfort, defensiveness, and emotion can skew both the delivery of the message and the filters through which it is heard. The wise consultant will prepare ahead of time for the conversation by writing out and rehearsing the message, trying different language and phrasing, anticipating reactions, and ensuring that he or she is prepared for a variety of responses. The goal is not to dehumanize the experience, but rather to minimize the opportunity for the conversation to derail because of misunderstanding and poor communication.

Extend the Benefit of the Doubt. Recognize that tough messages, even delivered well, have the potential to cause bad feelings. There's little that can be done to avoid this, but don't compound it by also making your client feel stupid. When clients make mistakes or behave in unproductive ways, on some level they probably know they have done so. Delivering moose messages with caring and compassion is likely to be much better received than messages wrapped in tones of "What were you thinking? Do you have any idea . . .??!!" Clients also need to know you believe they are capable of correcting mistakes and changing unproductive behavior. Delivering your recommendations with such benefit of the doubt can encourage them to take productive action.

Hold the Client Accountable

It may sound almost counterintuitive—the idea of the *consultant* holding the *client* accountable. But in strong relationships, there ought to be a built-in mechanism to ensure that agreements are kept. Inherent in the notion of a mutually beneficial and caring relationship there is an unspoken mechanism for accountability—and that is the innate desire of each one in the relationship not to violate the trust on which the relationship has been built. But even strong relationships experience missteps. And people are bound to avoid doing hard things, even if they agreed to do them.

When consultants do the tough interpersonal work for their clients, they aren't demonstrating courage; they are avoiding the risk associated with forcing clients to work the issues themselves. Some clients would love to delegate their responsibility for the impact they have on others around them to the consultant, to an executive assistant, or to anyone who will keep the machinery running as they continue to throw wrenches into the works. *Fixing problems for the client won't make the problems go away.* In fact, client behaviors may become worse if they believe that someone will always follow along behind them, cleaning up the messes left in their wakes. Marc didn't let Tom off the hook by stating that all mergers involve interpersonal issues or by offering to go to Fred and work out the issues on Tom's behalf. He made Tom do the work himself. Laura held Jim accountable for visibly leading the HR re-engineering initiative and for effectively managing the project team leader and head of shared services.

It takes courage to force clients to deal with their own issues. Chances are, the behaviors that are problematic have been problematic for some time. Clients may have strong and effective defenses against changing behaviors that they find rewarding, for whatever reasons. Consultants don't need to become therapists; they just have to insist that the behaviors in question change in order for the clients to be successful in what they are trying to achieve. It's a simple choice for the client: change or fail. Changing the behavior may be extremely difficult if it is deeply ingrained, but the choice to try is a simple one and, once made, allows the consultant to support the client's efforts.

Here are some points to consider as you work to *hold your client accountable.*

Establish Agreed-On Commitments. If you're going to hold the client accountable, it has to be made clear from the beginning what exactly she is agreeing to be held accountable for. In your contracting process, it is essential that roles, work commitments, and deliverables be discussed and concurred with. If you will need access to certain people or information, support from the client at specific pivotal points of the project, or decisions made in certain time frames in order to deliver your pieces of the project, then the client and you must set the ground rules for how this will happen. Having clearly established agreements, in and of itself, can serve as a mechanism of accountability, and it certainly is essential to have when you need to go back and discuss when a commitment has not been kept.

Use Metrics. Make sure there is some type of barometer in place that can let you and the client know how things are going. That way, you're not just using a subjective viewpoint to push the client for new behavior or actions. Make sure that whatever you agree on at the outset can be monitored and tracked. That way, you can quickly intervene at the earliest sign of things beginning to move off course. You can let your client know your concerns and, ideally, have her take action immediately, avoiding unnecessary major setbacks. If you and your client agree that she will be responsible for communicating with key parts of the organization as the change progresses, then put a mechanism in place that can take the pulse on the degree to which that part of the organization is hearing and understanding how the change is going, what it means for them, and what they should be doing about it.

Provide Nonjudgmental Feedback

The process of change starts with data in the form of feedback. The consultant can provide the data if no one else is willing to do so. When giving feedback, it's important not to pull any punches. The feedback needs to be complete, direct, and honest. It should be delivered with compassion, with attention to the receiver's ability to hear and digest it, and with continued support once the message is delivered (Nadler, 1977b).

Clients become angry when they feel pushed into a corner without a means of escape. They resent others criticizing their behavior if the criticism is intended to be hurtful or delivered without regard for the impact it might have on them or on the relationship. Delivering client feedback that addresses deeply ingrained behaviors requires skill. Consultants who are inexperienced in giving direct feedback to clients should practice their delivery with someone who can help them improve their technique before attempting to give the feedback to their clients. The truth is that many consultants, like most people, find giving feedback difficult. Because it is difficult and risky, they avoid it; and because they avoid it, they never get better at doing it. When the situation calls for the skillful delivery of difficult feedback, they are ill-prepared to do what is required.

One of the reasons that Marc was able to handle the situation with Tom expertly is that he practices giving feedback all the time. Marc's confidence and expertise in delivering the feedback made it easier for Tom to listen and to know what to do next based on the information he received. Marc was able to shift the focus from his own anxiety about giving Tom feedback to Tom's needs as the receiver of the information. Marc's combination of nonjudgmental feedback and skillful delivery made it easier for Tom to hear what he needed to hear without becoming defensive or angry.

Here are a few things to consider as you think about *providing nonjudgmental feedback* to your client.

Contract for the Privilege. Don't assume your clients actually want or expect you to provide your feedback and observations. Make sure that you agree at the start of the engagement that this is something they would find useful. Give examples of what types of feedback you might provide in the style in which you might provide it so they can make an informed choice about whether or not they see any value. Laura was careful to do this right at the outset with Jim, which helped when she confronted him. Although she had some negative feedback to share, she and Jim had agreed to give "the good and the bad."

Be Understanding. No matter how confident your clients may appear, they are still human. They feel insecure about how others perceive them, and your approval is important to them in some form. Separate your personal disappointments and judgments from the message so they understand you are not withdrawing your faith in their ability. However, being nonjudgmental doesn't necessarily mean being nonemotional. It can be helpful to allow your clients to understand your feelings. Just be sure that the emotions don't carry an edge that inadvertently has a blaming or punishing tone.

Ensure the Message Is in Their Best Interest. If you can't identify the benefit your client will derive from the conversation, don't have it. If the message is intended to benefit your client's colleague, boss, team, or someone else who hopes your client will change, you are simply acting as a middleman for others. Avoid this severely collusive role. Best interest doesn't mean the client will like the message, but it does mean that he can benefit from hearing it. Not all feedback is created equal. Applying the theory that "We all can grow from personal learning" is not always productive. In fact, if we tried to act on every single piece of feedback we all received, we'd spend all of our waking hours in therapy.

Use Timing Strategically. Most feedback rules stress the importance of timeliness. While it is true that putting off important messages too long can dilute their impact, it is also important not to rush them. Following your client back to his office right after a very tense meeting in which he may have displayed the "mooselike" behavior and debriefing on the spot isn't always productive either. Sometimes a little distance from tough circumstances helps to restore openness and a balanced perspective.

Marc didn't just offer some observations for Tom to consider. He told Tom that he would have to do something to change the situation if he wanted to succeed. Marc proposed a series of meetings with Fred, Joe, and Sam to address the issues, and Tom agreed.

It's important to note that Tom was in constant contact with Fred, Joe, and Sam before the meetings that Marc suggested. Tom could have talked to each of them at any time about the issues he was experiencing. The fact that he didn't is not unusual. It's fairly common, in fact, to find that senior executive teams are rife with interpersonal issues that are not discussed but that have an enormous impact on team effectiveness. Executives are no better at addressing interpersonal issues than other people are. In fact, because there is so much at stake, executive teams may have even more difficulty addressing issues than other groups do. Because they don't typically set norms of openness or practice giving and receiving feedback with one another, executives sometimes feel at risk when they attempt to deal with interpersonal issues. Having someone who can help them deal with the issues in a competent, relatively "safe" manner is often a requirement for them to make progress.

Marc provided the safety net that Tom and his team needed to proceed. By demonstrating confidence in the team's ability to deal with their issues and being present to facilitate their discussions, Marc was able to help the team tackle its problems. Sometimes, the consultant's insistence on action and display of courage are what is required to move clients in a direction they have known for some time they need to go. Courage is a catalyst to change.

In Laura's case, we saw how she explicitly contracted for the privilege to give feedback and observations. Particularly as an internal consultant, it is important to set the stage by contracting up-front. Superiors and/or those contributing to one's performance evaluation are typically not accustomed to having an employee give such direct feedback. It is necessary to define the internal consultant's role and expectation for success of the engagement. This gives the internal consultant license or permission to be explicit and act more as an external consultant.

Knowing how and when to deliver the feedback is an art, regardless of whether you are internal or external. Laura learned that she needed to pace the feedback depending on what was happening in Jim's day. It wasn't that she ignored delivering the feedback. She just was able to be more attuned to his receptivity and was able to use her time with Jim more effectively.

Not all issues that require courage on the part of consultants involve behavior on the part of their clients. Clients may need to be confronted about difficult business decisions they are avoiding, policies that aren't being enforced, practices that are unacceptable, or goals that aren't stretching.

Listen to our colleague Roselinde Torres:

"I worked with a CEO who was an industry leader and was very visibly accountable for correcting a major performance downturn in his company. His original improvement plan involved delegating a major reorganization and new process implementation to one of his senior vice presidents. Our assessment was that the performance turnaround required fundamental organizational DNA transformation, which needed to begin with the CEO.

"To truly improve performance, the company would have to undergo changes in multiple core processes, infrastructure, and competencies. Business presidents, who had different ways of doing the same things, would need to work with more consistency, discipline, and teamwork. It was also clear that the CEO had operated in a hub-and-spoke model. The organization revered his intuitive genius. There was no way he would accomplish the business improvement without changing his leadership and business model.

"I did not have an expectation that the CEO would automatically agree with the assessment, but I did want him to take the first step in acknowledging the magnitude of change required of him to play an active role in the transformation process. I took the risk that he'd take the change personally, not just as something happening to the company or to others in the organization. My first intervention was to enable him to see that he would personally need to own the change, not delegate it to the senior VP. We talked through some decisions and actions that would show his personal commitment and active leadership, not just symbolic sponsorship.

"I also engaged him in articulating his vision, any risks, and expectations for others. As he thought about others, he started to see the broader network of people and processes that would be impacted. During the conversation, I was conscious of showing respect for him, but not reverence in the way others within the organization had interacted with him. This was risky because it was countercultural, but I knew a collegial relationship between us would be necessary for me to have license to raise the 'undiscussables,' including issues having to do with his performance as a leader.

"My intuition told me that change of this magnitude for him and the organization would require several moments of truth between us over a number of years. I took several risks over those years. On some occasions he acted on my advice in the moment. During other times, he disagreed with me, ignored my input, or acted on the advice long after it was originally offered.

"Throughout my years in working with him, I tried not to take the consultation personally. I understood that it had less to do with me and more to do with his level of competency, emotional readiness, and the degree of resistance he was getting from others. I also had to manage my ego and ensure that it was his vision that was being enacted, based on his aspirations and capability. I was facilitating the emergence of his transformation, not doing it for him or crowding his stage.

"I acknowledged the emotions he might be feeling in a nonthreatening way. I always made it a point to reinforce at least one thing he had done well. This helped reinforce a foundation of success from which to take additional risks. I identified controversial organizational and personal patterns that I saw and engaged him in dialogue on whether these matched his frame of reference. I also asked for feedback on how the firm and I were working with him and the organization. I often asked, 'Is there anything we should be doing to be more effective in this particular organization or in working with you?' As the client, he expected to give me feedback on my/the firm's performance. I also provided feedback on my experience working with him. These two-way feedback exchanges were new to him and at first uncomfortable, but over time these candid exchanges strengthened our relationship. They also provided him with one model for feedback exchanges with others.

"I knew from the length and depth of our conversations that I was getting through. He would discuss topics with me that he had not discussed with anyone else in the organization. I was very discreet with confidences. He admitted confusion over what to do or times when he felt he blew it. He would excitedly tell me something that had worked well. He thanked me when he acted based on my advice and saw progress.

"By gaining confidence that he could change and by showing others, he enabled people to see that they too could abandon the old way of working and move into the new paradigm. The company exceeded its performance targets. There was external recognition from analysts, shareholders, and the media for their performance turnaround."

Roselinde's client, when asked to reflect on her courage in working with him, had some remarkable things to say about the nature of their relationship:

"Roselinde was very thoughtful and patient. She took time to learn about the business at first by just sitting in meetings and observing. She didn't hurry to give advice. She showed me that she really wanted to understand the situation, which I appreciated. It took courage for her to say at first that she wanted to just sit and listen. Initially, the team objected. They wanted to know what she was doing there and felt that we couldn't discuss things openly with an observer in the room. They quickly got over it. In fact, we have learned from this that it is OK to invite people to sit in on meetings for developmental purposes and now we do it all the time.

"Eventually, she told me that if the business was about to change and I was the founder, the change would be more profound for me than anyone. It was as if she was telling me I had to go on a diet; it wasn't pleasant to hear. She was being prescriptive, but in a very thoughtful way. I agreed with her about how difficult it was going to be for me to learn a new set of skills. What was really hard for me to hear was that some of my people might not be able to lead the change initiatives that were necessary.

"She said that she thought I could make it, but that some of my people might not. Seeing myself from her perspective was hard at first. Seeing my people differently was even harder.

"She told me that people were agreeing with me in meetings, but then would disregard our agreements outside of the meetings. She told me to be more sensitive to how people were feeling in the meetings and to check with people to see whether they really agreed with what I was saying. I discovered that I had been broadcasting messages that people weren't receiving. I also like to use analogies; she told me not to use more than one at a time because it tended to confuse people. Rather than admit that they didn't understand something, they would simply resist doing what I said.

"She also suggested that I acknowledge my errors in judgment in front of the group. There's a vulnerability I had shown with individuals, but not with the group as a whole. She thought this would help people respond differently during the meetings. When I did this, I got notes from people saying, 'I can't believe you said you were wrong in front of the group.' The group dynamics improved. She told me to use some active listening techniques—to go around the room and ask people individually what they thought. It forced people to verbalize what they were really thinking.

"She built a relationship where I trusted her because she just spent time listening. It would be easy, I suppose, for some clients or consultants to just focus on the problem right away. Roselinde was different. The more time she spent, the more I believed she was really committed. I would ask her a question and she would say she needed time to think about it for a few days. She didn't give me flip answers; she really thought about things. If the consultant isn't patient or you're not patient, you won't get to the real issues. You need to spend the time, develop the relationship. People who look at consultants as a cost don't see the real value. I would tell any CEO that he or she has to make the commitment in time to develop trust with his or her consultant. The consultant, in turn, can't just show up with an answer.

"With Roselinde, the relationship grew deeper over time. We could work on things that were increasingly personal and more difficult. I could press her for criticism, and she would give it. She built my trust by not pushing me farther than I was prepared to go at the moment. She would say, 'If you don't want to talk about this, I understand.' That made it my choice, which made me more comfortable with her.

"We didn't always agree, and she often disagreed with other people on my team who were advising me. Her independent opinions made her more valuable. I saw it as courageous at the time. There were times when she disagreed with me and I was right; in those cases, she would openly admit that she learned something.

"My advice to consultants would be to say to their clients that they aren't interested in giving out quick prescriptions because it doesn't work that way. Consultants should say that they are health care managers, not the emergency room. The good ones are like old-time family doctors."

Do good clients make good consultants, or do good consultants make good clients? Clearly, as this story indicates, it's a bit of both. From the client's end, there need to be patience, openness, and a willingness to invest in building a relationship that can yield true value. From the consultant's perspective, there needs to be more than just technical competence. Consultants must care deeply about their clients, invest in building a relationship, and have the courage to offer advice that isn't always easy to hear. How many consultants would take the time to just sit in meetings and observe before offering their advice, as Roselinde did? How many clients would understand that in order for their consultants to help them, they needed to make the investment and take the risk of building a personal relationship with them? Doing good work requires courage on the part of both parties. Without courage, we're just shoe salesmen and our customers feel cheated when their shoes don't fit.

If, as the consultant, you show fear of a topic or a tough issue, it's likely that your clients will have little confidence in your ability to help them work through those issues. If you are able to demonstrate the courage element of rQ, as Marc, Laura, and Roselinde did with their clients, your impact can be profound. Let's look at what this can help clients accomplish.

▶ Change Enablement

How Courage to Confront the Moose
Builds a Leader's Openness to Tough News

Most leaders are smart enough to realize that, at some level, the information they have access to is going to be filtered, biased, even manipulated. And the higher in the organization a leader is, the more this is true. The problem is, they don't know what information is the truth and what is not. They have to treat the reliability of what they are hearing from various internal and external constituents with caution. Often frustrated by never knowing when they will step on a land mine, leaders remain on the lookout for the unexpected news that will tell them, often in hindsight, what land mine they could have avoided. Although this is probably hard for them to admit, they also know on some level that a portion of the information they receive about themselves is also unreliable.

Until leaders can receive reliable information and perspectives that give them the whole, unadulterated picture, the confidence they can have in their decisions will always, on some level, waver. Yes, there will always be those narcissistic leaders who believe they can do no wrong. But the average leader in most organizations has some sense that he or she needs reliable data sources beyond the traditional management processes in place. Having a confidant who will give it to you straight—the good, the bad, and the ugly—is a major asset to leaders who want to implement fundamental change in their organizations. The pinch that comes from hearing about "the moose" that has been in the middle of the table for so long, but never acknowledged, is a catalytic pinch that provokes a leader to consider real versus cosmetic change.

It's also likely that the leader will appreciate the risk you take to raise issues and concerns that nobody has raised before. He or she will understand the courage, and the care, embedded in your choice and will be more inclined to listen. Sure, some will become defensive, even angry. But you shouldn't cower. Talk about what you are feeling, the risk you took, the reactions you are seeing, and the fact that, like it or not, the data is what it is. Help your clients move beyond their reactions to positive action. Help them channel the energy that you infused by drawing attention to the moose into making concrete choices in the direction of positive change. ◄

Table 4.1 provides a summary to help you build and assess courage in your relationships.

Table 4.1. Summary of How to Build Courage

Practices	Behaviors	Self-Assessment
Have Confidence to Call the Tough Questions	Confront personal avoidance of rejection and conflict	I am willing to address conflict with my client/internal collaborators
	Pick and choose your battles wisely	I confront my clients on issues that are critical to the success of the change effort
	Rehearse the messages	When delivering key messages, I spend time preparing what I will say and how I will phrase my questions
	Extend the benefit of the doubt	I gather enough data before I attribute cause or assign blame
Hold the Client Accountable	Establish agreed-on commitments	I work with my clients to define clear expectations about our projects
	Use metrics	I collaborate with my clients to create project plans
		I work with my clients to identify the measures of success of our projects
		I let my clients know when they aren't contributing enough to the project
		I ask my clients to show visible signs of commitment to the work we are doing
Provide Nonjudgmental Feedback	Contract for the privilege	At the beginning of the relationship, I set expectations on providing feedback to my clients
	Be understanding	I put myself in my client's shoes before disclosing negative feedback
	Ensure the message is in their best interest	I am aware of the power of feedback and how it helps my clients
	Use timing strategically	I prepare my clients to receive feedback from me on an ongoing basis
		I carefully select opportunities to give feedback to my clients

(5)

Someone in Your Corner: Advocacy

FEWER CIRCUMSTANCES ARE MORE CHALLENGING in a leader's life than initiating dramatic organization change in the face of staunch resistance. During a complex change initiative, the phrase "lonely at the top" can take on a whole new meaning. While we talked about courage and the need to sometimes push clients past their comfort boundaries in the last chapter, it is also important to let clients know that you are on their side. Effectively, you must become the client's advocate. To see how this advocacy element of rQ can work, let's take a look at how I [Ron] supported a client in making and implementing a very difficult but necessary decision.

"While I was working with the CEO of a large, global retail company, it became quickly apparent to me that his impressive career as a respected leader, his genuineness and deep integrity, and his breadth of knowledge about his industry could serve as the foundation for a terrific relationship. At the same time, I could also see that nothing in his career had prepared him to lead radical transformational change. He did realize it was required, and he was able to acknowledge the challenge his lack of experience presented. Neither of us was prepared for how much the organization's resistance to change would continually test his resolve though.

"One of the most painful parts of the engagement came when he needed to terminate one of the organization's most visible senior leaders. The two of them had worked together for many years, and their relationship was very personal. He wrestled with the decision for months, avoided it, entertained temptations of easy outs, and lost a fair bit of sleep. But the progress of change was significantly impaired until he came to the place where this decision could be made.

"I spent hours with him working through his personal struggle with the decision, his contributions to the failed relationship, and the inevitable judgments that would come from the leader's supporters in the organization and on the board. We talked about his discomfort with conflict, his paternalism, and the inevitable pain of further wounding this relationship that would ensue from ending the executive's decades of employment. We also talked about the significant consequences and threats posed to the transformation process by this person's retention. I was deeply moved by his genuine struggle with the decision. I told him how much I respected his courageous willingness to wrestle with such a complex and unique choice for him. I told him I admired his integrity to take responsibility for his contribution to the decayed relationship and to face the consequences of public judgment that would follow the decision. For a while, I was concerned that the client would back away from the decision."

Nothing is more frustrating for a consultant than to have a client back away from key decisions or initiatives owing to a sudden lack of confidence. Given the stress of the change process, it is likely that our clients will become caught in gusts of self-doubt along the way. The questions for you, the consultant, are (1) Can you see the self-doubt coming? and (2) What should you do about it?

Organization change must be approached as a marathon, not as a sprint. It will test a leader's endurance and perseverance as well-grooved patterns of comfort and familiarity are dismantled and it begins to feel like all hell has broken loose. The seasoned consultant will build into her relationship with a leader an allowance for such storms and establish herself as an ally and an advocate. The natural impulses to ease the pain and return to feelings of normalcy will intensify as the turbulence of change tests a leader's tenacity and commitment.

"Once the decision was announced, I used my 'hallway' time to check in with key members of the senior team, whose condemnation and scorn were visible. I listened to their hurt and their sense of loss, but challenged them to take a broader and long-term view. I reminded them of the competitive challenges the organization faced and that the transformation process wasn't an option, but a necessity for growth given their highly saturated, mature markets. Some were moved to reconsider their position; others dug their heels in. But I still felt obligated to push them to see a different point of view. They knew I was talking about the decision on its own merits as I saw them—I wasn't giving them the party line. But I felt, having watched my client struggle with such a major decision, that part of my role in seeing the decision supported was to influence the organization however I could to embrace it, despite their pain."

One of the most common phrases I [Ron] use with my clients is, "At times, it will feel like I'm your biggest critic. But those who know that I'm advising you need to understand that, if I'm going to be your biggest critic when we're together, then I will have earned my right to be your 'biggest fan' when we're with them." The organization needs to see tangible effects of a trusted advisor's advice in the form of changed behavior. That way, when the time for the consultant to help champion the leader's views and decisions in the organization comes, there won't be concerns that the consultant is merely colluding with the leader.

There are four components of offering leaders the support they need to stay the course:

- Help Leaders Acknowledge and Explore Their Apprehension;
- Provide Genuine Encouragement at Critical Crossroads;
- Help Leaders Stay the Course During Implementation; and
- Help Clients Recognize When They Have Exhibited Highly Effective Behavior

Let's examine each in detail:

Help Leaders Acknowledge and Explore Their Apprehension

There is good reason to worry if a leader never feels uneasy during a major change process. The challenge is helping leaders to acknowledge their uneasiness and to recognize the potential pitfalls it might lead to should they buckle under when the change process gets tough. Most leaders face their greasiest skids of apprehension the moment they begin to see the faces of those around them wince at the thought of significant change. In the beginning, there is always great excitement about a new initiative. Visions of competitive superiority, soaring stock prices, the admiration of analysts, and journalistic attention paid to great feats—all swell in a crescendo of optimistic energy as the trumpet signals "charge!" But then the discussion moves from theory to reality, and people actually have to do something. This is a different story altogether. The heat of protracted, often radical change brings an onslaught of "Yeah, buts," and "Don't forget abouts," followed by comments that distance the speaker from the change process and its consequences. That's when leaders can get a tad weak in the knees.

These are the moments when a trusted confidant's advocacy can make a significant difference. In the case above, I [Ron] felt it was important to acknowledge the CEO's clear struggle with the decision he faced. Some of his key leaders, and even members of his board, were displaying great resistance to his decision. We spent a great deal of time talking about the pros and cons of his options to prevent him from becoming paralyzed by his sense of torn loyalties and isolation. We kept focused on the vision he had set for the organization's growth and on what was going to be required to get there. We spoke about where he would have support for his decision, about how to leverage key leaders who recognized the complexity of the situation, and about the need for tough action. When he was ready, he made the decision.

In order to step into the role of advocate, you need to be able to have the sort of conversation with a client in a tight spot that will enable him to choose the best course and give him the strength to stick to it. Let's look at how our colleague Roselinde Torres talked candidly with a CEO client dealing with his own apprehension and staunch resistance in the face of significant change.

"The CEO feared that, if he gave an executive vice president candid performance feedback, the executive would react negatively and leave the company or stay and harm the business. This executive was widely known throughout the organization, well-connected with key customers, and visible to external parties. The CEO did not want to be second-guessed or blamed if the guy walked out. Also, the executive was responsible for a major part of the company, and the CEO did not want the executive to be distracted or demotivated in a way that might jeopardize key businesses.

"At the same time, the CEO understood that, if the executive continued his negative behavior, it would undermine his relationships with his peers and subordinates, also resulting in poor business outcomes. Left unattended to, the subordinate's performance would likely impact the individual's current and future career trajectory. Once the CEO recognized the executive's negative behavior, we both concluded that the CEO had to confront the executive. Despite the logic of the decision to act, the CEO pushed back by saying, 'We might have the perfect feedback session, but I won't have accomplished much if he quits.' For the CEO, initiating the performance feedback felt like opening Pandora's box.

"To enable the CEO to initiate the conversation with the individual, I engaged him in a lengthy dialogue to surface all of his fears and concerns. This was essentially a data-dump of all the things that could go wrong. We then talked about potential positive outcomes, which included a discussion of benefits to the individual executive, as well as a discussion about how the CEO would feel if he had a productive conversation. I also helped him to see that his intervention did not have to occur in just one magical conversation with the executive.

"One of the CEO's concerns had to do with 'not surprising' the executive with negative feedback. We developed a way to position the conversation and also used a disciplined process for communicating and working the feedback. We used data-based scoring instruments (self and other) that would allow a two-way feedback exchange. We also agreed to offer the executive a coach who would help him prepare for the conversation with the CEO and any developmental action planning. As part of the process, we scheduled a clarification session, which occurred after the CEO and the executive had met. The clarification session included the CEO, the executive, his coach, and me and was intended to ensure that messages were accurately sent and heard between the CEO and the executive.

"During the first part of the session, the executive heard the feedback but did not take it very seriously. It was not clear whether the CEO was soft-pedaling the message or if the executive was in denial. When the CEO confronted the issue directly in the clarification session, the executive internalized the message, became emotional, and asked if the performance issue was a fatal flaw and therefore required him to leave the company. This reaction from the executive validated for me that the CEO had the right instincts and had accurately predicted the executive's behavior. Often, clients have legitimate fears, and we should not, as consultants, underestimate or minimize them. They know their businesses and players much more intimately than we do. I always assume my clients are telling me the truth as they are experiencing it.

"The systematic feedback process was designed to both anticipate and manage the executive's reaction. Because of the preparation we had done, the CEO was able to respond in the moment and put the negative feedback within the context of other data. The executive was able to see how addressing this performance issue could enable him to have greater impact and to be more respected as a senior leader. The executive heard the message and has been actively working on the issue with his coach and others.

"I sent a follow-up note to the CEO commending him on stepping up to a difficult issue and citing what he had done well in the process. I also asked him to reflect on anything he would have done differently. My intent was to reinforce the learning so he would be better equipped and more confident to face a similar situation in the future.

"Following the clarification session, the executive positively acknowledged the CEO for having the willingness to engage in this level of candid conversation. The executive indicated that it could not have been easy for the CEO to have this type of dialogue and was grateful for the CEO's personal investment.

"The CEO was pleased with the outcome on multiple levels. His view was that the disciplined approach we used allowed for the quality and impact of the conversation. He was also pleased that the executive was visibly working the issue. He seemed to be most emotionally satisfied with the fact that the executive was genuinely appreciative.

"As I reflect on this example, it's clear that sometimes clients are apprehensive about acting in unfamiliar territory or when they don't know what to do. Situations that are emotionally charged appear the most unpredictable and can make the client feel 'out of control' and therefore hesitant to act. One role we can play as consultants is to enable clients to see the broad patterns, have a process to guide them, and trust their own natural instincts. The courage to act doesn't come from being 'in control' so much as in feeling confident and ready for whatever happens."

Provide Genuine Encouragement at Critical Crossroads

Many people fall prey to the naïve assumption that leaders at the top of organizations in positions of great influence have unwavering confidence and tenacity. "What have they got to feel insecure about? Look where they are!" go the hallway suppositions. Nothing could be further from the truth. My [Ron's] client needed to hear me say, "I know this is tough, and I can see how painful this is for you, but you've got to do what you know is right. No, it won't feel good at first, and the backlash might be a little heated for awhile. But if you really want to get to where you say you want to go, there really isn't any way around this. If I didn't think you could pull this off, I would have told you a long time ago. But I believe you can do this, and I believe you can do it successfully. You're just going to have to start with a really tough first step."

Encouragement can come in many forms. Depending on the personality of the leader, and the context in which he or she is attempting significant change, it is important to choose an approach that best matches the needs of the client. Otherwise, you risk genuine good wishes being interpreted as saccharine, condescending, gratuitous, or presumptuous. Here are some thoughts on how to provide different types of appropriate encouragement a leader might require.

When the Organization Is Resisting a New Direction Set by the Leader. In this case, the leader may be feeling either doubt about the viability of the strategy or doubt about the capability of the team to accomplish it. The first step in this situation is to find out which of these issues is causing the leader to waiver. If the leader is concerned about the viability of the strategy, encouragement could take one of several forms: (1) reminding the leader how he reached the decision to follow this course of action; (2) probing the nature of the leader's concern and helping her take steps to collect more data from the organization or benchmarking other organizations that have been through similar changes; or (3) simply sharing examples from your experience with other clients you have helped through similar situations. If the leader's concern is about the team's ability to implement the change, needed encouragement may come in the form of a conversation, where you make it clear that you know how to assess the capacity of the team and how to deal with any shortcomings that arise. Or, as in Roselinde's example, you may need to help the leader come to grips with an individual team member's performance. As leaders create new visions for their organizations, they also become more aware of the things that are getting in the way. They may need to think through what's needed from a senior team member and how current executives measure up against these requirements. Are there individual fatal flaws that are impeding individual or team performance? Have these flaws been dealt with directly and plainly? Dealing with people issues is never easy, which is why leaders tend to put it off longer than they should. Many CEOs will look for reasons to procrastinate. Some will go to practically any length to avoid "pulling the trigger" and terminating an executive. There are several reasons why so many smart, capable CEOs will go to such extraordinary lengths to avoid removing one of their direct reports. In Table 5.1, ten common reasons that stop leaders from acting are summarized.

Table 5.1. Ten Reasons CEOs Do Not Take Action

Narcissism	CEOs love to be loved. Terminating an executive does not usually generate love, admiration, and respect from the person being terminated or from others around him.
The Big Fall	Most senior executives have enjoyed a history of success, not failure. Delivering a first message of failure can feel as though a leader is destroying a career, a life, and a family. However, it is useful to remember that the vast majority of executives have actively sought higher and higher levels of responsibility, knowing that the risks increase proportionately.
The Failed Rescue	Many CEOs have unrealistic notions of their own ability to change people and solve problems. Executives are products of years of personal and professional experiences that shape their personalities, behavior, skills, and management style. To think that one can reverse all of this is, as one CEO put it, "the height of arrogance."
The Burden of Guilt	CEOs sometimes feel immense guilt—from the selection and staffing decisions they have made to failing to rescue. Clearly, there is no guarantee that every appointment will be a success. Indulging in guilt only stalls action and the opportunity for the organization and the individual to move on.
The Rusty Sword	Having moved out of line management some time ago, some CEOs are out of practice with dealing with these situations. However, making this tough decision is not an activity

Table 5.1. Ten Reasons CEOs Do Not Take Action, Cont'd

	that can be delegated. The only person who can act on it is the CEO.
Kremlin Watching	Forced departures from the senior team are very visible and may prompt some to speculate about instability within the organization. Soon enough though, people realize that stability is not threatened, particularly when carefully thought out communications and succession plans are executed.
The Essential Link	Executive team members sometimes cultivate close ties with outside groups, such as customers, community leaders, the press, or the financial community. They come to be viewed as links to the outside world. Fear of a backlash may prevent the CEO from replacing a problematic subordinate who was the darling of the stock analysts. But large organizations always seem to weather the departure of these important figures when they finally occur, and the ramifications never turn out to be quite as severe as everyone had feared.
The Irreplaceable Cog	This is the internal version of the essential link. Over time people become enshrouded in corporate myths that cloak them in an aura of near-invincibility. People come to believe that the place will grind to a halt without the special talents of these chosen few. The truth is that, in all but a handful of rare cases, their talent or expertise is never as crucial as it seemed. It often turns out that the organization they were leading runs better once the executive is removed and rational business processes replace a disorganized cult of personality.
The Incomplete File	Situations in which definitive empirical data clearly demonstrate that an executive should be sacked are the exception rather than the rule. CEOs who keep hanging back, waiting for more and more information, will almost certainly wait too long. By the time that kind of information surfaces, the executive in question will have caused measurable damage to the organization.

Table 5.1. Ten Reasons CEOs Do Not Take Action, Cont'd

The Empty Bench	As much as the CEO would like to get rid of someone, there is no obvious replacement in sight. CEOs have to ask how long they, the team, and the organization can continue to tolerate inadequate performance or disruptive behavior. Hiring from the outside is a gamble, but inherent in gambling is the potential for a big win.

From *When to Pull the Trigger: Individual Performance on the Executive Team.* New York: Mercer Delta Insights, 1998.

The most obvious way to prevent such serious situations from sneaking up is to keep a close watch through recurrent assessment. CEOs ought to employ a wide array of assessment techniques—surveys, 360-degree feedback tools, outside consultants, frequent appraisals tied to specific objectives and deadlines—in order to stay on top of the situation. The work of senior executives is simply too important for poor performance to go unnoticed or unaddressed for any significant period of time. In this context, providing encouragement to face these issues can be one of your most valuable contributions as a change agent.

When Others Are Questioning the Leader's Capability to Succeed. Personal rejection is at the heart of this circumstance. In this case, leaders need to receive strong, objective feedback about their legitimate strengths and their "flat sides" to ensure they don't fulfill the prophecy of the critics. Some of the criticism may even be public in the media.

Leaders, like all people, do have flat sides. Encouragement doesn't mean pretending that the leaders' flat sides don't exist. On the contrary, real encouragement comes when you get close enough to the leader to acknowledge the flat sides and can provide coaching on how to overcome them. There are several things you can do.

First, you can help the leader identify strengths he or she can use to compensate for the weakness. A leader who isn't a great public speaker, for example, may be having trouble motivating the troops. If the leader is a good writer, or is willing to accept help from others, a series of memos can help people feel the urgency and need for change.

Second, you can advise leaders to surround themselves with others who complement their weaknesses. A leader who tends to be indecisive may appoint a strong-willed champion of change to push the agenda forward. A leader who can't pay attention to details may need the help of someone who loves to make certain that every "i" is dotted and every "t" is crossed. Rivero and Spencer (1997) reported that in the past twenty years there has been a shift in the distribution of leadership responsibilities at the top of corporate organizations. Part of this shift has included the movement toward design and deployment of the executive team. With the increasing emphasis on the executive team's responsibility for governance, a need has emerged to more clearly define and structure the role of the team leader. Leadership responsibilities, which typically have been described as pertaining to a CEO, have changed hands, and different geometric models of leadership have appeared. While some organizations have created a position of COO to manage internal operations, others have assigned COO-like responsibilities to the executive team. It is important to note that neither governing role ought to preclude the importance of the other; instead, appointment of a COO is meant to alleviate a CEO's burden, allow her to focus on the proper agenda items, and open the door to dual management benefits.

Third, you can catch the leader at his best; that is, you can point out times when leaders demonstrate the skill in question and help them "connect the dots." If she has done it once, she can do it again. Encouragement in the face of criticism can take many forms. Just think about what is helpful to you when you need this kind of encouragement and try providing that for your clients. Helping your clients through these rough spots can do wonders for their confidence and for your relationship with them.

When There Are Unexpected Setbacks. Inevitably, something will go wrong in the process of change. Because nearly every change requires new behavior, it's to be expected that there will be some missteps. Some of these missteps may even be taken by the leader, which, in turn, could invite the ridicule of others, as discussed above. Learning to be resilient in the face of honest mistakes, learning from them, and getting up and moving on is essential for leaders during change, but easier said than done. People are often surprised by how difficult it is to loosen up after a very public gaffe. It erodes their self-confidence and can often set an ugly cycle in motion. More mistakes lead to more personal doubt, which in turn leads to more mistakes. A trusted confidant can help nip this in the bud at the first sign of hesitancy after a misstep.

What do you do when your clients foul up or lose confidence? It's a sure bet that this isn't the first misstep they have taken in their careers. Remind them that they have stubbed their toes before and that, while it hurts a lot for a short time, they will get over it. Help them think about how they would want their employees to respond to making a genuine mistake. Become paralyzed by inaction? Definitely not. Provide advice on what to do next—not in the next months or years, but immediately, *right now.* Make up a list of five things to do—people to call, a memo to write, an action to take, a decision to announce, a statement to prepare for the press—that would acknowledge the mistake publicly but also demonstrate a resolution to succeed. The specifics have to be tailored to the situation, but the idea is immediately to replace doubt or regret with positive action, the surest cure for the dreaded "Don't I look stupid?" disease.

In this next example, our colleague Dennis Tirman shares with us an account of a client facing severe scrutiny and feelings of self-doubt and the choices he made to offer encouragement.

"My client was a senior VP within a distribution company, entrusted with growing a current segment of business in a new way with an expanded offering. He asked for my help to redesign the organization. When we began the organizational design work, it was clear my client had reached the end of his patience and was extremely frustrated by the lack of support he thought he was receiving from his peers and the president and COO of the company. I had also been working directly with the president to build his leadership team, of which this client was a member. So I was able to work with and observe my client in a number of venues—with peers, superiors, and direct reports. I also knew that the president of the company vigorously supported the growth of this new offering, but somehow my client was unable to see this.

"My client was bright and understood the requirements of the new business model better than anyone else in the company. In fact, much of his frustration was due to his perception that others did not feel the urgency he felt, given the strategic imperative of growing this business. He could 'reason out' numerous aspects of growing this offering, including analyzing the potential business returns, identifying a graduating set of skills and capabilities required to sell and operate the offering, and designing and developing a training program to support implementation. But even with all this support made available to the local business leaders, he could not understand why they would hesitate to grow this offering aggressively.

"By the time we began the organizational redesign, my client was ready to resign. He was convinced that there was a lack of real strategic support for what he had been asked to do. He also began to question whether the strategy itself made sense for the company given his perception of the resistance to growing the high end and differentiated part of the offering. His intellectual nature could not make sense of the resistance to this opportunity to help the company do exactly what it needed to do to have greater financial returns, nor could he figure out how to work with the resistance.

"My relationship with this client grew out of his real frustration and the impact it began to have on his self-esteem. He wanted help, as he would openly raise the question with me as to whether he was the right person to lead this business. We discussed this in depth and arrived at an assumption that, regardless of his abilities, if he continued to question his own capability, he certainly would not be a good candidate. We did discuss clearly the areas in which he felt capable and comfortable and areas in which he was frustrated and felt a growing sense of defeat.

"The breakthrough that occurred with this client was a reframing of the task he was engaged in to grow the business. While he knew clearly that he could not accomplish this on his own, it was difficult for him to see how to build support with his peers and others who were responsible to execute the business locally. I pointed out to him that, since he had the best grasp of this business in the company, what he needed to do was be more of a coach to help bring others up to speed. He also had to do this in a way that was not perceived as condescending, which was an existing perception of him.

"The role we agreed he could play was one of capacity builder. During the data-collection process for the redesign, it became abundantly clear that a large part of the difficulty in growing the business was the lack of leadership at the local level. This lack of leadership was a result of general managers not being familiar or comfortable with the new offerings and concerned that it would end up taking resources away from initiatives they were more familiar with. He had already built much of the capacity-building infrastructure, and now his task was to bring the style of leadership that would engage, energize, and enable others to learn and support the new offerings.

"The approach I took was to be very open with my client about the behavior he should display and the impact it would have on others. One example occurred during a presentation he was giving to the lead management team of the company in which he was trying again to raise awareness of the opportunity connected with the new offerings. He had made this presentation more than once, so it was frustrating for him to be plowing the same ground over again. It was also obvious that many in the group were also becoming frustrated or tuning out. On a break, I talked with my client about my observations, and we discussed some ways for him to move away from forcing change toward partnering with the leadership team.

"I was as authentic as I could be with him and shared how his behavior was impacting me, as well as observations of the impact on others. I also encouraged my client to hear or understand in a different way what others were saying or doing with regard to supporting the growth of the new offerings. Instead of hearing questions and concerns as only resistance, he could begin to use these questions from his peers to help build more commitment and better approaches to implementing the model. While he had to stand firm on some 'nonnegotiable issues,' he could use their input and get farther faster.

"I also pointed out to him the obvious strengths and commitment he had displayed in the face of some clear resistance. We were able to get to the point where he recognized that the majority of resistance was not aimed at him personally but was directed at what some managers feared or did not understand. Over the course of about five months, it became clear to my client that he had not been hearing the full range of reactions and responses to his efforts, especially the more supportive ones.

"Evidence of my client's individual change came during the presentation of the new organization for his business to the business leaders of the company. The new organization was widely accepted and is currently being implemented. This acceptance was in large part due to the idea my client had to meet individually with each of the three regional business leaders to explain the new organization and understand any concerns they had. While it is clear a significant change process will need to be planned to achieve the full potential of the new organization, it appears my client is now more capable to lead it in concert with his peers and the president and COO of the company."

Dennis' client has this perspective to share on the story.

"Dennis provides me with encouragement in many ways. It is clearly through the diagnosis of situations that Dennis supports me. My personal growth comes through how Dennis is able to talk to me about the examples where I do well and where I do not do well. We are able to talk about the differences between what works well and what does not. It is always a good experience. Sometimes I know I will have to talk to Dennis because I 'blew it' in a meeting or a presentation. But through Dennis' help, my awareness of where I blow it is increasing over time.

"The most valuable aspect of the relationship is clearly Dennis' ability to ask the frank questions that everyone else will dodge. He says, 'I'm just a dumb person from the outside, but what was the rationale for this decision.' He never says this in a pejorative way, but in a more inquisitive fashion. It is through his ability to go back to the third-party observer to diagnose the dynamics and the issues at hand. I have learned that my biggest problem is always in what a person does not say versus the person who says what is on her mind. Dennis helps me to look at what people do *not* say and *why* they do not say it.

"Sometimes I feel so comfortable with Dennis that I talk about things that are very personal in nature. I feel as if I am out jogging with a friend. It is a fine balance between sharing what is personal and what is needed for business success. Sometimes I feel guilty I take Dennis' time, but I also know that I need to work through some of those feelings to be effective. Dennis is an excellent sounding board.

"The difference in this relationship versus relationships with other consultants is that Dennis grew to understand our business but also balanced his learnings from other client situations. He always asks, 'I experienced this situation with a client; is it similar?' Dennis does not presume that he knows the answer and that he is right. He always questions whether or not the situation is similar if he believes it is. Other consultants want to tell us the answer. Dennis does not presume to know the answer. Another aspect of the relationship is built on Dennis' masterful job of follow-up with notes and presentations that are both clear and concise. The clarity and brevity are extremely important to me. Other consultants just want to tell us the answer and go on and on."

Practice Positive Reinforcement with Another. Find a consulting partner (or a willing friend or significant other) and try out your advocacy skills. Try being an advocate by asking the person to tell you about something that he or she has been trying to accomplish. Listen carefully to what the person says, probe the barriers to success, and find out the things he or she has done that have been most effective to date. Then, use your knowledge of the person to reinforce his or her ambition and ability to do the job. Remind the person of things he or she has done well in the past and make the connection to the initiative being undertaken now. Remind the person of his or her positive qualities and help the person think about how to use these strengths to succeed. You should not be falsely positive about the person's strengths or overly optimistic about his or her success. The goal is to provide genuine advocacy and reassurance. When you are done, ask for feedback on how well you did.

Then, ask your practice partner to play the part of someone resisting the change being undertaken. Your role is to convince the other person that the change is worthwhile. Your partner's job is to make your job as difficult as possible. He or she will get into it, and you'll find that your skills as an advocate of change are strongly tested. Again, ask for feedback on how you did and what you might have done differently to bring the person around.

Help Leaders Stay the Course During Implementation

The third aspect of advocacy is to work with the leader to get the change embedded as deeply as possible into the organization. This becomes especially important in places where there is inherent resistance to, even rebellion toward, change—especially in outlying locations. In the example at the beginning of the chapter, I [Ron] felt it was part of my role to seek out those key leaders who were clearly unsupportive of the CEO's decision to remove the problematic executive. My goal wasn't to be an ambassador for the CEO, but rather to be an outside voice of reason to challenge perspectives that were based on flawed assumptions. In some cases, my interventions "moved the needle" and helped initial resisters through their sense of loss and into a place of acceptance. In other cases, people just wouldn't budge.

Many leaders, on the heels of initiating major change, will prematurely declare victory and minimize the need to pursue the rest of the change agenda. Then, when they are blindsided by some significant event that signals that the change is faltering, the leader embarks on an appeal campaign that usually only undermines his credibility. In despair, the leader may reverse course and find some face-saving way to raise the white flag, usually under the guise of "responding to more immediate strategic needs" or "re-evaluating priorities given current business conditions." The sad consequence of such failures is that the organization is now further disabled from future change.

The proactive consultant will help her client anticipate those places where change is likely to struggle for survival and develop a plan to head off any significant threats of sabotage. Together, client and consultant work to find ways to leverage their respective roles as leader and change expert to build the organization's commitment to, understanding of, and ownership of the change. Here are some considerations that will enable the consultant to help the client stay on course.

Do a Stakeholder Analysis. One of the first things to do is to make sure you have a map of the territory you are helping your client explore. If you don't already have one, work with your client to put one together. The map should be an analysis of the various groups and individuals who influence your client. These groups and individuals can be internal or external. For each group, make certain you and your client understand what each group wants: better stock performance, more job security, greater recognition, a bigger job, or whatever. Take some time to understand how your client views these demands. Are they reasonable or unreasonable? Which are most important?

Then think about the change you are helping your client undertake. Where will the greatest resistance come from and why? Who needs to be educated? Who needs to be included in decisions? Who needs to quit whining and get on board? Finally, ask yourself how you can be helpful. Which of the people or groups can you speak with personally? What could you say or do that would be helpful? For the groups you cannot address, how can you help your client prepare for the struggles that are certain to come? This kind of analysis will do two things: (1) it will help you be a more effective advocate for your client and (2) it will help you avoid surprises that could knock the wind out of your client's sails. Table 5.2 provides a template to accomplish this task.

Table 5.2. Stakeholder Analysis Matrix

Objective	Use the Implementation Team to plan specific actions that will improve the effectiveness of the change initiatives or enhance the speed or sustainability of the implementation effort. An integral part of implementation efforts for each initiative should be a specific plan of engagement for each of the stakeholder groups. By involving stakeholders throughout

Table 5.2. Stakeholder Analysis Matrix, Cont'd

	the change process, they are more likely to own the work and enhance their capability to sustain the change over time.
Pre-Work	Each Implementation Team member should complete a matrix for each major initiative for which he/she is responsible. Start with the initiative that is the most pressing or involves the most risks/issues to address, and then assess others.
Stakeholder Groups and Names	Your initiative may involve others or different groups. List all relevant individuals of the stakeholder group.
Issues and Extent of Impact	What are the key issues or problems? How critical are these issues, and what is the potential impact of these issues if they are not resolved?
Barriers to Change	Describe the barriers to change and, if possible, why they exist. Examples include lack of: clarity or understanding of direction/change, agreement on direction/change, ownership/commitment to drive the change, capability to change, alignment between this group and other stakeholders, and so forth.
Change Management Leverage Points (Enablers to Change)	Describe the enablers to change: What is currently working well and to what do you attribute that? What aspects of the change process need more attention?
Actions to Take	Describe recommended actions to enhance the change effort. Include ideas to engage the stakeholder group (or individuals) to effectively raise and resolve the issues and drive the change.
Implementation Team Work	The initiatives will be reviewed and discussed in the meeting. The team will select an initiative and use a structured approach to better understand the issues and develop recommended approaches/interventions for the initiative. Finally, the team will prioritize the approaches and discuss and agree on action steps (who, what, when, follow-up mechanism, and so on). Repeat for the other initiatives.

With Those Who Lose and Those Who Remain. Often the harsh reality of change can leave behind a sense of grave loss for those whose jobs, power base, resource control, or organizational "clout" are dramatically altered. Their anger is aimed directly at the leader who initiated the change that brought about the loss. Further, when severe change requires a reduction in headcount, those who remain have a cold sense of "survivor syndrome," often characterized by anxiety, guilt, and grieving. In these cases, the consultant can be a force for renewal in parts of the organization where the leader may be viewed as the adversary.

With Remote Offices and Subsidiaries. In many global organizations, those on the geographical outskirts—most distant from the leader of change—can feel excluded from, out of touch with, or dangerously unaffected by the change. Without directed efforts, the change could take years to find its way to these remote corners of the organization, if it does so at all. In this instance, the consultant can focus on finding ways to engage these distant groups. While exploring strategies to reach people who are geographically dispersed, it is important to think about their change-related concerns. Kim and Mauborgne (1993) studied twenty-five multinational organizations to find out what most motivates managers of remote offices to execute the global strategies formulated at headquarters. They found that these managers were most concerned that the global, strategic decision-making process employ due process—an open process that would be consistent and fair and allow for their input. When applied to change management, due process is likely to mean (1) that top leadership is familiar with all remote office concerns and situations regarding the change agenda; (2) that a two-way communication is present in the decision-making process of change; (3) that top leadership show some relative consistency in making change decisions across geographical units; (4) that remote units can legitimately challenge top leadership's views and decisions regarding the change agenda; and (5) that the rationale for final decisions is communicated to all offices across the globe.

With Threatened Executives. There will always be a few leaders for whom the change represents exposure of some kind. New technologies may represent the obsolescence of individual skill sets; new strategies may herald the arrival of fresh talent, relegating existing leaders to the "day-old" bin; new structures may introduce a shift in power bases and the requirement to share the limelight. In each of these instances, where these executives are likely very visible and their behavior toward the change a strong barometer from which many will take their cues, the consultant can play a unique role.

Our colleague Peter Thies has some ideas on how to extend advocacy to leaders and their constituents during large scale change.

"In the summer and early fall of 1999, Janice, my CEO-level client, was thinking through her approach to leading the acquisition and integration of several international organizations. The existing company had a very traditional business model, with a focus on entirely different markets, and a long history in a small company town.

"This was going to be a complex transaction and integration, dubbed a 'triple merger' by those closest to the deal. In addition to the considerable financial complexities, the political, cultural, and organizational issues were staggering. The new organization needed to be a peaceful union of organizations based in the United States, the United Kingdom, Europe, and Asia. If that weren't enough, the parent company believed the acquisition should become accretive in the second year of operation. By all accounts, this was a high-degree-of-difficulty dive.

"Between the spring of 1999 and the summer of 2001, Janice and I spent countless hours in various locations thinking through her transition into the role of president and CEO and how she wanted to lead the integration process. As we discussed her approach, she remained steadfast to the idea that the transition from separate entities to one global organization would be open, transparent, inclusive, and engaging. This idea captured her core values, and she never wavered in her commitment to them.

"Janice's deeply held beliefs about leadership and change reflected the notion that 'people own what they create.' She knew intuitively that, for the organization to become one integrated global company, change had to be embedded throughout the fabric of the new organization—all locations, all levels, all functions, all lines of business. As a result, she thought very carefully about the best way to involve people. My role as an advocate focused on helping Janice and her team implement an integration process that reflected her values. In short, we helped Janice build bridges to the organization's myriad components. Because Janice had always intended to embed change as deeply into the organization as possible, our advocacy for her agenda included bringing tools, methods, and approaches for combining geographically disperse organizations into one integrated global company.

"Our support for Janice's bridge-building effort has taken many shapes and forms over the past two years. For example, we worked with Janice to create a transition council to provide oversight for integration activities after the close date. She selected members to manage the change process who she thought would effectively represent perspectives from all parts of the new organization.

"Janice also created a governance body composed of 130 senior leaders from all parts of the company and locations throughout the world. This leadership team meets twice a year for several days to discuss a myriad of topics from strategy to communications. We saw that social integration didn't occur during the meetings. It happened when groups of leaders were laughing and singing at a medieval feast in Europe or playing "crazy" golf. To monitor the progress of integration, Janice and the transition council charted a transition assessment and "pulse check" surveys. The assessment collected candid feedback on how the transition was going so adjustments could be made along the way while the surveys were administered quarterly to collect data from the leadership team to view the progress and compare results.

"While each intervention is unique, there is one constant: Our shared belief with Janice that building bridges among geographically disperse units is a matter of bringing together real people with real data using a well-designed process."

Building bridges happened within the client system and also between the consultant and client organizations. The teams from both were able to truly partner as Peter's client, Janice, told us:

"Our relationship really developed out of our need to accelerate growth. We were not in any pain and were doing quite well at the time. However, I recognized that to get the growth, we would need a set of leaders who really would become change agents. We would need to make major changes, and we needed someone to provide us with a nonemotional viewpoint but at the same time help us.

"What has been most valuable in the relationship has been the impact on the total organization. Peter has brought a style that is direct, open, honest, and challenging without being confrontational. His strengths have been in the organizational design and the multiple varieties, the different nuances, and in getting to know the senior leaders who would lead the organization. Peter understood what their strengths were and where they would play positively in the organization. What the team did was to help the organization and individuals work together as a group to drive change. They helped us get our mindset correct.

"For me, Peter acts as a sounding board. Early on, Peter provided me with a written document that outlined the CEO/COO role. Throughout, he provided me with feedback from the rest of the organization. Peter was able to tell me my strengths and where I needed development. He never expressed it in terms of 'This is what you must do.' Instead, he would say 'This is what we recommend for you to be more effective.' He understands what we are trying to do and will provide thoughts, suggestions, and recommendations. Sometimes those recommendations are accepted, but he knows when to back off when they aren't. Peter knows that it is not about reformatting me. It is about enhancing what's already here.

"We had an exceptionally complex set of business deals in combining separate companies from Europe and America into one larger American company. We had organizational, geographical, and cultural differences. We had never built bridges among the companies before. We knew we would not get anywhere unless the leadership team at the top crossed the bridge first. The Mercer Delta team put a structure and process around what was coalescing as the new family. They helped us as a leadership team to be willing to change; they defined a shared experience that allowed us to define those 'nonnegotiables' for the organization that would most definitely change—and those areas of flexibility. They helped us put a communication structure in place. I cannot stress the importance of the communication structure enough. There is no such thing as over-communicating when you are bringing about change in an organization.

"What was fundamentally different about Peter and his team was that their objective was neutral. They had no vested interest in who would be winners or losers—whose viewpoint would rule the day. It was, and still is, only about the organization's success. What the consulting team did was gain the confidence of both the top leadership group and middle management. When people spoke their minds, it never came back to haunt them. There was never retribution. The middle management layer looked to see what the leadership team did with the information. The data presented was focused on where the problems were and on how to start fixing them. A critical turning point for our success was in how we built bridges with the middle managers. They were now being heard, and solutions were being developed with their input.

"I'd say the keys to success for Peter and his team were in how they created a format, a process, and a proposition that showed value. Peter has been able to sustain that value. I'd recommend to other consultants that they not be afraid to lose the account. When you become afraid, you lose your value. Be true to the value proposition you bring into the situation. If the client is not taking information or recommendations, press it and come back to it. Do not compromise the value that you demonstrate. If you can develop a personal relationship that is beyond the borders of what is happening in the office, great. But if not, it does not matter. It all comes back to the value you provide.

"Over the course of our work together, Peter and I have developed a true friendship. It is not feigned. He has not compromised and he has provided significant value."

As we look at this story, we see the deliberate ways in which bridges were built and in Peter's advocacy of Janice. Two things stand out as we reflect on this relationship. First, at every point, Peter trusted his instincts and declared his point of view, whether it supported existing views or not. Peter called it as he saw it, and Janice saw this style as being challenging without being confrontational. Peter did not have to agree with Janice to have a productive and effective relationship. Peter worked under the assumption that he would share points of view with Janice, debate them rigorously as needed, and then move on with a shared perspective.

Peter and Janice also periodically stepped back to look at their experiences and progress in working together. As they did this, both acknowledged the changing nature of their relationship over time, what and why they were working on something, what each brought to the party, and what needed to change, both for the organizational transition and in their relationship. Acknowledging where you are at any point is an important component of deepening a relationship.

Trusting and Being Trusted by Internal Collaborators. Since we as consultants are close to what's happening, we can become "outside insiders." We can see things others can't, we can share insights from other companies, and we can say things that would be difficult and/or too risky for others to say. But there are limits to this role, including lack of first-hand experience in the operations of the business and no full-time presence at the client site. For these and other reasons, we rely on "inside outsiders"—those who are there every day, and in particular those who are very confident in their positions in the company (that is, "bullet proof"). Without internal collaborators, nothing has sustainability. In addition, the internal collaborators give us a perspective on what's going on that our clients don't see. They also provide insight into the "general state of things" in the business and the emotional state of key players in the organization. In Peter's case, members of the transition council played this role.

Use a Checklist. Here's a short checklist to help remind you of things you can do to be an advocate for your client:

- Spend time with your client at regular intervals just to talk about the change effort and how your client is feeling;
- Engage your clients when you sense that their energy or confidence is waning;
- Reinforce positive change leadership behavior when you see it;
- Make a list of your client's strengths so that you can use them in advocacy situations;
- Provide specific examples of how other leaders have handled similar problems;
- Coach your clients on positive steps they can take immediately to deal with setbacks;
- Talk directly with people who are resisting the change;
- Analyze the groups and individuals who influence your client;
- Identify the goals/objectives of stakeholders; and
- Recognize and work with the supporters and resisters.

Help Clients Recognize When They Have Exhibited Highly Effective Behavior

Amazing as it may seem, clients often don't recognize their own strengths in leading change. Being an advocate involves helping them understand when their actions are having the intended impact. When a client makes a key decision, gives an impassioned speech, deftly handles a difficult situation with a subordinate, chooses to involve others appropriately, or calls attention to the need for metrics to assess progress, it's important to let him know he has done something right. Behavior that is positively reinforced is more likely to be repeated. Calling attention to things that clients do right encourages them to demonstrate behaviors that produce change in the future. What's more, positive feedback restores self-confidence during times of doubt. Clients are more likely to "stay the course" if they are being complimented for the difficult steps they have taken. We are not talking about insincere flattery or other obvious ploys to engender closeness. We are talking about complimenting clients when they really deserve it.

There are a few things that you can do to ensure that your clients focus on what they have done well. First, you can adopt the military's After Action Review (AAR) process (Baird, Deacon, & Holland, 1998), with special emphasis on what went well throughout the change effort. Or, secondly, another good fit for advocacy is the Appreciative Inquiry process (Cooperrider, Sorenson, Whitney, & Yaeger, 2000). Of course, you can also provide spontaneous feedback whenever it's appropriate. We will take a moment to define these ideas and then provide an example of how Bill used one of these techniques.

The AAR is a structured way of debriefing, making certain that the different perspectives of those involved are given voice. The goal of an AAR is to learn what worked and what did not. In the context of providing positive reinforcement, the goal would be to help leaders hear and pay attention to what they did well. The AAR provides a perspective on this through the eyes of subordinates, peers, and other stakeholders. Gathering information in a structured way makes the data more complete and objective, lending even more support to those things that are called out as superlatives. Since AARs typically look at what worked and what did not, it's up to the consultant acting as advocate to make certain the client is hearing the positive news. Inevitably, clients tend to focus on the negative. It's admirable, but it doesn't help their motivation or self-confidence. Making a special effort to highlight the good news is more likely to produce the kind of energy clients need to take that next step.

The goal of Appreciative Inquiry is to find and intensify the positive forces that already exist in an organization related to a change that needs to take place. At Avon Products Inc., for example, Appreciative Inquiry was used to explore instances of men and women working together effectively as a way of stimulating more tolerance of diversity (Watkins & Mohr, 2001). As a form of advocacy, Appreciative Inquiry can be used to help clients understand when their leadership has been at its best. Once in touch with what works, clients can formulate what are called "provocative propositions" or hypotheses about things that they could do consistently to make their leadership more effective. Working from positive examples, rather than from instances of failure, provides clearer clues about the right things to do. When clients focus on failures, they may not know what they could have done differently. When they look at successes, they already have an idea of what works for them.

Using an AAR or Appreciative Inquiry to bring more structure and intensity to the review of what the client has done well does not take the place of real-time, direct feedback. The best feedback is immediate because it helps the client make the link between the positive feedback and the behavior they just exhibited.

"I [Bill] was working with a client who had struggled for months to engage his team in a change effort. As the pressure for change escalated from 'It would be a nice thing to do' to 'We've got a crisis on our hands,' the client called his team together for an offsite, which I attended. He was patient in hearing their concerns; in fact, he was much more patient than I would have been in his shoes. Nevertheless, the effect was positive. The team set a new agenda for themselves that they were highly committed to and generated creative action plans for accomplishing the needed changes.

"After the meeting, I complimented the leader on his willingness to commit the time of his people to this work and on his style in leading the meeting. We then spent the next half-hour talking openly about his victories and defeats, as well as his concerns going forward. The time was well-spent. He hadn't been receiving much reinforcement from his team or from others, and my feedback came at a good time. By the end of the conversation, he was talking with more energy about the future and the things that he needed to do to help his team succeed. I felt that I had helped him in a genuine way to reaffirm his commitment and vision for the team and to regain some confidence that he could lead the team to the future he desired."

Is there a lesson here? Never underestimate your clients' need to know that you are on their side. If you have earned enough of their trust to give them the bad news, you must also work hard to bolster their spirits when their determination begins to waver. Let's take a closer look at this.

▶ Change Enablement

How Advocacy Helps Leaders See the Change Through

We tend to think of all leaders as courageous, strong, committed, and persevering like Mother Theresa, Winston Churchill, or Franklin Roosevelt. However, not all leaders are like that. In fact, *most* leaders have good days and bad days, times when they feel like quitting or giving up, or periods where they feel unappreciated for the efforts they make on behalf of others. Most leaders *don't* give up, but they do need reassurance from time to time.

Supporting your clients and being an advocate on their behalf is important because it expands the energy clients have for change and the degree of risk they are willing to tackle. Leaders usually have very few true advocates; they have subordinates, who are sometimes supportive and sometimes skeptical. And they have peers, who are willing to lend a hand when asked. A few very fortunate leaders have mentors, who guide them through difficult decisions and come to their aid without being asked to do so. But most leaders are lonely at the top.

Advocating on behalf of your clients with others makes the work of leading change easier for your clients. Rather than having to deal with every instance of resistance or misunderstanding, your clients can reserve their energy for the most important battles. Instead of hearing a stream of attacks against their plans and questions about their leadership, they instead are more likely to hear ideas from those brought into the fold on how to advance the cause. Leaders thrive on the energy of their subordinates. When subordinates are excited and committed, leaders become more positive and hopeful. Leaders dream of being in situations where they have to pull in the reins instead of flogging their subordinates across the finish line. You, as their consultant, can help by acting as a sounding board for those with concerns or a sparring partner for those who insist on debating every issue. As a consultant, your job is not to decide the direction of change or to replace the person leading it, but it is to help leaders to be successful by supporting good decisions they make. Change, especially when it's important and radical, will have its enemies. Involving others in helping to shape the change should always be the first step in managing resistance. For some, involvement may not be sufficient. The change may be too threatening, the fear of the unknown or the potential consequences may be too great, for participation alone to build support. A little advocacy, mixed in with an understanding of how to influence others, can be a helpful complement to participation in some of these more difficult situations.

Consultants who are advocates for their clients benefit directly and indirectly from the efforts they expend to support their clients when needed. They benefit directly from the increased likelihood of success for the change efforts they are undertaking and they have stronger client support. Consultants also benefit indirectly from deepening their relationships with their clients. Even though your client's self-assured leadership and support of a change effort may not be seen today, it will almost certainly be needed eventually. Building a stronger relationship with your client is important for both short-term and long-term reasons. Winning the battle in the short term feeds the positive cycle of risk taking, reward, and continued risk taking. Building a better relationship for the long term means that efforts to improve an organization will probably continue for greater lengths of time, making deeper and more significant changes possible. ◄

Table 5.3 summarizes some of the ways to show advocacy we've discussed here.

Table 5.3. Summary of How to Show Advocacy

Practices	Behaviors	Self-Assessment
Help Leaders Acknowledge and Explore Their Apprehension	Help leaders to acknowledge their uneasiness	I spend time talking with my clients about the pros and cons of their options
	Recognize the potential negative effects of leaders' apprehension	I recognize times when my clients lose momentum or are getting worn out
	Acknowledge leaders' clear struggle with the decision they face	I help my clients keep their focus on the vision they have set for their organizations
		I review with my clients where they have support for their decisions
		I talk with my clients about how to leverage key stakeholders who recognize the complexity of the situation

Table 5.3. Summary of How to Show Advocacy, Cont'd

Practices	Behaviors	Self-Assessment
Provide Genuine Encouragement at Critical Crossroads	Find out which issues are causing leaders to waiver	I remind my clients of how they reached their decision to follow the courses of action they are now on
	Provide encouragement in the face of adversity	I offer to benchmark other organizations that have been through similar changes
	Share with leaders some objective feedback about them	I share examples from my own experience with other clients I have helped through similar situations
	Prepare leaders for possible setbacks	I help my clients come to grip with shortcomings that may arise on their executive teams
		I provide objective feedback to my clients about their strengths and weaknesses
		I help my clients identify which of their strengths can help compensate for their weaknesses
		I advise my clients to surround themselves with others who can balance their weaknesses
		I point out times when my clients demonstrate needed skills and help them "connect the dots"
		I encourage my clients to think about how they have gotten over hurdles in the past
		I help my clients think about how they would want their employees to respond to making a genuine mistake
		I provide advice on what to do next immediately rather than in the long term
Help Leaders Stay the Course During Implementation	Work with the leaders to get the change embedded deeply into the organization	I help my clients anticipate where change efforts are likely to meet resistance
		My clients and I find ways to leverage our respective roles as leaders and change expert to facilitate change

Table 5.3. Summary of How to Show Advocacy, Cont'd

Practices	Behaviors	Self-Assessment
	Cultivate trust among internal collaborators	I encourage my clients to engage organization members in remote offices or foreign-based subsidiaries
		I help my clients prepare for dealing with resistance from critical organization stakeholders
		My relationships with internal collaborators help me develop a perspective on what's going on that my clients don't see
Help Clients Recognize When They Have Exhibited Highly Effective Behavior	Help leaders understand when their actions are having the intended impact	I let my clients know when I think they have demonstrated the right kind of behavior or made the right decision
		I use processes such as AAR or Appreciative Inquiry to help my clients recognize what they have done well

One Plus One Equals Three: Combining Capabilities Through Collaboration

CONSULTANTS WANT PROSPECTIVE CLIENTS to believe that they will take on the role of a strategic partner—one who shares in the problem solving, risk, and ownership of the solution. The websites and promotional materials of all the major consulting firms emphasize this partnership stance, and in many cases consultant behaviors bear this out. But in others, the partnership is in name only. Blending the best of two knowledge bases, skill sets, perspectives, and ideas into a unified effort on behalf of an organization change effort is much more complex than it sounds.

Much of what happens in today's world of partnerships is really nothing more than parallel play—a consultant and a leader working *alongside* one another, guiding their respective sets of activities. Or it is a *serial* partnership; that is, "I did my part of the collaboration, now it's your turn to do your part." Nevertheless, there are fundamental differences between "expert models" (I did my part, now you do yours) or the "extra pair of hands" model (parallel play) and the true collaborative efforts we have in mind when we think about the combining capabilities element of rQ. The most important difference is in the ownership for the outcomes, which *must* be deeply embraced by the leader. As soon as the consultant starts to care more about how things are going than the leader does, we no longer have collaboration, but an unhealthy dependency that will prevent change from ever happening.

Our colleague David Wagner faced a challenging engagement where he worked the process to ensure that when things were done, the client deeply owned the outcomes.

"The first really tough work with the chief administrative officer (CAO) and the chief information officer (CIO) involved crafting the case for change that the IT organization would use to define its vision and a new architecture. The CAO wanted to delegate the work and the writing to the CIO and me, but I knew this would never work since he had such strongly held views about what IT could and should be. On top of that, the CAO had experienced some organizational failures with IT that had resulted in a write-off of about five million dollars and had almost cost him his job.

"I had to push back quite firmly on his desire to delegate this work, and we talked at length about why I thought it wouldn't work. I emphasized that when he talked about the IT vision, he had to use words and phrases that he was comfortable with. I emphasized that the only way people would get on board is if they believed that he was firmly committed to both the vision and the CIO's capability for leading it. Then I asked him to talk about why he didn't want to do the work, and it became clear that it was something that he wasn't very comfortable doing. Based on this discussion, I proposed a work process that would accomplish the objective, but would not be uncomfortable or frustrating for him.

"I scheduled a series of meetings with the CAO to discuss, review, refine, and have him articulate his vision for IT, using materials the CIO and I had crafted jointly. I soon realized that the CAO would not do the work without me actually in the room reviewing it with him, so I captured his comments, pushed for clarification, redrafted, and refined the documents each time I met with him. I also challenged some of his thinking by offering alternative models of how IT could be structured to deliver more value across the entire enterprise, not just within each division as it currently existed. This uncovered the CAO's strong bias against centralization and required us to work through alternative models and descriptions of an end state that he was comfortable with. In the end, he could talk clearly about the rationale for change and some key parameters and boundary conditions for an IT vision.

"Another major contributor to developing trust with the CAO was the progress we made with the IT organization and its top leadership. When we started, the IT leaders from different divisions could not understand why we were bringing them together, as they had been decentralized for the past eight years. Over the span of six months, we were able to forge a strong team that was committed to a new vision and had several alternative organizational designs in mind. When the CIO and his team reviewed these with the CAO, the CAO was amazed at how far they had come in their thinking and how aligned they were as a team. The CAO was a bit in awe of what we had done to achieve this, and he was a bit scared because the team had pushed their thinking beyond what the CAO was ready to embrace.

"I gave the CIO feedback about what he was doing well or could do more effectively to lead the change and about how he needed to proactively engage with the CAO on his role in sponsoring the change. The CAO played a crucial role, since the CIO was relatively new to the organization and he reported to the CAO, I recommended that the CIO work closely with the CAO to ensure that the vision and rationale for the changes were articulated in a way that represented his ideas and expectations.

"One example was the talking points I drafted for the CAO for one of his first sessions with the leaders of the IT organization. While the CIO, the CAO, and I had worked on the talking points jointly, the CAO said during his remarks, 'Well, I guess I'm supposed to say. . . .' I gave him some pretty harsh feedback about how people could easily interpret his behavior as a lack of personal commitment to the effort and the negative impact that might have on the work they were about to do. At first he brushed it off, but I didn't relent and insisted he needed to come back at the end of the day to reinforce his commitment to what they were doing and ask if there were any questions. The CAO agreed, and it was actually a turning point for him and the group because some difficult questions were raised. He addressed them straight on, based on the work we had done to better articulate his views and assumptions.

"Over time, the CAO shared his deep and personal concerns about individuals. I knew we were making breakthrough progress when, as we were talking about personal issues and changes he knew he needed to make, he said, 'I've never told anyone this.'

"He also committed to his own personal change agenda and faced issues and took actions that he never would have done without my personal support and encouragement. This included a number of one-on-one meetings with peers of his to better understand his behavior and how it was impacting the team, the organization, and his relationship with the chairman. In at least three of these, the level of candor and constructive feedback truly amazed his colleagues and created a new foundation for him to carry out his role.

"Another great compliment was that he would frequently tell me and others, 'You aren't like other consultants.' He meant this both in terms of how we work and in terms of the impact we had."

We asked David's client, the CAO, for his perspective on the four-year relationship. In the paragraphs that follow, the CAO describes what made this relationship different from ones he had with other consultants.

"The difference is that the objective of the original assignment, and subsequent assignments, was what was at hand. David never treated us as a revenue source linking his firm to the next revenue stream. This helped establish a trusting relationship. What we were trying to do at present was more important than what came next. As senior executives, we are used to people sucking up to us and looking for more money. I never felt he was pushing the commercial side to get another assignment. It was about dealing with the issues at hand, which formed the basis for ongoing dialogue.

"The relationship first started with the objective evidence based on an interview process. The data brought out what people were truly thinking and saying. I could not refute the data; it was what it was. The data hit me like a two-by-four. I felt like I had been kicked by a mule. We had organizational issues, but there were also personal leadership changes needed. David's job was to lead me through a self-discovery process of personal change. I first had a choice—to make up my mind to change or leave things the same. The data made me uncomfortable.

"David provided guiding support. He made me feel comfortable in an uneasy situation. It wasn't just about changing the IT organization. I needed to make major changes in the way I managed. He has been in the same situation with other leaders in other organizations, so he was able to give me comfort in that he knew what I was feeling and going through. David helped me realize that my feelings were real and normal. David helped me take that step through the chasm. Taking that step was built on faith; and that faith didn't appear overnight. For me it started with that first investigative work and how David presented the information and revealed the truth.

"It is really easy not to do the personal change stuff. Once you peel away the title, executives are dependent on our egos, on our own motivations, and on our level of comfort with the way things have been. Transformational change is about human behavior and beliefs.

"It wasn't about one step in front of the other. It was two steps ahead, one back. David had done this before, and he was able to put the right steering on it to guide me and us. He did not need to know the specifics of our business. I needed to be the master of the content. David needed to know the range of behaviors that we would experience and what was acceptable. He let us go three steps forward, one back. He knew how I and others would react and allowed us to see where we needed to go.

"I learned the human behavioral side was just as important as the structural change. I've installed systems before, but I realized that people will just use the new tools to do the same things they used the old tools for. We needed to change behaviors and beliefs. People needed to feel strongly that it was the right thing to do. While it was uncomfortable, it was a process. David had the ability to get us to see what we needed to do, how to do it, how we felt and would feel, and how we could be successful both on the organizational level and the personal level.

"The key was blending the fact-based, objective views of the situation with the subjective approach. It was really, 'Hey Mac, are you willing to deal with this?' and then providing me with the guiding support through it all."

There are several things that stand out in David's case. First, it took time to do. There is no blueprint for building client ownership overnight. It also takes time to get a certain rhythm going to enable mutual respect for one another's value to emerge. Second, there were results. David's license to push the client was based on clear evidence that the process was working and that the results were "sticking." And they were sticking because the client and his organization were taking responsibility for *making* them stick. Finally, David clearly had no need to be at the center of the glory, nor did he push for future work. Instead, he worked to ensure that his client was successful. David calibrated the progress by watching for the gradual shifts in his client's behavior and outlook, not by the volume of accolades the client was offering. The praise from the client was an expression of gratitude for how much more capable he had become in the process.

These are the six skills that we, as a firm, have embraced over the years to define our views on building collaborative relationships. We will discuss each in turn:

- Understand client requirements;
- Create a shared view of desired outcomes;
- Build client ownership throughout the engagement;
- Build client capability through learning;
- Design work to guarantee synergy; and
- Discuss expectations regarding working relationships.

Understand Client Requirements

Understand One Another's Motives. The defining and distinguishing feature of a truly collaborative relationship is mutuality—it is a two-way experience. There is an inherent paradox in this point when you consider collaboration between a consultant and client, where one is clearly in the service of the other. So how do you establish mutuality in the context of roles, where one is primarily *serving* and the other is primarily *being served*? The answer lies in understanding what each person in the relationship will ultimately gain from the experience—beyond just achieving the intended results.

Focus on Making the System Work. Clients have good reasons for undertaking organization change efforts. Whether the need for change grows out of industry events or is part of a strategic plan, clients clearly recognize that change efforts should only be undertaken when the need to disrupt the status quo is clear. "If it ain't broken, don't fix it" is such a commonplace phrase that consultants sometimes argue with clients, "If it ain't broken, break it" in order to focus attention on opportunities to improve organizational performance. What most clients want is a system that works well, and they want that as quickly, cheaply, and easily as they can get it. Praise for being a forward-thinking, risk-taking model of good leadership is important to some clients, but making the system work well is fundamental to all.

Be Aware of Your Own Aspirations. Consultants have some desires as well. We want to help leaders succeed in improving their organizations; without that, nothing else can be gained. Beyond that, we aspire to have successful engagements, a modicum of recognition from our clients, and positive regard from others. Many of us are motivated by a deep desire to help others grow, change, and lead more meaningful lives. Still, none of this is possible without success from an organizational standpoint.

When we take a step back and think about it, we realize that our general aims are actually quite closely aligned with those of our clients. What's strange is that either or both parties sometimes question whether or not this is true. Here's an example from my own [Bill's] experience:

"After working for almost two years on a project with a branch of the U.S. military in Europe, we realized that the end of our government-sponsored engagement was upon us. Recognizing that there was room for further improvement in how the organization operated, my colleagues and I worked long and hard to develop the most effective approach we could imagine to transfer the capability for continued improvement to people in the organization, none of whom were trained in organization development. Eventually, after a tremendous amount of effort and using all of our available creativity, we designed a program to enhance internal capabilities to lead change.

"At the end of the second day of our three-day offsite, it was obvious that the energy in the room was low. People were talking about baseball, politics, and anything but organizational improvement. It was obvious that our effort was failing. Suddenly, I jumped up as I heard a crash on the floor next to me. One of my colleagues had thrown his notebook on the floor and was now screaming at the people in the room at the top of his lungs, visibly upset at their behavior. Effectively, the fellow said, 'We put in months of work and came thousands of miles to do this—the least you could do is try to act like you care about what happens to this organization!!!' (My colleague expressed himself in more emphatic terms, but I've left out some of the more colorful language here.)

"I was shocked. They were shocked. I figured our workshop was about to end a day early. Then, out of the deafening silence that ensued, came a voice from one of the lower-ranking military personnel in the room, 'I'm sorry. We didn't know you really cared about us. We thought you were like all the other government contractors who are just looking for a paid vacation to Europe.'

"Until then, we had assumed our interest in improving the performance of the organization had been mutual. The work had been difficult, and we were well aware of the learned capacity in military units to simply wait out a change that you didn't like until a new commanding officer came along. Still, we thought we had a mutual connection when we did not."

The key to making a connection in this instance was a genuine display of emotion. Far from getting us fired, my colleague's emotional display made us real people. With hindsight, I wish we had done it sooner. What this lesson taught me was that (1) you shouldn't simply assume that your desire to create a more effective organization is shared by your clients; (2) connecting with your clients around what you are trying to accomplish is fundamental to progress and may be harder than we think; and (3) being aware of your emotions and sharing them openly is both legitimate and vital in creating more collaborative relationships.

Create a Shared View of Desired Outcomes

Be Very Clear About Where You Are Going. The Cheshire Cat said, "If you don't know where you're going, any road will get you there," and that quote has become infamous for good reason. Organizations will embark, with astonishing frequency, on major initiatives, expending enormous energy and resources and getting people whipped up in a frenzy of activity, all toward very ill-defined, highly vague, and ambiguous ends. Some change processes have clear goals from the outset, such as the total quality and re-engineering programs of the 1980s and 1990s. At the other extreme are change processes that begin with a diagnostic phase that is intended to clarify where change is needed; neither the client nor the consultant knows in advance what will follow.

In more open-ended types of interventions, it's easy to understand how client and consultant aspirations can become disconnected. The client may have had an idea of where the change process was headed before ever calling the consultant in. The consultant, on the other hand, is interested in addressing the right problems, not just their symptoms. After a diagnosis, the consultant can become sold on the client's view of what needs to change, while the client is still back where she started. An example of this from my [Bill's] experience was in work that I did with a colleague in support of a CEO who wanted to change his organization's culture:

"The CEO wanted a culture that focused more on speed, growth, and customers than the existing culture, which tended to be slow to market and internally focused. After speaking with a number of people at different levels of the organization, my colleague and I fashioned a series of interventions to change the culture. These ranged from large group interventions to making sure that each of the top sixty leaders had a personal action plan for improving the culture of his or her unit. The CEO said he supported these initiatives, but, as time went on, it was clear that what he had in mind was more along the lines of 'intervention by exhortation.' That is, he wanted to give speeches about changing the culture, but didn't hold people accountable for actually doing anything that would produce culture change. When we confronted him about this, he insisted that he was dedicated to creating a new culture, despite his lack of obvious support for the interventions we created. It was, in his mind, up to his people to decide what specific actions should be taken to change the culture.

"His approach might have worked if his subordinates were convinced that changing the culture was essential. Instead, they sensed that the CEO wasn't really as concerned about the culture as he was about controlling costs. Culture change activities took time, cost money, and made people in this traditional company uncomfortable. If the CEO wasn't going to champion the change, it wasn't going to happen.

"In this instance, our relationship with the CEO wasn't strong enough to allow us to keep pushing back on him. We had delivered our advice, pointed out the consequences of his behavior to him, and been up-front with our feelings about the effort we were involved in. We knew we could continue to work with a few leaders in the organization who were naturally inclined to pursue culture change in their units. We also knew that many others would continue to resist doing work to change the culture, even if we were able to demonstrate positive results through pilot experiments. The chances of changing the culture of the whole organization were slim."

There's a saying that you can lead a horse to water but you can't make it drink. In this case, the horse thought it was thirsty, but when we led it to water, it still wouldn't drink. This will happen in engagements from time to time. As a consultant, you don't get to make decisions about what is best for the organization. You can perform diagnoses, make recommendations, point out the consequences of inaction, highlight positives when you see them, call attention to benchmarks, have peers offer their perspective, call on your past experiences, get permission to try pilot experiments, initially work with those who are positively inclined, cajole, challenge, urge consideration, and do whatever else you can to influence decisions. Ultimately, however, the decisions are up to your client.

As a rule of thumb, the best time to clarify where you are going is as soon as you possibly can. A corollary to this rule is that the best time to discuss a change in direction with your client is as soon as it happens. You should try to avoid taking a broad charge from your client like "help us to improve our culture" and then running with it on your own. As we pointed out in a Chapter 1, the contracting phase of an engagement is vital. That is when consultant and client have an opportunity to define together respective roles, outline processes, and define scope and time boundaries that will help clarify the direction of work (Schein, 1987). Just because the client trusts you to provide help doesn't mean that the responsibility for decision making is now yours. The client is still in the driver's seat and needs to know the destination.

Find Common Ground in One Another's Values and Aspirations. Relationships need some type of glue to keep them intact over long periods of change, beyond the content of the initiative. Those participating in the relationship must feel they are connected by something greater than just the work, or eventually the work will become a chore—and potentially even drudgery. Knowing that each person collaborating in the relationship feels drawn toward the work by some unique sense of purpose or believes in the efficacy of the work because it drives toward some larger good creates a powerful energy. This energy can be a great source of wind in the sails when the intensity of the work feels draining. Dennis Tirman saw this clearly as the relationship with a client unfolded:

> "The relationship had a wonderful excitement to it for both of us. I think most of that had to do with two characteristics: We had a great respect for each other's view of the world and philosophy of organizational life, and both of us had a genuine interest in learning."

Search for this kind of intersection with your client. Think about what interests you in doing this work; make a list for yourself if necessary. Then think about your client. Which of the things on your list is likely to be an interest of his or hers? Experimenting with new approaches to leadership? Helping people in the organization realize their capacities? Kicking the stuffing out of the competition? Creating some intellectual capital together? Find the common ground and use it to support the evolution of your relationship. Move beyond single interventions that stop and start abruptly to an ongoing relationship that continues to attack these higher order goals from multiple perspectives. Try new things together; learn together; spend time together talking about things that are important, beyond the crisis of the day. Good relationships that enable change have "legs" that support them for the long run.

Consultants who focus on one intervention after another have transactional relationships with their clients: "I do something for you; you pay me." The trouble with this is that, as soon as the intervention is over, so is the relationship. Then each time an intervention is needed, haggling over the price of the intervention happens all over again. Consultants who share higher level goals and interests with their clients develop sustainable relationships, in which there is a feeling of partnership.

There are marked differences between transactional and long-term partnership models (Carucci & Tetenbaum, 1999). Basically, long-term partnerships are characterized by:

- Maintaining Trust;
- Meeting the Needs of Both Partners;
- Completing Tasks While Strengthening the Relationship;
- Mutually Owning Outcomes;
- Having Deep Personal Investment in the Relationship;
- Being Committed to Respective Development; and
- Building a Common Ground from Shared Values

Then new interventions almost take a back seat to the longer term mission. Certainly, there is less starting and stopping, less haggling over price. Ultimately, there will also be more opportunities to make significant changes in the organization, as the client shares your passion for achieving success in the areas you have identified together. The change process becomes jointly owned, rather than a project or program the client buys off the shelf.

Build Client Ownership Throughout the Engagement

Ensure That the Client Is Involved at Every Step. All too often, people in organizations who hire consultants or who garner the services of internal change practitioners somehow slip into passive roles, deferring to the expertise and direction of those whom they believe know what they're doing. Nothing could plant the early seeds of failure more effectively than having the leader slowly check out as the consultant conceives, directs, orchestrates, and drives the initiative. Although this might seem obvious, it happens with surprising regularity. Usually the consultant is too caught up in the energy of making progress, feeling valued, important, and in control to notice. The problem, of course, is that the control is only an illusion. As long as the consultant is seen as the ringmaster, everyone else around adopts the role of spectator, unable to fathom how they will actually *live with* the work once it's finished. Bob Saracen, a senior partner at Bishop Partners, a consulting firm that specializes in executive search for CEOs and senior executives, comments:

> "It never ceases to amaze me how much ownership clients are willing to forfeit for some of the most important decisions they have to make—selection decisions to the senior ranks. They somehow believe that having the final say in a decision translates into having ownership for that decision. If I don't include my client and relevant members of the client organization in every step of the process, I know that the leader who finally enters the organization as 'the choice' will have that much more difficulty successfully assimilating and making an impact. It's essential that consultants view their role as helping to facilitate successful choices on the part of our clients, not making the choices for them. If, after we leave the picture, the good work we did fades into the woodwork, we didn't do our jobs. The decisions and actions we help clients take must outlive our presence for our work to be considered successful and helpful."

There are many types of decisions that clients should make regarding your work together. Here is a list of some, which you can doubtless add to based on your own experiences:

- How much improvement is needed, and how will it be measured?
- Who should be involved in the diagnosis?
- Should external stakeholders (customers, analysts, and regulators) be consulted?

- What should the breadth of the change effort be? How many issues should be addressed simultaneously? How many units and which geographies should be involved?

- What should the depth of the intervention be?

- How many people should be directly involved? How much should be spent on their participation?

- How much lost time is acceptable given the investment in change or in developing people?

- How much disruption in customer service or performance capabilities is permissible, if any?

- What changes are acceptable? Which processes need to be fixed? Who needs to be replaced?

- Who should serve on committees or task forces that are driving the change?

- How should communication about the change take place, internally and externally?

- What role should the leader play in communicating?

- What's the most effective way and best time to involve people in shaping the direction of the change?

- How should resistance be dealt with? How much pushback is acceptable?

- How long should it take to implement the change?

Thinking seriously about the points you add to this list is an important part of confronting how collaborative you really are in engagements. Each of us, at one time or another, has been tempted to make one or more of these decisions *for* our clients instead of *with* our clients. The more we take matters into our own hands, the less investment the client will have in the process and the outcomes. If you make these decisions for your client, your client will view you as an operative, that is, as someone who has assumed the role of a subordinate, who has taken on the responsibility for the success of a project or program.

The client's relationship with you, in this situation, will be the same as that with other subordinates. If you make good decisions and do good work, you will be rewarded appropriately. However, you will not necessarily have a relationship with the boss that goes beyond the current project. If instead you make these decisions *with* your client, the responsibility for success will still rest with him or her, and your relationship will be less like that of a subordinate and more like that of a trusted advisor.

Ensure That the Client Understands the Process. Leaders in organizations can usually be relied on to have a fairly strong understanding that something needs to change. But *what* to change and *how* to change it are another story. In our experience, leaders tend to woefully underestimate the amount of time, energy, effort, and resources it will require to get fundamental change to happen and to have it stick. It is essential for the consultant to spend the necessary time on the front end of an engagement building the client's understanding of what it is likely to take to pull off the initiative at hand. Inevitably the client will resist. Reacting to the instinctive impatience organizational leaders come equipped with, they will usually want the work done in half the time, for half the resources and effort. And they will likely be fairly certain that what they are asking for is possible. By using examples of similar initiatives, building plans that lay out the work to be done, and employing applied theory of how organizations *actually* change, the consultant must help leaders embrace a more realistic picture of how to achieve what they aspire to accomplish.

At the same time, it's important to be sensitive to your client's expressed needs and to respond appropriately. If Rome is burning, you shouldn't propose taking several months to put together a team that will find the optimal way to fight the fire. This happened to me [Bill] recently as I went on a call with a colleague to a major client.

"In our first meeting, the client told us of the need to restructure the organization and change the top leadership team. I started to describe the process we would normally use to accomplish a change of this magnitude, which would ultimately affect hundreds of thousands of people and the corporation's future. As I laid out the six-month plan, my colleague picked up on the client's increasing frustration. She jumped to a whiteboard and started sketching out the changes that she heard the client suggesting. He corrected her on several details, but agreed with the overall synopsis she presented. The CEO issued a memo the next day outlining the organizational changes and presenting the new top team.

"It took several months to fully implement the changes, of course, but the client got what he really needed: immediate action to bolster the confidence of employees and investors. Rome was burning in this instance, and a long-term approach just didn't fit the client's needs. Once the fire was out (or at least the flames had died down), the client was more ready to hear what changes would be required to stop the fires from starting up again. My colleague and I were both right. Real change in the organization would take time; but unless visible short-term actions could be taken to buy time, there could be no long-term change."

Nadler (1997a) describes this point as the immediate need to shape the political dynamics of change. The leader takes action to assure buy-in from key stakeholders, using symbols and strategic communication tools, while at the same time defining the point of stability without which the lengthier change process would not be sustainable.

Being in a relationship with your client doesn't mean that he or she is always right. Many times, clients want to do something that is cosmetic and expedient, rather than what is really required to produce lasting change. However, being in a relationship with your client doesn't mean that you are always right either. Almost by definition, being in a relationship means that you will try your best to educate one another and formulate appropriate strategies together. Consultants who are like short-order cooks, trying to do whatever their clients tell them to do without ever pushing back, will always be kitchen help. Consultants who never listen to their clients' needs will eventually exhaust their clients' patience and interest. Consultants who help their clients understand what it takes to create effective change but who also work creatively with their clients to respond to their most pressing needs will find themselves in satisfying, long-term, productive relationships.

Build Client Capability Through Learning

Uncover What the Client Hopes to Gain from the Experience Beyond the Intended Outcomes. Every change effort presents an opportunity for leaders to fulfill some additional aspirations they might have for themselves or for their organization. Sadly, these secret hopes often go unvoiced in the haste to get the work up and running. The anxieties of initiating change are great enough, and leaders will naturally be reticent to disclose the greater hopes they have. Some leaders may hope to use the work to build greater credibility for their organization. Others may hope to use the work to advance the careers of key, high-potential leaders in their organization. Some may hope, as a by-product of the change, to forge a new set of relationships among key leaders or functions. Rarely are complex organization change efforts uni-dimensional. The opportunities to effect multiple changes on multiple levels do exist, but sometimes those that leaders hold most dear may need to be ferreted out, wrestled with, and better understood so the leader can feel proud and confident about pursuing the opportunity.

Over the years, a number of executives have tried their hands at writing about organization change, on their own or in collaboration with their consultants. David Nadler's work with David Kearns (1992) at Xerox produced a joint book, *Prophets in the Dark*, which outlined their approach to reversing Xerox's fortunes in the early 1980s. More recently, Jack Welch (2001) has chronicled his many efforts to remake GE. Other CEOs who have tried their hands at writing include Alfred Morrow (1972), Bill Gates (1999), Jeff Papows (1998), Max DuPree (Spears, 1995), Andy Grove (1999), and Jean-Marie Messier (2001).

Most of our clients are interested in understanding how to change their organizations and, once they have learned something about it, they're eager to share their knowledge with others. Organization change is difficult, complex, and important. It presents a worthy challenge for any leader, and mastering it is a vital requirement for an executive to be thought of as a great leader. Our clients are bright, inquisitive people, or they wouldn't be where they are. When consultants play the role of experts and assume the responsibility for planning change, they leave executives on the sidelines watching the parade go past. Wise executives will fight to retain control over the change effort in their company because they sense that leading change is their responsibility and something that they need to learn for themselves. When the group of consultants formulating GE's Workout™ program first proposed its design to Welch, Welch made several significant changes that ultimately made the program more effective (Tichy & Stratford, 1999). Even though he had the advice of a hand-picked team composed of some of the country's best consultants, Welch didn't simply turn over the reins to them. Our clients like to think, and many of them would welcome the opportunity to think with us about the complexities of change. The more that you can pose options and ideas for your clients to consider, the more they will join you in the intellectual work that leads to effective change.

Identify Specific Aspects of the Work That Could Lead to Stretching Client Capability.
Equally as important as understanding what the client aspires to accomplish is to identify *for the client* areas where you believe the organization can build capability as a result of the change effort. Organizational blind spots will become exposed during the process of change. An important way to add value is to identify limitations of the organization that leaders might not otherwise be inclined to pay atten-

tion to and to deliberately use the initiative to fortify the organization's capability in that specific area.

During change, for example, the inability of members of the senior team to communicate effectively to the organization may become apparent. This in turn may lead to a broader discussion of their ability to provide inspirational leadership. Some further discussion and diagnosis may uncover that senior team members have managed well through periods of stability, but have never led a major transformation of the business. Combining these data for the CEO may make obvious the need for a customized leadership development program to address these issues.

On a broader scale, how often have you encountered deficiencies in an organization's IT systems or compensation plans during the implementation of a new process or organizational design? More often than not, these support systems lag far behind the aspirations we help leaders create for their organizations. Unless addressed, they act like brakes during the implementation process. Sometimes, they can even stop implementation altogether. It's no wonder that large IT and HR consulting firms exist; there's little difficulty in finding evidence in most organizations that these critical systems need to be fixed.

Even though these and other areas may be beyond your scope, calling attention to the need to address them is important. Your work can't fully succeed unless the environment surrounding and supporting change initiatives is aligned with the outcomes you are trying to achieve. Nadler and Tushman (1997) refer to this as creating organizational *congruence*.

In the average organization, at the time you walk in the door there are probably between fifty and one hundred separate initiatives underway to improve organizational performance in different units, departments, and remote offices. Because many of these initiatives are started locally, there's a very high probability that they aren't coordinated or aligned in the outcomes they are trying to achieve. Getting a handle on what's already going on is one of the first things you should do, because those initiatives will compete for energy and resources with the effort you are about to undertake. It's difficult to achieve organizational congruence or improved performance when each element of the organization is being pulled in a different direction. Help your client identify, assess, prioritize, and focus efforts where change is needed most. Your work will be more successful, and people will thank you for taking things off their plates that are overloading their capacity to function effectively.

Design Work to Guarantee Synergy

Have Candid Discussions About What Each Person Brings to the Table and How These Combined Capabilities Can Create a Unique Level of Value for the Initiative.
Knowing that a client is doing all he can to ensure success of the initiative, and knowing that the consultant is doing everything within her ability to make a meaningful contribution to the initiative still doesn't ensure optimal success. In fact, such efforts can still be considered *parallel,* rather than collaborative. It is at the *intersection* of a client's and a consultant's contribution that true collaboration and synergy exist—where one plus one equals three. It is where the leader's intuitive understanding of the organization's unique idiosyncrasies joins with the practitioner's insights about the anxieties of change that are born with powerful interventions. Remember David Wagner's client, who commented that he was the master of the content—David's area of mastery was in knowledge of the range of behaviors. The work process undertaken by the leader and practitioner must be synergistic *by design.* That means identifying the problems, exploring the merits of numerous options for solutions, facilitating discussions during critical meetings, and designing implementation steps must all bear the fingerprints of *both* players.

Companies hire consultants because they bring capabilities, expertise, and perspectives that are not as well developed internally. The consultant's presence in the system should help leaders accomplish things that they could not accomplish by working alone.

During the 1970s, when the big automakers in the United States were under attack for the first time from their Japanese competitors (Shimokawa, 1994), a colleague attended a conference where several of the CEOs laid out their plans to respond to the situation. Our colleague came away unimpressed with what he heard. The more he thought about it, the more he realized that *if these leaders had known what to do to fix the situation, they would have already done it.* Of course, their answers were incomplete and shallow. They were just figuring it out for themselves. Many years and many consulting hours would be expended before better solutions would be developed and tested.

Just because people are in positions of leadership doesn't mean that they are ready to face every challenge laid at their doorstep. The world of business is full of unexpected change and competition that comes at you from unanticipated quarters. As Adrian Slywotsky, a partner in our sister company, Mercer Management

Consulting, says, it's rarely the established big competitors that radically transform an industry. Industry upheavals are almost always started by companies with nothing to lose that destroy the established business model: the smaller, hungrier firms that are trying to find enough light to grow in the shade of their giant, slow-moving counterparts. It's sometimes difficult for leaders to acknowledge that they don't have things figured out, but those leaders who recognize this first and get the help they need are likely to last longer and be more successful than those whose mirrors tell them they are still the fairest of all.

Consultants are not immune to sudden attacks of overconfidence either. Just because a method or technique has worked before, even worked many times, doesn't mean that it's right for every organization. Giving advice without careful diagnosis is like committing plagiarism. Clients who feel that you don't really understand their needs and are just lifting passages from work with other clients will soon seek help elsewhere.

The ideal situation, as we've implied, is one in which the client and the consultant are combining their experience and wisdom to fashion the best possible course of action for the company. Neither has all the answers, but both have important things to contribute. Jack Welch had worked at GE for many years before he became CEO. Still, he didn't know at the time that he became CEO that he would help GE become a "boundaryless organization" (Ashkenas, Ulrich, & Jick, 1998). Deciding that took time, diagnosis, and discussion with his advisors. At first, Welch just knew that there were too many barriers to getting things done in the company. Over time, he and his consultants began to understand the nature of those barriers and what should be done about them.

In a similar vein, Cisco didn't begin with a highly developed and effective process for acquiring companies as its engine for growth. Developing that engine took time and external support. John Chambers' true wisdom wasn't in knowing all the answers; it was in recognizing where he needed help and finding it in order to make his company successful (Goldblatt, 1999). In fact, one could make an interesting study of the role advisors have played to great leaders throughout history, in truth and legend: Merlin to Arthur, Machiavelli to Lorenzo di Medici, Anna to the King of Siam, Harry Hopkins to Franklin Delano Roosevelt, Henry Kissinger to Richard Nixon and Ronald Reagan. The art of giving and taking advice in a relationship involving a leader and advisor is one that each party should strive to better understand.

Have Open Dialogue About Preferred Working and Learning Styles. Untested assumptions about how you and your client prefer to work and learn can become insidious obstacles to the change effort. If a consultant isn't aware that her client prefers to spend time reflecting on input before making a decision and the consultant has a strong bias for action, she will appear to be very impatient and pushy to the leader, whose frustrations will grow as more complex decisions emerge. It's better to ensure such preferences are discussed from the outset of the relationship rather than let them be discovered through trial and error. Relationships are difficult enough to build under the best of circumstances. Contracting at the beginning for how best to incorporate your client's ideal working and learning approaches can help avoid unnecessary glitches when the process faces the inevitable bumpy parts of the road. Listen to how David Wagner describes how he learned to adapt to a new relationship in the context of the earlier case:

> "The CAO was not an easy person to get close to. He intimidated many people in the organization. His training was as an accountant. He had risen through the organization to become CFO, and he tended to think more linearly and concretely. I realized early on that I had to change my expectations of him and how we did our work together. Even if I sent him a document to review ahead of time, he rarely read it or reacted to it. I had to reorient how we worked together, focusing on just a few key things in great detail, capturing his input, assumptions, and reactions, and then using that information to revise our work."

As a consultant, you need to figure out what the client needs and where he is, accept where he is, and work from there. It often means refining the content of what you put in front of clients so it more directly connects with their thinking, and it may mean adapting to how they like to work, take in ideas, make decisions, and commit to actions.

As we mentioned in a previous chapter, the first of Herb Shepard's (1975) "rules of thumb for change agents" is *staying alive.* By that he means working with the client in such a way that the client can continue to tolerate your presence in the system as you work toward change. If the consultant pushes the client too fast or too hard or suggests interventions that make the client exceedingly uncomfortable, the change effort may be stillborn. The onus for adapting one's style is on the consultant, at least at first. Once the consultant has gained the leader's confidence, it may be possible for the consultant to push harder or to ask the leader to do things that the leader would not normally do. Until then, staying alive means paying careful attention, looking and listening for signs of discomfort, and regularly asking the leader how he is feeling about the way the effort is proceeding. It's really no different from any situation in which one person is trying to help another learn to do something new. Whether it's learning to play tennis, ride a horse, or climb a mountain, good instructors pay attention to how quickly their clients are assimilating what they are being taught and to whether or not they are comfortable performing each new skill. So it is with relationship-based consulting. Rather than "doing a number *on* the client," the consultant interested in establishing a sustainable relationship "does the number *with* the client." The consultant adapts his or her approach to the preferred style and pace of the leader and works gradually to make more of his or her own perspective and approach available to the leader for consideration.

Establish Regular Intervals to Monitor Progress. Even with solid contracting on the front end, it is still important to take the pulse of the relationship throughout the engagement, more so early on. Asking for feedback on how the relationship is working is crucial to monitor how the leader is absorbing the consultant's input, to see whether there are any unmet needs that require better understanding, and to continue to learn more about one another.

Check-ins can be formal or informal affairs. As we discussed earlier, it's good to have a mixture of both. If it becomes obvious in the course of an intervention or workshop that the leader is agitated and uncomfortable with what is going on, it doesn't make sense to wait to discuss her thoughts until your planned check-in in a couple of weeks. On the other hand, planning and sticking to check-ins at regular intervals helps the leader to reflect on what has or has not been accomplished and on how that fits with his or her expectations of where things should be.

Often, consultants huddle together to strategize their next steps in working with clients. The results of recent efforts are discussed, ideas are thrown around, and new proposals are developed for the client's consideration. In her work with a client system, Roselinde Torres initiated a regular series of client strategy meetings at which the next steps of the intervention were planned. What made these meetings interesting was that they included the client. Not only did the consulting team have a chance to brainstorm ideas to help the client, but they were able to hear reactions to their ideas from the client himself. Before long, the client was throwing out ideas for the team to consider. As time went on, the client and consulting team found this a more natural way to work and questioned why they had ever done it differently.

Discuss Expectations Regarding Working Relationships

Put the Client First; Don't Let Egos Get in the Way. Many of the consultants we interviewed and studied felt strongly that we must never let our own egos get in the way. Roselinde Torres comments:

> "Keep the clients' best interest at heart. Help them change while acknowledging and reinforcing their strengths and talents. You have to feel genuinely connected in order to both support and challenge them. If you look forward to your time with them, it's a better outcome for the relationship. If they get the sense you are just another consultant with smart ideas who cares more about the task than about them, they will value the work on the task but not you."

Janet Spencer's views build on this point:

> "Always remember—this isn't about you. It's about your clients and what they're going through, and about the company and how it will behave/react, et cetera. Park your own issues and insecurities at the door. Recognize your feelings as you have them, and even discuss them with your client—but don't make building a relationship about what you need."

Agree on Roles, Procedures, and Interactions. In every consulting assignment, there are times for leaders to lead and consultants to fade into the background. Some consultants have a need to be on stage more than they should. They take over the role of the leader: giving speeches to the troops, communicating bad news to individuals about their careers, or drafting letters to investors. In their desire to be helpful, or to ease their frustration with the rate of progress, consultants can cross the line from consulting to managing. It's important for consultants to understand that their job is to build the leader's capability to lead change, not to replace him or her as leader.

When consultants take over, a number of bad things happen. People lose confidence in the ability of their leader. The leader loses confidence in his or her ability to lead. The consultant gets smarter about how to lead change in the organization, but the leader does not. The consultant feels ownership for the change effort, but the leader does not.

For all these reasons and more, it's important that the leader and consultant discuss their roles at the beginning of their relationship. Having this discussion sets an important benchmark for later reference. If either the leader or consultant starts to step out of line, the initial agreement can be recalled. Later, if it makes sense to change the agreement, it's always possible to do so. Just like the initial agreement, changes should be made explicitly and not by one party simply assuming a new role.

The same goes for how processes related to the change will be carried out. The consultant may have a preferred way of involving people in change, such as using Appreciative Inquiry, large group interventions, or focus groups. It's important that the client have input into these important decisions so that, when issues arise, the client understands the reasons behind the procedures that have been selected. Consultants should make their clients aware of the range of choices available and the pros and cons of each. Argyris (1970), in his classic work, *Intervention Theory and Method,* points out the importance of creating free, informed choice for clients. Today, too many firms thrive on selling methods or approaches that offer the client little or no choice in how the work is done. Predictably, clients usually have a big problem committing to the solutions recommended by these firms.

In one engagement, our colleague Caryn Kaftal faced the challenge of working with a senior executive who was entering a new role as a senior vice president of HR, establishing her credibility as a trusted advisor to senior management, and quickly building a function that would be a force for change in the broader organization. Let's see how Caryn describes how she helped the executive define her own expanding role in the organization:

> "We focused completely on helping her define her personal agenda and laying out the details. This included creating a vision of success for both herself and her function, developing the requisite skills, putting a plan in place to close existing personal and organizational gaps, and elevating the HR function to the level of strategic business partner. We worked together to develop a detailed action plan and then worked over an extended period of time on each component of that plan. We met frequently and did regular check-ins. We revisited and updated the plan on at least an annual basis.
>
> "It was in our contract from day one that I would help her build her organization and her point of view on the function, as well as craft the interventions her function would initiate as part of leading change in the organization. We reached critical turning points as we got into building her capability. I had a chance to help her develop her skills and point of view as an HR executive, as well as position her function as a strategic partner in leading the business.
>
> "Having 360-degree feedback data to work with also gave us more revealing material and an opportunity to address fundamental gaps in capability, confidence, and perception. This executive was an aggressive learner, was willing to

acknowledge areas for improvement, and was willing to take advantage of plans put in place to close apparent gaps. In partnership, we created a place where she could be 'whole'—where strengths could be readily identified and weaknesses could be put on the table and dealt with. Our objective was to keep our eye on future potential—where she wanted to take her function, who she wanted to be as an HR executive, the reputation she wanted to build for the HR function, and the impact she wanted to make.

"We bore witness to her success and could therefore reinforce it. We were there for major speeches, were responsible for aggregating important feedback, helped design major change interventions, and measured their effectiveness.

"In all probability, the most significant element was finding very visible stretch opportunities and helping execute them effectively, with this executive in the lead. There is nothing like a big, visible success to build a relationship! The HR organization moved from being a peripheral and second-class function to being a strategic business partner. In little more than two years, the CEO created a seat on the executive committee for this executive and visibly put HR at the top of the organization. She was also later promoted to president of an operating unit. This is all evidence that she established the credibility of the HR function and herself as an important business leader."

The relationship Caryn developed with her client shows how combining the capabilities of two people brings about greater results than just relying on one person. Read along as Caryn's client describes their relationship:

"The relationship has been ongoing for three and a half years now. It formed quickly, and just got tighter with time. It was a good, comfortable fit right from the beginning. Caryn was trustworthy and credible from the outset. I came to rely on her more heavily over time as she helped me build my own capabilities and those of my organization.

"What led me to know that she was trustworthy and credible was that I never felt she had a personal agenda. Our work was about my success and how to make my function viable. She never took credit where it was not due; she had no ego in this. Caryn's interests were about me. I had been a lawyer prior to taking on the HR function, so I had knowledge in the area. We never substituted Caryn's knowledge for mine. She supplied me with information and engaged in the decision making, but the decision was always mine. Caryn's credibility was heightened by the fact that she also had a vast store of knowledge in the area.

"In a world arrayed with no HR infrastructure, Caryn helped me determine priorities and how to move on those priorities. That was the most valuable aspect of the relationship. As a lawyer, I would see a problem, I would keep people up-to-date, I'd move through to resolve the problem. But as an HR leader, I needed to get people's buy-in along the way. I credit Caryn with showing me how to get buy-in to the priorities and how to make it a process such that we could then move quickly. I did not have a staff at the time, so I know it would not have happened without Caryn. One success then allowed me to do other things. It was because of her that I moved into other areas of the business.

"We did spend a fair amount of time in the beginning talking about roles, but over time it became ingrained. It was a natural part of who we were. I knew what to expect. I like Caryn as a human being and care about her as a friend. I know for me that, if there is not a personal connection, I will not be able to build a trusting relationship.

"Caryn's interpersonal skills are incredible and there was an immediate bond. I would not have made the time on my calendar if there had not been that bond. You have to want to see your consultant. I did not see our time as another chore in my day. If I can't enjoy the person, I am not going to make room in my day. I found our sessions intellectually stimulating, along with being reflective.

"One of the keys to the level of trust we had was that Caryn felt strongly about my ability to develop in-house capabilities. It was not about becoming dependent on Caryn and consultants. It was about creating institutional capability. Caryn never made any bones about it. She told me I needed a high-level internal OD person. That statement showed me that she was willing to cut revenues to her firm. It was a clear example of the selflessness of her work.

"One of the things I learned about myself was understanding the impact of how people perceived me in the organization. I was just me, but I learned that people looked to me, looked at what I was doing. Leading an organization had not been in my repertoire before. I would not have learned how to lead as quickly without Caryn. Caryn helped me look at how I wanted to be perceived in the organization, how I was actually being perceived, what the gap was, and then what I needed to do differently to close that gap. At first I was extraordinarily insecure and afraid. Caryn helped me to overcome my fears. She helped me realize the strengths I had that would help me and what the perceived weaknesses were. We worked together in changing those perceived weaknesses.

"My recommendation to others wanting to develop a strong client-consultant relationship is that you need to not only listen, but to bring your viewpoints forward to help. Being a little pushy with those viewpoints helps to create a certain sense of urgency for follow-through on the priorities. Understanding what will meet the needs of the organization and making sure the client also understands is the lubricant for getting things done. This helps the client's own personal growth and answers the needs of the organization. The consultant needs to help the person set his or her own priorities and then get the person to work fast.

"What makes Caryn different than others is her sense of selflessness and commitment to follow-through. She also has a very diplomatic manner about her. She can give you constructive feedback but say it in a way that you can actually hear. It is important for consultants to be frank and to be honest, but you must say it in a way that is not hurtful or condescending. Caryn made a real effort to work with everyone in my organization, not just with me. She was who she was with everyone, not just for me—the boss. There was no sense of hierarchy."

Caryn's visible focus on making her client successful, helping develop her confidence and credibility, and ultimately, helping her build a powerful presence in the organization—with both a significant voice as a business leader "at the big table," as well as a respected HR function—were hallmarks of this initiative and underpinnings of its success. She worked hard to ensure that there was maximum ownership on the part of her client for the sustainable success of the HR function. Caryn's client clearly acknowledged the value of that hard work to make sure she and her organization developed capabilities. Let's look at how this ownership component fits more broadly into the rQ collaboration element.

► Change Enablement
How Combining Capabilities Through Collaboration
Builds Maximum Client Ownership and Commitment

This chapter has been about combining consultant and client capabilities to build maximum ownership and commitment to change. The reason that Jack Welch was so committed to the program of change at GE is that his fingerprints were all over it. At the same time, he didn't invent the program himself. He called on a large team of consultants to give him their best thinking and then worked with them to make it even better.

Busy executives who want to hire consultants to do their jobs for them and egotistical consultants who are all too happy to oblige may deserve one another. The problem is the work they do together will be less effective than it could be because of their poor collaboration. What we assert, and what we hope the examples we have provided demonstrate, is that combining capabilities leads to better thinking about how to change the company and greater commitment on the part of the client to making those changes work. It's probably easier for both parties not to collaborate: It takes less time, involves less debate, and lets each party just focus on his or her job. Consultants and clients need to fight against this natural tendency.

Think about the accomplishments in your life for which you feel most proud. In tracing the path to the achievement, can you not see a mosaic of many people's thoughts, ideas, and input? It's likely that none of your achievements were the result of any single effort. While highly independent in nature, clients and consultants who work well together come to appreciate that truly synergistic outcomes are the result of subordinating one's ego and need for control. Clients and consultants do themselves a great favor when they work against their independent streaks in pursuit of a greater creative process that can come only as a result of combined capabilities. ◀

Table 6.1 provides a summary of how to combine capabilities through collaboration.

Table 6.1. Summary of How to Combine Capabilities Through Collaboration

Practices	Behaviors	Self-Assessment
Understand Client Requirements	Understand one another's motives Focus on making the system work Be aware of your own aspirations	Early in a project, I spend time getting to know the members of the client system and their personal aspirations I encourage my clients to share their perceptions of how my work is contributing to reaching their objectives I tell my clients how I feel about their commitment to the work we do together

Table 6.1. Summary of How to Combine Capabilities Through Collaboration, Cont'd

Practices	Behaviors	Self-Assessment
Create a Shared View of Desired Outcomes	Be very clear about where you are going Find common ground in one another's values and aspirations	I keep my clients informed about the direction and progress of the work I am doing I stay closely connected with my client throughout a project, even after we agree on the work to be done I make a list for myself during each project of what interests me about the work I am doing I look for common ground between my personal aspirations and my client's
Build Client Ownership Throughout the Engagement	Ensure that the client is involved at every step of the engagement Ensure that the client understands the process	I do not get so caught up in the work and the progress made that I neglect to update my client I like to involve the client in all phases of the project I remind my clients of the decisions they need to make I help my clients recognize the potential ramifications of their decisions
Build Client Capability Through Learning	Uncover what the client hopes to gain from the experience beyond the intended outcomes Identify specific aspects of the work that could lead to stretching clients' capability	I encourage my clients to define their objectives beyond the current project I encourage my clients to find ways to reaffirm for others their leadership roles in our work I encourage my clients to explore areas for development revealed through our work together I help my clients assess and decide where change efforts are most needed
Design Work to Guarantee Synergy	Have candid discussions about what each person brings to the	Before starting a project, I take the time to explain my working and learning styles to my clients

Table 6.1. Summary of How to Combine Capabilities Through Collaboration, Cont'd

Practices	Behaviors	Self-Assessment
	table and how these combined capabilities can create a unique level of value for the initiative	When I start a new project, I don't just use the same small set of intervention formats I have used on previous projects
		I recommend that my clients use interventions that fit their working styles
	Have open dialogue about preferred working and learning styles	I adapt my consulting approach to fit my clients' cognitive styles
	Establish regular intervals to monitor progress	I ask my clients for their feedback on how our working relationship is meeting their needs
Discuss Expectations Regarding Working Relationships	Put the client first; don't let egos get in the way	When I find that my client is becoming "difficult," I do not just go ahead and do the work by myself
	Agree on roles, procedures, and interactions	I describe for my clients the pros and cons of alternative ways to do the work
		I spend a substantial amount of time early in the relationship with my clients to discuss our respective roles
		When the work changes, I make sure that my clients and I reassess our respective roles

7

The Capacity to Influence: Interpersonal Agility

THE LEGENDARY ABBOTT AND COSTELLO ROUTINE *"Who's on First"* is one of comedy's all-time classics for a good reason. We can all relate to the frustrating feeling that we are being absolutely clear with someone during a conversation, yet despite our fervent efforts we find we have been misunderstood as the conversation disintegrates into a sparring match.

In the routine, Abbott, talking about a baseball team, explains that "who's" on first, "what's" on second, and "I don't know's" on third. Costello responds by trying to get Abbott to tell him the names of each player. Abbott continues to explain, very clearly he believes, that "who," "what," and "I don't know" are the players, and he can't understand why Costello doesn't get it. Costello, in the meantime, is becoming increasingly frustrated by what he believes is either Abbott's ignorance or his inability to name the players.

This example illustrates how miscommunication and misinterpretation can lead to impaired relationships. Every exchange with another person is a potential building block in the unfolding relationship. The exchanges between consultants and

159

leaders—whether insights, ideas, feedback, concern, empathy, admonishment, or even idle chit-chat about the weekend—all matter. Each is an opportunity to leave the relationship better than it was.

Consequently, it behooves consultants to avoid complacency about the style and manner with which they communicate and interact with their clients. There is never a "one-size-fits-all" approach to interpersonal relationships. Because consultants play so many different roles for leaders—friend one moment, adversary the next; wise advisor in one meeting, fellow inquirer in another—they must have the interpersonal agility to span these roles with the requisite skills and behaviors to play them all effectively. Developing the interpersonal agility element of rQ takes enormous capability and continuous development on the part of consultants.

A high degree of interpersonal agility enables consultants to accelerate clients' adoption of new ways of thinking and behaving. The sooner you "click" with clients, the sooner your clients' views of themselves and the organization—and the corresponding behaviors—will become responsive to your efforts. We believe there is a core set of practices that enable a consultant to be *interpersonally agile*:

- Exceptional Listening Ability;
- A Broad Range of Personal Styles;
- Signal Detection;
- A Light-Hearted Sense of Humor;
- Humility;
- Dexterity with Different Methods of Communication;
- Ability to Convert Experience to Relevant Wisdom; and
- Knowledge of How Clients Learn and Accept Help.

Let's take a closer look at each aspect of interpersonal agility.

Exceptional Listening Ability

Chances are you laughed, or at least smiled, when reading *Who's on First*. When it comes to human misunderstanding and misinterpretation, the odds are high that *hearing* without *listening* is a major culprit in the disconnection. Many readers are aware of the threats to effective listening between two parties. These include such things as:

- Hearing only what we expect to hear;
- Hearing things that agree with our points of view; not hearing things that contradict our points of view;
- Projecting feelings or emotions into a current relationship that are left over from a previous one;
- Stereotyping the communicator and prejudging what he or she is about to say;
- Filling in gaps with what we assume the person would have said;
- Being distracted by other things going on and not paying full attention to, or clearly hearing, the message;
- "Stepping on" what the person is trying to say as we rush to make our own points;
- Ignoring what the person is saying as we formulate our defenses or proposed solutions; and
- Inferring motivations for what the person is saying that are not really there.

Thus, hearing is not the same thing as really *listening* to what a person is trying to say.

David Wagner comments on the importance of listening in the context of a client engagement:

> "I listened carefully to the things my client was concerned about, asked probing questions to better understand the issues, reflected on what I heard, and often made strong suggestions about what I thought he should do and why. In subsequent meetings, I would often follow up to ask him and others about what actions had been taken, what the impact was, and how he was feeling about the progress (or lack of it), which then led to more listening, reflection, reaction, and coaching on my part."

From David's view, there is an ebb and flow of listening and advising. David never assumed that he understood his client without checking to make certain that they were on the same wavelength. Imagine what might have happened if David had rushed to action based on an incomplete or incorrect understanding of what his client said. David would have wasted time, caused his client to question his competence, and put himself and his client in the position of having to go back out to the organization and change the direction of the intervention. Changing direction would have likely caused friction between David and his client, which could have taken considerable time and energy to resolve. Looking back with this list of potential disasters in mind, the effort David spent in making sure he understood his client seems an especially wise investment.

What makes good listeners? One example that comes to mind is the physician who listens before making a diagnosis. After asking patients what's wrong with them, any good doctor will listen attentively to the patient's words and note any unusual reactions. While registering what ailments are "going around," doctors listen so as not to jump to any conclusions. After integrating all the available information, the doctor is in a better place to make an accurate diagnosis. That's what good listeners do naturally. However, the reality is that, for many people, listening is a skill that requires constant sharpening. Here are some strategies that can help fine-tune one's listening ability:

Make an Effort to Control Outside Distractions. Start by giving your client 100 percent of your attention when you are engaged in a discussion with him or her.

Repeat What You Hear. The intention is not to mimic, but to understand and clarify what was said. Periodically, it may be necessary to remind yourself not to dismiss an idea before considering it fully. Individuals with a penchant for being self-absorbed need to learn that they don't have to agree with others in order to listen.

Focus on What the Other Person Says. Avoid trying to figure out what the person is going to say; you may miss what he or she actually says.

Never Interrupt. Interrupting is offensive and rude. Also, it sends a subtle message that you are not serious about listening, possibly cutting off the flow of dialogue.

Seek Only As Much Information As You Actually Need. If you feel that priorities are changing along the way, then explore further. While it is often thought to be desirable to get the overall picture, it can sometimes be overwhelming, and it can cause you to appear unfocused.

Remain Calm. Avoid overreacting to highly charged words and tones. Hear the person out, then respond. Most people will cool down and begin to talk calmly once they vent their anger and frustrations.

A Broad Range of Personal Styles

The individual personality of a consultant helps set the tone of a relationship with a client. Knowing the assets and liabilities of one's personality can go a long way to making a connection quickly with different clients. If you are an intellectual type—quiet, reserved, and analytical—there will be some clients with whom you connect quickly, others with whom it may take more time. If you are a high-energy type, showing enthusiasm and passion for the work, the same will be true. There is a wide range of options when it comes to interpersonal style, and it can be a great asset for the consultant to have a proficient repertoire at her fingertips for the variety of clients and client needs she will encounter. Roselinde Torres comments about the range required of her in the context of one relationship:

> "I had to listen, was empathic, and tried to reinforce positive intentions, even if the client couldn't get it 100 percent right. I expressed emotions—excitement when he/the organization had a win; concern when I thought they were going into a hole; frustration when they ignored my advice and then had the predictable problems occur. I took risks—calling the question even if it risked ending the relationship; expressing my respect and regard for him as a person, not as a CEO or exalted leader."

Great actors have the ability to play a wide range of roles. Great consultants should be capable of playing a wide range of roles as well. Clients are unique, as are the situations we encounter as we work with clients on change. Each client and each situation deserves a unique and appropriate response. Consultants who are limited in their repertoire need to recognize, at a minimum, that a client's needs or a situation may not match their abilities. If this is the case, the consultant should recommend others who are better prepared to provide support. All of us have flat sides; even John Wayne left the dancing to Gene Kelly.

Here are some thoughts on how to broaden your style:

Know Your Current Style and Its Limitations. Think about your style. What are your overused strengths? What are your under-leveraged talents? What are some aspects of your style that beg for improvement? Knowing your own style is the place to begin when improving your agility. Think back over your consulting engagements. Is there a pattern of success or failure under specific circumstances? For example, have you done better when you are following a predetermined approach or when you are forced to invent the approach as you go along? Do you work more effectively on your own or in teams? Do clients appreciate you for your brain, your heart, or your technical competence? The more you can get to know yourself, in terms of both strengths and limitations, the easier it becomes to see opportunities to stretch your capabilities and broaden your agility.

Keep in mind that you are likely to gravitate toward styles that have worked for you in the past, that you are already comfortable with, and that reflect your personal preferences. If you tend to be analytical and calculated in how you offer advice, you may want to consider how to introduce your heart into the mix—talk about the emotional implications behind the analyzed data. If you tend to be quite animated and expressive, you may want to modulate by introducing a more pensive and contemplative style. Overusing a style means that you are likely to use it at times when the situation may call for something different, and you may be missing the signals. Know when your dominant, preferred approaches work best, and when they do not, and adjust accordingly.

Emulate the Styles of Others Unlike You. Once you know your own strengths and limitations, identify two or three people who seem to have mastered the strengths you wish to develop. Think about what they do and how they do it. If you can, interview them so that you understand what they keep in mind as they exercise the particular strength you wish to emulate.

When dancers want to learn a new step, they frequently begin by emulating someone who already has the move down. You can do the same in your consulting work. Find someone you can learn from, observe his or her moves, work with the person if possible, and hold yourself to the same standard as other performers—don't go live on stage until you have mastered your moves in rehearsal. Start by choosing someone who seems particularly effective with a style you know you need to develop. Jot down things the person does, phrases he or she uses, how the person engages his or her clients. Take particular note of the positive effect the behavior has on the client and the situation. Out of the different methods you have observed, what can you immediately incorporate into your own repertoire?

Experiment with a Variety of Language, Tone, and Nonverbal Communication. To a significant degree, people perceive us by how we present ourselves to them during conversation. When people use the phrase scintillating conversationalist to describe someone else, they aren't usually referring to someone who drones on in a soft monotone voice, with his hands by his side and eyes looking at the floor. Like most people, clients are drawn to good storytellers. Try recording yourself on videotape as you describe the work you did on a recent project. Is the tape interesting? Do you vary your tone and volume? Do you use gestures to punctuate your points? Is your language both interesting and professional? If not, it's time to pay more attention to this fundamental skill. If you try to improve but have difficulty doing so, a personal coach may be in order. Since the success of most consulting work depends on how our messages are received, our delivery needs to be effective.

Signal Detection

Ever walk into a room where you instantly felt that things were just a little off kilter? Nothing anyone said or did told you this specifically, but somehow, in your gut, you just had the sense that something was amiss. Every time we enter a room where a client is, there are signals that tell us the "temperature" of the relationship, of the client's outlook that day, and, in general, the mood of how the work is progressing. The ability to pick up and accurately interpret these signals is a vital capability in the context of building strong client relationships. Each of us has the ability to sense signals that others are sending. Navis (1990) recommends that, after each substantial client interaction, a consultant make brief entries in her journal about the things that people said, the general gist of the conversation, and any other incidental behavior. She should also note significant events that will help her sense patterns in the signals detected.

Early in our relationships, we are less able to interpret these signals than we are later on. Initially, we can read only the clearest signs of disinterest, anger, frustration, or excitement. We need to calibrate our signal-detection skills with others as we learn about the variability of their responses to different stimuli. At first, we might read too much into a smirk or gesture; we may take these small signals to mean that we are experiencing a meltdown in our relationship, when in fact there is nothing to worry about.

Later, as we get to know others, even very small cues can indicate matters of huge significance, especially when we learn to associate those small cues with the underlying feelings that accompany them. You can observe this in meetings among people who have worked together for a while. People will react strongly to things that others do, without any words being said. People will sometimes state what they think other people are feeling, without others having said something that would indicate they were feeling anything at all.

What's important about this to us in client-consultant relationships is that, however we do it, we must become better at communicating what is really going on. If we can improve our signal detection, it will allow us to formulate probes that will help us ascertain the validity of our observations. Ultimately, it is not whether we guess the other person's feelings correctly that counts; it is that we picked up on *something*—and that we bothered to check it out.

One of our colleagues offers this advice about watching for certain cues from clients:

> "If you feel uncomfortable, the client probably does too, which means that you are onto something. Watch out when people change the topic really quickly; it probably means that they are avoiding something. They may not even be aware they are doing this. When the topic is a difficult one, allow for plenty of silence. The client will say something meaningful."

Here are some thoughts on detecting important signals:

Listen to Your Gut. The expression "listen to your gut" means to get in touch with your own reactions to what's happening around you. We often feel tension in our stomach; hence the expression. You may feel tension elsewhere. Where do you *feel* success? Closeness with your client? Anger? Confusion? Chances are these mental and emotional states show up for you in a physical way. While we're not recommending that you consult while wired up to a biofeedback machine, we do know that our ability to frame appropriate responses to situations is sometimes aided or hindered by our affective state of mind. If you can pay attention to physical clues that signal strong emotions, you're halfway there. The other half is learning the steps to deal with each emotion as you experience it. Once you know you're angry, what can you do to turn your anger into constructive action? If you're confused and you know it, can you instigate an inquiry that will help you feel more in control? If you can feel what's going on and respond, you are less likely to find that strong emotions lessen your effectiveness.

Be sure to also pay attention to when you are denying your own reactions. Listen to the tape that plays in your head. If it's telling you that that funny feeling you have isn't real or that you're just over-reacting, this is important to note. You may be inadvertently self-censoring, and thus missing opportunities to point out important insights to your clients. If you're having a funny feeling in your gut, you're having it for some reason. Pay attention to it and find out why. It may well be what leads to a solution or insight that has eluded you and your clients.

Detect but Do Not Overinterpret. We are often puzzled about another person's moods or reactions to a specific event. When that person is the leader of an organization, attempts to make sense out of every signal that he or she sends, both verbally and nonverbally, can quickly get out of hand. We will frequently second guess ourselves—to our detriment. If a consultant goes too far in interpreting the leader's behavior without checking out his assumptions, he can twist himself into knots for no good reason.

> "I [Bill] was meeting with a client about an important decision that needed to be made about the direction of change in his organization. This client, who is normally very highly engaged in our discussions, seemed withdrawn and disinterested in the conversation. It would have been easy to read his lack of enthusiasm as dislike for what I was saying and, for a moment, I did. I started to think about what I must have overlooked in preparing for the meeting or what it was about what I was saying that could be so far off the mark. I stopped the conversation and said something like, 'This doesn't seem to be what you were expecting to hear. What did I miss?' The client then told me that his reaction had nothing to do with our conversation. He was still puzzling over a conversation he had with his boss, which had left him dissatisfied. If I had not stopped the conversation to ask what his signals meant, I might have gone back to the drawing board on my proposals for no reason at all."

A Light-Hearted Sense of Humor

The emotional drain of complex organization change can render leaders stressed, anxious, and often—in the chaotic throes of the work—cynical. They carry these tensions into rooms with other members of the organization and often unintentionally spread the negativity. One of the best tools in a consultant's arsenal can be a sense of wit that, when appropriately deployed, can turn the mood of a room from tense and somber to upbeat and optimistic.

Peter Thies has learned to rely on humor, as he says:

> "I will try humor early in a relationship when I see the environment is too serious. I want to learn if the client is able to see the lighter side, and I use it as a

barometer. In the case I spoke of earlier [Chapter 5], we had already conducted the transition assessment and now we were doing the CEO assessment. In my conversation with the CEO, she asked me, 'So, on a scale of 1 to 10, where would you put me?' My response was, '5.1, just to the right of average.' She snickered and then said, 'I'm glad you said that because if you hadn't, you would have lost credibility. I put myself at a 2, so you were being generous.' I knew I needed to show some humor because she was appropriately concerned with all the things that she had not done up to this point in the transition and with her leadership. It was time for some levity.

"I believe the use of humor with CEOs levels the playing field to show we truly are peers. I will frequently use it when there is negative feedback. I want to have the message heard, but without it being a slap in the face. My clients and I will rib each other back and forth. It is about give-and-take. They give me feedback too and will also use humor. It shows we can poke at each other."

Janice had this to say about Peter's use of humor:

"I'd describe it as a friendly biting banter. It is our organization's nature and there-fore can be used appropriately. Peter will use humor to lighten the atmosphere, particularly when he recognizes it will be an intense day during which emotions will be high and that we will be making tough decisions. Peter has actually used the soccer (football) analogy with the referee whistle, referee shirt, and the use of yellow or red cards just like they do in a real game. It has worked great."

Poking fun at yourself can be especially effective, letting the client see that, while you take the work seriously, sometimes it helps to be lighthearted about it. When clients are wound up like tight springs from the intensity of the change, they can become ineffective without realizing it. They become curt, self-absorbed, inse-cure, and edgy in ways that diminish their positive influence on the organization—whose support they need for the change. Making sure that clients are not burdened from the full weight of the change process by demonstrating a sense of levity can keep needed energy accessible to them for influencing others. It also helps ensure that, when exciting moments of learning happen or when tangible evidence of progress appears, they have enough emotional stamina to celebrate the small wins.

Management consultant Robert Sabath (1990) suggests that humor provides a fundamental competitive edge. It makes you different from your competitors, even if they use humor too, because your brand of humor is unique to you. It connects you personally with your audience, and it starts them laughing with you. Manfred Kets de Vries (1990) looked at the critical role of humor in organizations by drawing an analogy to the historical figure of the king's jester. With a license to be outrageous in the pursuit of humor and no fixed position at court, the jester could tell the king important things with a candor no other person could risk. Through naïve questioning, self-depreciation, and satire, consultants are allowed to explore the boundaries of the unspeakable and bring their clients to face reality in a somewhat less threatening way.

Here are some thoughts on using humor:

Make Yourself the Target. Humor is an effective vehicle for accomplishing a number of important objectives, such as relieving tension, inspiring creativity, and increasing closeness. In a professional setting, humor needs to be both tasteful and appropriate. To ensure that your attempts at humor don't miss their mark, make yourself the target at least some of the time. You don't need to be self-deprecating, but you do need to show a little humility. The person who jokes about others but never himself or herself is soon either distrusted by others or perceived to be overly arrogant. Using humor is a great tool for adapting to difficult circumstances in our work with clients; it can be all the more effective if we use it to show that we don't take ourselves too seriously.

When you make a harmless mistake, through either a particular idiosyncrasy that is a trademark of your personality or the proverbial spilling of coffee, you have an opportunity to add levity to both your and your client's day. It also helps ease the awkwardness that can accompany moments during which people might otherwise feel embarrassed for you. So enjoy a good laugh at yourself occasionally. It will show a human side that makes you more endearing to your clients and that sets them even more at ease with you.

Use Discretion. Despite years of experience, we never fail to be amazed by how insensitive some consultants are to their clients' reactions. This shows up very clearly in the area of humor. Some clients are deeply offended by jokes told by consultants who fail to notice and go from one joke to the next as if the world is their stage. Left unchecked, this behavior can jeopardize everything consultants are trying to accomplish in building relationships with their clients.

One way to assess the appropriateness of humor is simply to observe how clients interact among themselves. If clients are quick to tell a joke, it's probably fine to join in. Jokes can help break the ice, but it's important for the consultant to avoid being viewed as a comedian, especially early in the relationship with a client. Given a choice, we would recommend establishing competency first and levity second.

Let Them See You Laugh. Having a sense of humor doesn't mean that you have to be able to tell a joke at the drop of a hat. Relationships can grow deeper by just sharing laughter during a humorous moment. Laughter is a natural human reaction. It's what psychologists call a psychogenic reaction; in the same way that we yawn when others around us yawn, laughter evokes a natural physical reaction that causes us to laugh along. There's usually no harm in doing so, providing that the laughter doesn't come at someone else's expense.

Laughing with others is a sign that we enjoy their company. It says that we enjoy a common reference point, that we are part of the same culture and history. Think about the last time you visited a foreign country and how difficult it was to feel natural there; even knowing when to laugh was probably hard. Laughing along with others says, "We're all in this together," "I understand you," and "I'm human too." These subtle understandings among people open doors to deeper and more personal relationships.

Another important aspect of laughter is that it gives others permission to do the same. How often have you asked yourself about your clients, "I wonder if they ever have any fun?" Sometimes our clients become so mired in the intensity of their daily battles that they seem to lose any sense of levity and joy. Moments that invite a spirited laugh seem to pass by unnoticed. Be sure to laugh as a way of helping your clients climb out of the morass of their challenges and enjoy a moment of joyful relief.

Humility

Part of influencing leaders to adopt new ways of thinking and acting is to model for them your own sense of fallibility. Clients need to see us learning and changing, subjecting ourselves to their influence, if we are hoping they will willingly subject themselves to ours. If clients begin to feel that we are there to rescue them or fix them, they will resist our influence and resent what will feel to them like arrogance. Dennis Tirman shares these thoughts:

"Be humble about the power of human relationships. Keep your own blinders off as much as possible, both with respect to your clients and also yourself. Continue to simultaneously look at the situation and look at yourself in relationship to the situation. Know your limitations, and get help if you need it."

True humility enables us to talk comfortably about both our strengths and our shortfalls. It also provides an innate sense of what is appropriate in a given moment. Humility is a double-edged sword, however. False humility is as off-putting as arrogance, creating just as much discomfort. No humility, on the other hand, raises the defenses and umbrage of clients as they brace for our next self-congratulatory remark. In the middle is a healthy sense of who we are and who we are not.

Some thoughts on balancing your own sense of humility:

Stay Focused on the Client's Needs. Given a choice of listening to people talk about themselves or talk about you, which would you choose? Most of us are mildly interested in what people think of themselves and intensely concerned about what others have to say about us. As people, we are naturally interested in ourselves. The mistake some people make is to believe that others are as interested in them as they are in themselves. Especially in consulting work, most conversation needs to be focused on the client. The consultant needs to talk about the client, the client's concerns, the client's organization, and the client's team. If we spend too much time talking about ourselves, we won't be of much help to our clients, and our relationship with them will falter.

At the same time, talking about our experience with other clients and our own theories and views is important when what we are saying is linked to the client's situation in a way that is clear to the client. When in doubt, checking to see whether or not our input is understood and useful is more effective than going on to the next example.

Use Yourself as a Reference—Good or Bad—Sparingly. Clients want to know that their consultants are experienced and that their knowledge is relevant to the problem at hand. It's important that we convey confidence as consultants and that we back up our words with examples of deeds. Nevertheless, there is a limit to how much we should say about our own expertise. Clients will usually ask for more evidence of our competence if they need it. Once they have accepted our offer to help, we need to shift the focus to them and away from ourselves. We can draw on our experience, but always in the service of our client's needs.

Pay Attention to What You Tell Yourself About Youself. "Humility challenged" consultants may be individuals whose self-view is distorted. As we mentioned above, listen closely to the tape in your head as it tells the story of how others experience you. If you hear messages of inadequacy, you may be provoked to overcompensate for that message by drawing attention. On the other hand, if you hear messages of magnificence, you may give in to the urge to broadcast these messages so others can enjoy them with you. Having a healthy sense of self and self-confidence are critical aspects to a healthy sense of humility. Be sure to get a reliable handle on where your sense of yourself stands and make appropriate adjustments to ensure it is balanced.

Do Windows. We often take notes at meetings, offer to draft letters for our clients, and in other ways carry some of the load of the work associated with change in any complex organization. We don't do this because we think we're better at typing than anyone else; we do it to demonstrate that we are committed and that we want to share in the effort to make the engagement a success. Clients notice small efforts, especially when they are unexpected. Our own behavior models what we hope others on the management team will do: Pick up the weight and carry it forward.

It is not uncommon for consultants to feel that certain tasks are menial and therefore beneath them. After all, what do others think of us as paid advisors when they see us transcribing flip charts after a meeting? In our experience, clients see that we "do windows"—that we are so committed to the client's success that no task is beneath us. This enhances our credibility and the humility with which we are seen. Serving is an essential part of consultant-client relationships. Clients can be exhausted by people in their organization who are motivated by a sense of entitlement and status. When we are willing to roll up our sleeves and jump in to do what it takes to get the work done, they deeply appreciate it.

Dexterity with Different Methods of Communication

With the unprecedented volume and speed of information that we all deal with, the successful practitioner must have many communication arrows in her quiver to stay connected with clients. The many points of contact available to client-consultant relationships can be a clear advantage if harnessed correctly, and each requires its own approach and style. Conversation, presentation, e-mail, voice mail, written documents, memos, brief notes attached to relevant articles, symbols, and metaphor all provide "glue opportunities" to strengthen relationships. The more adept you are at creating and using these communication tools, the more likely you will build relationships of depth and richness.

> "I [Ron] recently had an experience of building a relationship with a potential new client via e-mail. We had trouble connecting by phone, so I took the risk of sending a slightly humorous e-mail to my potential client based on a brief exchange and laugh we had during our initial meeting. He responded immediately with an e-mail that took my humor one step further. I replied again, continuing the light-hearted exchange while reinforcing my hope that we would be able to work together. Over the course of several months, I was able to offer insight for his highly political and complex dilemma. The use of fun, creative metaphors enabled me to deliver some tough messages to someone I barely knew. I was able to quickly establish a strong rapport that conveyed my commitment to his success. Eventually, he did agree to work with me, and we started our work with a bond we would not have had otherwise. This experience proved to me that staying in touch across distances with clients however you can is crucial. The trick is to use the medium the client prefers."

Clark and Brennan (1991) evaluated seven common communication media and their qualities in helping establish a common ground between individuals. They found that different media provide different opportunities for coordinating activities and establishing understanding. For example, videoconferencing can be useful primarily to support conversation among participants and allow presentation of objects or artifacts in real time. Chat boxes and video whiteboards can be received simultaneously or separated by other activities. Electronic messages and other computer records and data can be reviewed and revised, but don't foster the feeling of being in direct contact with another individual or group. Based on their own findings, Daft and Lengel (1986) recommend that, independently of other considerations, you should always choose the channels that most effectively reduce uncertainty and equivocality in communication. Providing combinations of various media gives you choices that would otherwise not be available. Extra channels for communication have been found to be reassuring and psychologically important (McCarthy & Monk, 1994).

Consultants who need to communicate regularly across national borders must be particularly careful about adopting new technologies that alter the context of their interaction with people in other countries. Consultants must be careful, as misunderstandings can occur if people with a different cultural background decide that new communications procedures are not suitable substitutes for face-to-face interaction. In some countries, for example, videoconferencing is considered to be an unacceptable medium for conducting business. In many situations, the selection of mutually acceptable communications media must first be agreed on, before voice mail, e-mail, or fax can be used as a substitute for a person-to-person meeting. Gundling (1999) provides a list of relevant questions to consider when trying to select the appropriate communication methods that can be applied to our discussion (see Table 7.1).

Table 7.1. Criteria for Selecting Communication Media

Criteria	Questions to Ask
Availability	To what extent are various communication technology options readily available to the client?
	Which technologies can be used regularly without putting the client at a disadvantage?
User Skills	Is the client adequately skilled and comfortable with the different modes of communications considered?
User Choice	Have you asked your client how he or she would prefer to communicate?
Cultural Variables	Is the communication taking place with a client in a low- or high-context culture?
	Are there other cultural requirements or preferences?
Level of Rapport	How well do you know the client you wish to communicate with?
	Does rapport or lack of it affect the level of needed context?
Importance of Message	Is the message of sufficient priority to dictate a high-context medium, or will a low-context form of communication be sufficient?

Table 7.1. Criteria for Selecting Communication Media, Cont'd

Context	Are there means for creating greater context to enhance participation, such as in-person meetings, multiple media, and facilitation techniques?
Communication Pattern	Is there some sort of agreement that indicates when your client can expect messages and in what form?
Time Windows	Do you know and respect the most convenient times to send and receive messages across time zones?
	Are there ways to share private contact numbers that will improve communication while respecting people's personal lives?

Adapted from E. Gundling (1999), How to Communicate Globally. *Training & Development, 53*(6), 28–31.

Communication is more effective when it takes advantage of multiple methods. Any form of communication can become dull if it is overused. We like to help our clients express themselves in a variety of ways. The effort that comes from varying communication methods adds to the clarity and creativity of the messages we help our clients convey. We find it especially effective to help clients play with ideas they have not used much before. Videotaped skits or debates that can be shared with others are examples of this. Find out what methods your clients overuse and underuse; help them learn to vary the medium and the message.

Know Your Clients' Communication Preferences. We find that some clients prefer to think through a written document before an important discussion. Others prefer to be shown a slide presentation with no pre-work. If you don't know your client's communication preferences, ask. Clients prefer to work in ways that feel comfortable to them. The consultant's challenge is to communicate in the way that is easiest for the client.

Understanding your client's preferences doesn't mean that you should play exclusively to them, especially if that means reinforcing bad habits. If your client prefers to communicate predominately by e-mail because that enables him to stay behind closed doors, away from people with whom he desperately needs to interact, then you must also find ways to draw him out of that comfort zone with other forms of communication that build new muscles for him. Be up-front about this, of course, but balance how you demonstrate respect for a client's preferences with how you help broaden his or her capabilities.

Know What Thoughts You Are Forming. Chris Argyris made clear the value of recording our reactions to an ongoing conversation. By writing down what we are thinking and feeling as others are talking, we become clearer about the theories and hypotheses we are formulating. Then, when it's time to share our thoughts, we have something to say. We shouldn't assume that our hypotheses are correct; we should test them with our clients. By doing this, we come to a deeper understanding than we would have otherwise.

Some people have delayed reactions to situations and therefore have more completely formed thoughts upon reflection a few hours—or even days—after an event. If you recognize this pattern within yourself, then be sure your clients understand that sometimes your most valuable insights may come after a discussion you've had with them, and not necessarily during that discussion. *That you are forming thoughts,* however, *during* the discussion is important for your client to know. That is why thinking out loud and sharing your observations and preliminary thoughts is important as well.

Know How Best to Capture Your Thoughts. Because a lot can happen in a single meeting or conversation, it's a good idea to develop a disciplined way of capturing important thoughts as they occur to you. Using a notepad is only a starting place; having a convention that forces you to capture notes in a variety of categories can help ensure that you are tuned into what is happening on several levels. For example, you might section your pad into quadrants that deal with the stated problem, the client's explanation, your own ideas about what is going on, and your thoughts about the relationship between you and your client. You can generate a list of interesting quadrants and vary it from conversation to conversation to see what works best.

Develop Multiple Ways to Convey Your Thoughts. More often than not, a picture or model is more effective in conveying our thoughts than are words alone. What's important is not how eloquently we state our message; what counts is that our clients understand us and that they are moved to action by what we say. To make this happen, capture your thoughts in the best way you can, whether in words or a picture, and then test how well your message gets across with those on the receiving end.

Know When to Convey Your Thoughts. Stand-up comics know that timing is everything. Your mouth needn't open every time a thought crosses your mind. Some of the most powerful consultants talk sparingly, preserving the impact of their messages for times when it really counts. Not saying something when you are asked can sometimes be more powerful than answering. Of course, timing and content go together. When a message should be delivered depends on what you are trying to say. One hopes we all know that feedback should be immediate, whereas advice should not be given until the person is prepared to listen.

Over time, you will develop a rhythm with your clients—a cadence that helps you gauge the pace, volume, and timing of when to provide your thoughts. Ultimately, *their,* not *your,* clock speed should dictate this cadence. Each client will be different, requiring you to calibrate accordingly.

Ability to Convert Experience to Relevant Wisdom

All consultants bring experience to their work, even if it's only the experience they have gained from living on earth for as long as they have. Good consultants are able to convert that experience to relevant wisdom in each new client situation. In other words, they find a way to link their own experience to the issues their clients are facing and pull from their experience relevant insights and advice to help their clients discover better ways to tackle the challenges before them. Listen to David Nadler talk about this aspect of interpersonal agility:

> "I get a piece of information and try to fit it into a pattern. You're given a couple of dots and you try to connect them. I then elicit information on what I think the next dot should be. If I can get enough information, I start to recognize a pattern. Then I say to myself, 'OK, this sounds like an experience I had with another client,' and then I begin to draw from that experience. I can begin to make some assumptions about the kinds of problems they have and then test what solutions they have or have not tried. It's a preconscious, organic process. I gather data, formulate hypotheses, and test them as I collect more data. As the picture begins to fill out, or not, I can begin to predict where solutions might lie."

There are several steps in converting experience to wisdom that are illustrated by David's story. These include:

- Demonstrating active inquiry,

- Recognizing patterns,

- Drawing on experience,

- Formulating hypotheses,

- Experimenting, and

- Zeroing in through successive approximation.

The process of converting experience to wisdom begins with active inquiry. Our first job as consultants is always to understand what is going on. We do this by asking questions, observing how people behave, reading analysts' reports about a company, digging up news stories, reading things the client sends us, taking a tour, noticing what's on the walls, and so forth. In fact, what we're doing is looking for clues that help us to figure out how to use our knowledge and experience to help the client.

We don't begin consulting relationships with an answer or a program in mind. We need to figure out what the issues are, what the client has already tried, and what kind of approach might fit the situation at hand. Often, we wind up inventing a customized approach that is tailored to the client's needs. Even these customized approaches are based on things we know or have seen work before, however. In our minds, we are constantly comparing the current situation to others and beginning to see how what we did elsewhere could be helpful in another situation.

Recognizing patterns is the key element here. Being agile means not seeing everything as a nail that can be pounded with our favorite hammer. It means understanding enough about what is the same and what is different in a particular situation to call for a unique solution. Instead of just using a hammer, we use our whole toolkit. Like carpenters who craft custom cabinets to fit the space in a kitchen rather than force-fitting pre-manufactured designs, we look for ways to apply our expertise in light of our clients' needs. Like good carpenters, we know our trade well and have ideas in mind about how things should turn out as we begin our work. We have built enough cabinets to know what questions to ask before we begin.

Experience matters in our work as consultants. The deeper and broader our experience, the more likely it is that we will be able to apply past learning to the current situation. Clients are reassured to hear that we have seen similar situations before and that we already have some ideas about approaches that might work. As we draw on our experiences, we begin to formulate hypotheses about what will or will not help our clients succeed.

Hypotheses are usually framed as "if-then" statements, that is, "*If* we do this, *then* things should get better." We can test these hypotheses with our clients. Has the client tried this before? Does it sound like a reasonable approach to him? Does it sound like we are making sense? Are the action levers we are about to pull likely to have a positive effect?

None of us can predict exactly how things will turn out in the course of an intervention. Organizations are too complex to permit complete control over all the dynamics and forces that will come into play as we test our hypotheses through experimentation. As Kurt Lewin said, "There's nothing so practical as a good theory" (Lewin, 1948). What he meant was that a theory that explains what is going on in an organization is useful because it helps us to direct our attention and resources to the right things. If we are simply taking a shot in the dark, our approach might work without our understanding why. We may employ the same approach again only to achieve different results. This tells us that we really don't understand what is happening at all. By formulating hypotheses and testing them through experimentation, we are developing a grounded theory of how the organization works so that we can intervene more effectively.

The more we experiment, the better our understanding of the organization becomes. We zero in on effective solutions to problems by successive approximation. We try what we think will work, check the results, think about how to do it better the next time, and try again. By remaining flexible and not prejudging the solution too quickly, we develop an approach that is right for the situation, rather than just force-fitting an approach that worked somewhere else under different circumstances. Once we succeed, we file away the memory of what we discovered for application in future interventions.

Knowledge of How Your Clients Learn and Accept Help

Experience and success build pride and, as the proverb says, "Pride goeth before the fall." Using interpersonal agility to increase our influence with clients requires that we view each client as unique, with different needs and preferred ways of relating to us as consultants. If we believe we've seen it all and that our job is to convince our clients as quickly as possible that we know the one right way to approach their problems, we will quickly alienate them and may find our relationships ending before we can have the influence we desire. If we don't pay attention to how each client learns and the ways in which he or she prefers to accept our help, consulting with him or her will feel like trying to shift into gear without using the clutch. We know what we want to do, but the harder we push, the louder the sound of grinding gears becomes. When we encounter resistance to our advice, the answer isn't to push our point of view even harder; it's to understand the client's clutch.

Here are some points to keep in mind about understanding how your clients learn and accept help:

Focus on Your Client, Not on Yourself. When consultants focus on their own anxieties or try to force through their own predetermined agendas, they are mostly aware of their own level of comfort or discomfort. The success of the meeting is gauged by their own satisfaction with the outcomes, not that of their clients. Self-awareness is a good thing but, when taken to the extreme, it blocks out awareness of others. At the end of each meeting, the goal should be for the client to say, "That was a good meeting; I learned something useful today" or "I enjoyed that. I'm looking forward to working on what we discussed." Clients are more likely to say these things when we adapt our approach to theirs rather than expecting them to adjust to us.

By focusing your attention on the client instead of yourself, you are bound to pick up more of the signals the client is sending about how he or she likes to learn. For example:

- Clients who are introverted usually respond favorably to pre-reading, agendas, and other things you do to prepare them for the meeting.

- Clients who are more naturally extroverted would rather talk things out; chances are, if you send them pre-work, they will not read it.

- Some clients like to take the lead, while others prefer to follow. Those who take the lead will wrestle for control of the agenda until they obtain it. Their interest is in getting the consultant to react to what they have planned, rather than being handed a plan by the consultant.

- Others want the consultant to formulate the plan so that they have something to respond to. Some clients have become masters of the critique; they have learned to review everything others put before them with an eye toward adding value and perspective. If your client fits this pattern, you should know that it's important to demonstrate your acceptance of his or her input before moving on to the next point.

- Some clients are detail-oriented, while others could care less about how things will be done. Clients who are micro-managers simply can't be comfortable until they know exactly how actions will be accomplished.

- Clients who are more strategic in their orientation will lose interest in action planning very quickly.

- Some clients are natural readers and learners, while others are self-taught. Clients who are hungry for information will ask for things to read or tell you how much they appreciated the article you sent. They may also appreciate information gained through benchmarking, surveys, or other methods that give them a glimpse into how others do things.

- Other clients couldn't care less what anyone else has to say. They believe strongly in their ability to be the best judge of what is right for their organizations and find articles or studies irrelevant.

Become Comfortable with a Framework That You Can Use to Analyze Individual Differences. The signals listed above are just a few of the ones you will pick up from your clients about their preferred ways of learning and receiving help. After working with a number of clients, it's possible to begin categorizing clients by their learning styles or needs so that adapting your style to theirs is easier to accomplish. Good models are available for this purpose should you choose to employ them.

The Learning Style Inventory (Kolb, 1976) classifies people into four types of learners, depending on whether they are (1) more active or reflective in their approach to learning and (2) more conceptual or applied in their thinking. The resulting four styles are easy to spot and to work with once you understand them.

Others prefer to use the four Myers-Briggs Type Inventory (MBTI) dimensions and the resulting sixteen styles to think about how to interact with their clients (Krebs Hirsh, 1985). We mentioned the difference between introverts and extroverts earlier. There are also important differences in whether people are intuitive or sensing, thinking or feeling, and judging or perceiving.

Develop a Repertoire of Teaching Styles. Regardless of the model you choose, it's important to be able to read clients' styles and to have the agility to respond to them accordingly. This can be practiced with peers and family members; understanding and adapting your style to their needs can result in significant improvements in your relationships with them as well. As you work to better understand how others take in information, you can also begin to experiment with different teaching styles. How many ways can you help others learn? Do you have an overused strength, or can you easily vary your approach to meet others' needs? Which approaches on the list below are you comfortable using?

- Verbalizing (lecturing),
- Writing,
- Creating experiences from which others can learn for themselves (simulations, experiential exercises, role plays),
- Networking (creating connections for others),
- Self-guided study with periodic reflection and discussion,
- Research (conducting a study, doing a survey, using focus groups),
- Action learning (joint projects),
- Socratic dialogue (This is a collective attempt to find the answer to a fundamental question. The question is applied to a concrete experience of one or more of the participants that is accessible to all other participants. Systematic reflection on this experience is accompanied by a search for shared judgments and reasons),
- Case studies, and
- Group discussion.

Developing agility in your teaching style will help clients learn more easily, because your approach will match their preferred styles of learning. But what if you have trouble figuring out what works? The simplest answer is to ask. Clients will usually tell you their preferences. Would they like to receive articles to read? Are they interested in spending time discussing ideas, or would they rather you write a letter summarizing your recommendations? Would benchmarking be valuable, or do they already know exactly what they want to accomplish? Given the choice, would they rather work on a plan with you alone or involve other members of their team? The more questions you ask, the less guesswork will be involved in adapting to clients' needs.

▶ Change Enablement

How Interpersonal Agility Accelerates a Client's Adoption of New Ways of Thinking and Acting

Never underestimate the intensity of the demands on your clients' attention. We are not the only voice in the din clamoring to be heard. The "survival agility" they must show in the face of so many relentless obligations is an intense challenge for them. So delivering the right message, by the right mechanism, with true understanding, in an uplifting and motivating way is an art that simply *requires* agility. If clients' absorption rates are already impaired by the environment around them, then we certainly don't want to further cloud their perspectives by delivering messages in ways that simply aren't helpful.

Becoming interpersonally agile can involve quite a bit of "weaving and bobbing." But if our clients are to become more adept at hearing, synthesizing, and acting on what we tell them, we must be the ones to ensure the packaging of our advice and counsel—in every interaction—is as close to the bull's eye as possible. Otherwise, we risk having what we offer being diluted by or, at best, marginalized in the bottomless pool of information deluging our clients every day.

When our clients are facing difficult decisions that could have severe performance implications, that will likely require one approach. When they need help with ensuring the time they spend with their leadership team achieves certain objectives, that's another. When they must confront their colleagues with issues that will invite difficult conflict, that's a third. When their own skills fall short and they must acquire a new capability to meet emerging challenges, yet a fourth approach is needed. If our clients are to be successful using our consulting in these varying contexts and if they are to do so in as quick a time frame as possible, then we must be prepared to "weave and bob" to find the optimal way to influence them in each circumstance. If they must struggle to grasp, absorb, and use our advice because we offered it in a way that, while meaningful for us, didn't fit for them, they will eventually—simply out of exhaustion—turn to other sources for help.

This isn't to say that, if we choose the right medium and approach, clients will simply turn around and apply what we tell them verbatim. They may still struggle with it. They may even still resist. But their struggle and resistance should not be due to difficulty with how the consulting was offered. Change will happen much quicker if we can avoid that struggle and get right on with the noble struggle of making change happen in the clients' organizations. ◀

Table 7.2 summarizes how you can develop interpersonal agility.

Table 7.2. Summary of How to Develop Interpersonal Agility

Practices	Behaviors	Self-Assessment
Exceptional Listening Ability	Make an effort to control outside distractions	I don't fill in the gaps with what I assume my client would have said
	Repeat what you hear	I actively listen for things that my clients say that may indicate their doubt or divergence from my point of view
	Focus on what the other person says	
	Never interrupt	I let my clients finish what they have to say before I respond
	Seek only as much information as you actually need	I avoid starting my responses with "Yes, but . . ."
	Remain calm	
A Broad Range of Personal Styles	Know your current style and its limitations	My observations of others help me decide how to work with them
	Emulate the styles of others unlike you	I can get along with all kinds of people
	Experiment with a variety of language, tone, and nonverbal communication	I am open to working with all types of people
		I am aware of my developmental challenges as a consultant
		I try to identify my strengths and limitations in working with my clients
		I take advantage of opportunities to learn from individuals who have strengths I wish to develop
		I carefully observe actions of individuals who have the strengths I wish to emulate

Table 7.2. Summary of How to Develop Interpersonal Agility, Cont'd

Practices	Behaviors	Self-Assessment
		When speaking with my clients, I pay close attention to my communication style, such as my choice of words, tone, and verbal/nonverbal signals
		I strive to use attention-grabbing language when talking with my clients
Signal Detection	Listen to your gut Detect but do not overinterpret	I regularly make brief entries in my journal about things people have said and other incidental behaviors, as well as significant interactions and events
		I pay attention to how key members of the client organization exchange information
		I restrain myself from seeing my clients' negative moods as a sign of my failure
		I keep my emotions in check when working with clients
		When I detect negative moods from clients, I find ways to understand the reasons behind them
A Light-Hearted Sense of Humor	Make yourself the target Use discretion Let them see you laugh	I use humor in conjunction with serious material
		I use humor as a way to help win over hostile audiences
		I encourage my clients to use humor with members of their organizations
		When using humor, I often use myself as a target
		I tend to make fun of myself if appropriate when working with clients
		Before using humor, I pay careful attention to its appropriateness to the client setting and circumstances

Table 7.2. Summary of How to Develop Interpersonal Agility, Cont'd

Practices	Behaviors	Self-Assessment
		I look for clues in my clients' environments to determine the suitability of using humor
		I laugh with my clients when encountering a humorous situation
		My clients and I share laughter in our working relationships
Humility	Stay focused on the client's needs	I acknowledge to my clients when something is outside my area of expertise
	Use yourself as a reference—good or bad—sparingly	I test work assumptions by seeking the opinions of others
	Pay attention to what you tell yourself about yourself	I believe that my clients' questions do not undermine my professional credibility
	Do windows	When working with my clients, I monitor the amount of time I spend talking about myself
		When talking about my personal experiences in my work, I make sure it is in response to my clients' needs
		I take on additional tasks to be helpful to my clients, even though that's not expected of me
		I volunteer to take on work that is on my clients' plates
Dexterity with Different Methods of Communication	Know your clients' communication preferences	I feel comfortable using a variety of communication media
	Know what thoughts you are forming	I use different forms of communication for different types of messages
	Know how best to capture your thoughts	I know my clients' preferred methods of communication, whether written documents or conversation
	Develop multiple ways to convey your thoughts	When working with my clients, I tend to adapt to their preferred methods of communication
	Know when to convey your thoughts	

Table 7.2. Summary of How to Develop Interpersonal Agility, Cont'd

Practices	Behaviors	Self-Assessment
		I keep track of my thoughts and feelings during an ongoing conversation
		I routinely write down my thoughts and ideas as they come up while working with my clients
		I use an organized approach to capture important thoughts when working with clients
		I use a variety of modes of communication when presenting ideas to my clients
Ability to Convert Experience to Relevant Wisdom	Demonstrate active inquiry Recognize patterns Draw on experience Formulate hypotheses Experiment Zero in through successive approximation	I look for clues in the client's environment that can help me envision future developments I make comparisons between my current engagement and past ones I maintain a dialogue with my clients during all stages of the work I don't prejudge the response to a problem too quickly I manage to transfer learning from one project to another, no matter how unique each may appear
Knowledge of How Clients Learn and Accept Help	Focus on your client, not on yourself Become comfortable with a framework that you can use to analyze individual differences Develop a repertoire of teaching styles Ask questions when in doubt	I tailor my approach to my clients' style and preferences I work with a variety of theoretical frameworks to analyze my interactions with my clients

8

The Future of Client Relationships and Enterprise Change

WE HOPE YOUR SENSE OF ADVENTURE AND URGENCY about the need to change the relationships between consultants and clients has been tapped as you've traveled through this book. We hope that you have honed in on one or two important aspects of your client relationships toward which you will direct your energy and attention. We believe this is an important, almost pioneering, kind of undertaking. Today's views on the consulting relationship, characterized by cynicism, greed, and ambivalence, are an unfortunate reality with which we must contend.

Simply talking about the need for change won't cut it. Leaders who depend on us are too sophisticated and—after receiving inconsistent value for their investment—too jaded and savvy for us to simply tell them we're different. We have to show them. The good news is that we know what it takes to show them. We know where and how they receive value in their relationships with us, and we know how enterprises really change. So the question left for us as consultants is, "Where do we begin?"

We'd suggest you return to the questions you answered at the beginning of the book and see whether what you've considered in the interim provides you with some clarity on where you can start your part of the journey. Include your clients in the process; let them know what you're working on and how you intend to think about your relationships with them. You don't want to surprise them, and needless to say, your new behavior may require complementary new behavior on their part. So you should work with them in the context of your relationship to plan for how best to enhance your experience together.

Your principal task as you move forward with your clients is to develop your own rQ as broadly as possible. As we look ahead at the tumultuous and uncertain times our global business community will navigate, the need for well-grounded, trust-based, client-consultant relationships is going to become more crucial. With an increasing availability of consulting help of all levels and an intensifying set of circumstances urging leaders to seek help, the need for reliable advice from credible consultants who know how to help enterprises change will only grow. We think there are several reasons for this:

- Globalization of the business community;
- Complex dynamics of markets and competitive landscapes;
- Pressure on leaders to deliver results; and
- Growing acceptance of leaders who seek help.

As we near the end of our time together, let's examine each of these factors individually.

Globalization of the Business Community

Over the last thirty years, business globalization has taken consultants who deliver their services to individuals and groups beyond their home country limits. There has been a plethora of books, articles, and training programs developed for people doing international business to introduce them to cultural differences (Adler, 1997; Hofstede, 1980; Laurent, 1983; Trompenaars, 1998). Management literature has only recently started to examine the consequences of globalization on consulting practices in the field of change management and leadership (Cole, 1991; Jaeger, 1989; Johnson, 1991). These authors agree that the issue of cultural differences is very real and that it can play out in many different situations: One has to look at the cultural identity of the individual (for example, a foreign-national CEO), the team (for example, a multicultural team), the organization (for example, a foreign-owned organization), and the societal context (for example, a foreign subsidiary). By combining these different levels, you will end up with a complex cultural matrix.

Starting at the societal level, some have already questioned the universal value of organizational development, a field primarily of American origin (Cole, 1991). In light of different administrative heritages (Lubatkin & Floyd, 1997), the cross-cultural viability of organizational practices has been questioned and controversy has arisen concerning the extent to which these practices are primarily applicable to the United States. Using Hofstede's (1980) cultural model (see Table 8.1), Head and Sorensen (1993) found that some organizational development interventions were more oriented toward certain cultural dimensions than others. For example, countries high on masculinity dimensions, such as Japan or Venezuela, might be characterized by task-oriented interventions, while countries higher on femininity dimensions, such as China, would be more inclined toward process-oriented interventions. Although these findings have to be applied with care, they nonetheless indicate that, as a consultant to organizational change leaders, you are likely to bump into different sets of assumptions and beliefs about change—and ways to implement it—in your clients as you cross cultural borders.

Table 8.1. Hofstede's Dimensions of Culture

Power Distance	The extent to which the less powerful members of institutions and organizations accept that power is distributed unequally. People in high power distance cultures are much more comfortable with a larger status differential than are those in low power distance cultures.
Uncertainty Avoidance	Refers to how comfortable people feel toward ambiguity. Cultures that rank low, compared to other cultures, feel much more comfortable with the unknown. As a result, high uncertainty avoidance cultures prefer formal rules, and any uncertainty can express itself in higher anxiety than those from low uncertainty avoidance cultures feel.

Table 8.1. Hofstede's Dimensions of Culture, Cont'd

Masculinity-Femininity	Refers to expected gender roles in a culture. The cultures that scored toward what Hofstede referred to as "masculine" tend to have very distinct expectations of male and female roles in society. The more "feminine" cultures have a greater ambiguity in what is expected of each gender.
Individualism-Collectivism	Describes the relationship between the individual and the collectivity in a particular society. The essential distinction is one of independence versus dependence. It is suggested that this dimension is associated with relational behavior—determining the relevance of others. For collectivistic cultures, the personal relationship prevails over the task, whereas the opposite is the case for individualistic cultures.
Long-Term/Short-Term Orientation	In his later work, Hofstede introduced a fifth dimension, "the extent to which a culture programs its members to accept delayed gratification of their material, social, and emotional needs." Long-term orientation is characterized by persistence; ordering relationships by status and observing this order; thrift; and having a sense of shame. Short-term orientation is characterized by personal steadiness and stability, protecting "face," respect for tradition, and reciprocation of greetings, favors, and gifts.

Reprinted from G. Hofstede (1980), *Culture's Consequences: International Differences in Work-Related Values.* Thousand Oaks, CA: Sage.

How do you find out what these assumptions and beliefs are? We think that you can uncover them precisely by referring to and relying on the competencies of your relationship intelligence (rQ). As a prerequisite to relationship building, trust is universal. How you establish it, however, is not. What will it take on your part for a particular CEO to feel comfortable sharing his or her objectives, fears, and hopes? When asked about their trans-cultural experience, some of our consultants shared their insights:

"I felt I had to do two things to prepare myself for working with my foreign client: first, learn about his culture through reading and talking to colleagues with experience in the same country. Second, with this information in hand, self-reflect and gain more clarity on where I thought my own cultural beliefs and assumptions were likely to sharply contrast with my client's. By doing this, I was able to show my client a willingness to 'speak his language' and become less of an outsider.

"With my Latin American clients, it was obvious I would not get anywhere near them until some connection had happened at a more personal level. At the onset of a relationship with a U.S. client, I may only briefly comment on the family portrait on the desk and more quickly move to business. With my Latin American clients, I tend to find that, unless there are discussions about family life, I won't get to move on to business."

These two examples illustrate the utility of self-awareness, empathy, and social skills, which are all critical components of emotional intelligence, itself a requirement to establishing trust. These examples confirm the universal value of trust while illustrating that different strategies are used in different cultures to reach this objective. This can apply to the other elements of rQ. Having skin in the game involves the strategic use of time to deliver messages, and in Chapter 3, we showed how planning social times can create the necessary bond with your clients. This tends to be a known requirement of relationship building in Latin cultures. Bourgeois and Boltvinik (1981) reported that Latin clients do not segregate work from the rest of life as much as their American counterparts do. Consequently, your Latin client will have to know you early on at a personal level and be convinced that you're willing to bring more than your tools and expertise to the table.

This cultural characteristic also has an impact on how you will be able to express courage in calling the tough questions: If you criticize the work, in some cultures you are also criticizing the person. The implications are significant, and any one of your interventions would not only affect your client's work role, it would also affect the person's whole identity. In most Asian cultures, saving face is also an important cultural given that needs to be factored into how you plan to give feedback to your client, especially in group settings.

Communication almost always comes to mind as a challenge to building effective cross-cultural relationships. Beyond the language barrier, there are some more profound differences in communication styles and patterns you will have to be aware of in your work with foreign-national clients. For example, Friday (1997) showed significant differences in discussion patterns between American and German executives.

A systematic examination of global differences in rQ's dimensions is beyond the scope of this book. We do want to point out, however, that the utility of rQ can be raised to the nth power when applied to cross-cultural consulting engagements. This resonates with what other practitioners have described as best practices in establishing effective client relationships at a global level (Gibson, 1998; Ratiu, 1985).

Complex Dynamics of Markets and Competitive Landscapes

The rules of business have changed dramatically in the last two decades, and competition is now ruthless. Leaders have become weary of trying to stay on top of their jobs because of failed acquisitions, technology, leadership, business fads that have come and gone without leaving much good behind, and the continually shifting competitive environments as players enter and exit markets nearly overnight. No sooner do they try one solution to a problem when a new problem creeps up, spawning a host of new options. And the time frames in which leaders must make decisions about these options have shrunk significantly. What used to take weeks and months to decide now must be settled in hours and days. While information technology has helped in some ways, it has also increased the challenge.

The availability of information to leaders today is utterly overwhelming. Boiling down piles of available knowledge into the concrete and manageable set of data needed to make the best possible choice, and doing that in short order, takes insight, breadth, and guts. Leaders simply can't do it alone. Separating the wheat from the chaff in the information pile, analyzing the pros and cons of available options, and recommending priorities and a game plan can often best be done with someone the leader implicitly trusts. This does not entail diminishing the leader's involvement, but rather leveraging it. The complexity and breadth of today's leadership role in organizations simply does not allow for a leader to have total control over all decisions. The biases and politics of those on the leader's team must always be considered when obtaining input from insiders. So the trusted outsider (even if you're an internal consultant, you still must be an "outsider" to be effective) is left as a unique and important source of advice, guidance, and expertise.

Pressure on Leaders to Deliver Results

The average tenure of CEOs is decreasing as investors, analysts, and the media continue to expect faster and larger returns. The level of public scrutiny of CEO decision making has increased dramatically in the last few decades. Much of what was once privy to only a few insiders is now public knowledge. Boards, representing the interests of shareholders, have also been put under microscopes to ascertain their fairness and objectivity. Fewer boards are composed of members who will support the CEO's every decision. Many ask to take a more active role in reviewing strategies and decisions that are likely to influence the long-term value of the company.

All of this puts a premium on improving performance as quickly as possible. The first one hundred days of a new CEO's tenure, a period made famous by the legislation passed during Franklin Delano Roosevelt's first one hundred days in office, has become an important measure of his or her performance. In the face of this pressure, more CEOs are turning to trusted advisors to help them execute change swiftly.

As the consulting industry has grown, it has become more common to see companies engage consulting firms in large projects that would be impossible to accomplish quickly, if at all, by relying strictly on internal resources. Leaders of many companies have recognized that internal resources either resist making needed changes or lack the critical expertise to carry out massive overhauls of business models, information systems, or organizational processes. Despite the sometimes enormous costs and risks involved, CEOs are counting on consulting firms to play a major role in organizational transformation.

Leaders are also retooling their enterprises through acquisitions and divestitures. Treating business units like holdings in an investment portfolio, leaders are seeking the best return on their investment for the shareholder, even if it means leaving familiar ground to set out for new territory.

As the pressure for rapid, significant change grows, so does the need to manage change efficiently and effectively. Time to think things through, make sure everyone is on board, and plan each move in detail has been greatly compressed. Change actions are not only increasingly sudden, but they are also increasingly far-reaching. CEOs, if they are to safeguard the interests of shareholders, cannot just roll the dice and hope for the best. They have to know how to change their companies quickly, completely, and successfully. It's a tall order.

It should come as no surprise that more CEOs rely on trusted advisors to guide them through the steps involved in organizational transformation. It's not uncommon for CEOs to be working with several advisors at once: one on strategy, one on communications with the financial community, and another on organization change. Investors and boards of directors expect CEOs to seek competent counsel in these matters and to be ultimately responsible for how things turn out. With so much on the line, CEOs choose their advisors carefully.

We have seen many technically competent advisors who fail to win a CEO's confidence. CEOs aren't unduly impressed with advisors who are technically competent; it's the price of admission. Given a choice among equally competent advisors with similar technical knowledge, what determines a CEO's choice? Brand name recognition certainly helps. It's easier to explain to the board of directors why a consultant was chosen if she or he is backed by a recognized firm or is a widely recognized expert on the issues. The same is true of people who come recommended through the CEO's network. In choosing a physician, we often rely on the advice of our friends, even though they aren't medical experts. The same applies to CEOs choosing consultants; if their friends have had a good experience, it's more likely that they will as well.

Beyond name recognition and recommendations, choices often come down to chemistry. The CEO may talk to a number of consultants to gain a sense of how they would work with him or her. If they appear equally competent, the choice is one of comfort or intuition that the person selected will get the job done. In this context, and in building a reputation, the consultant's rQ matters. CEOs are turning more to trusted advisors for help—but they aren't turning to just any advisors. Assuming that you are technically competent, mastering the skills outlined in this book will position you to be among the chosen few.

Growing Acceptance of Leaders Who Seek Help

As leaders' jobs become more difficult, the business community is increasingly accepting the fact that leaders need to seek help. Twenty years ago, leaders could look forward to long tenures in a job. They could control their environments, indulge in lengthy planning sessions, and direct things from a desk high atop a large office building. Those days are long gone. Today, leaders are lucky to have time to think about next week, much less next year or the year after that. They can expect two or three major career changes in the course of their work lives. Instability is now the norm, and navigating unpredictable and unprecedented terrain simply requires help to avoid disaster and get the job done.

A new generation of leaders who seem to thrive on the perpetual vortex of change is emerging. And they seem quite comfortable asking for help along the way. Younger leaders, rising to big jobs more quickly in today's talent-starved environment, are far more inclined to grab as much advice and knowledge from any source they can reach. In contrast, many of today's most senior leaders grew up in an era characterized by rugged individualism that perpetuated the notion that asking for help signaled weakness. If an advisor was needed, it meant a shortfall in one's intellect, courage, knowledge, or character. Even these leaders, despite their conditioning to be self-sufficient, are finding themselves in broad roles spanning global organizations for which they feel ill-prepared. They too are reaching out for help.

The challenge all these leaders face is that the quality of help they can receive from consultants varies widely. With each industry boom, consulting numbers escalate rapidly. It's hard to imagine a large organization today not engaging consultants for some purpose. Given the spate of consulting-bashing books and articles over the past few years, however, it appears that not everyone has felt good about his or her consulting relationships. Leaders are not likely to stop using consultants any time soon, but they probably will be more careful about choosing which consultants they employ.

Leaders will find themselves asking, "Where can I find someone I can trust, who has my best interest at heart, will tell me the truth, and knows what I need her to know to help me with the complex challenges I'm facing?" And the first name to come to mind will belong to the trusted consultant who has built a relationship with the leader that is markedly distinguished from the crowd of consultants that came before.

Conclusion

As we look at the challenges leaders are facing in an increasingly complex global business environment, we can see the challenges for ourselves as consultants. On the one hand, leaders are compelled to lead such complex, multidimensional business lives that in many instances they simply must seek the help of a trusted advisor. Business culture is shifting in a way that recognizes and supports a leader's need to seek this help. In a way, this is good news for us in that leaders are increasingly open to the sort of help we can provide, regardless of whether we are internal or external consultants. On the other hand, the same pressures that drive leaders to seek us out also compel them to gain optimal value from us or move on if we cannot deliver support quickly. In the same way that corporate boards dismiss underperforming CEOs, so clients are apt to dismiss consultants who underperform.

Consultant "underperformance" can take several guises. As we pointed out at the beginning of this book, it is possible to spend a lot of time and effort only to see a change initiative fail. Remember your answers to the questions posed in the preface of this book. Perhaps the most important concept you take with you as we conclude this book is that the reasons change initiatives fail are embedded in the elements of rQ. Think about your own experiences in this context. What went right with successful change initiatives? What types of relationships were involved? How did these relationships change over time? What kinds of situations were you in? What emotions came into play? Who was involved? What roles did they play? What sort of personality characteristics were involved?

Now think about initiatives that fell short of their projected outcome. Did a change effort fizzle during implementation? Was a leadership team simply unable to address an issue too sensitive for anyone to confront? Did the client become too dependent on you? Or were you never able to get close enough to the client to impact his or her thinking in a meaningful way? As you think about your consulting work in the context of rQ, you'll see how each of the elements fit together to create your relationship intelligence. We encourage you to take the next step by designing your individual development plan. We have provided a comprehensive rQ self-assessment in the Appendix of this book. It will give you a base on which to build. As you work, remember that we developed this concept as a result of our reflections on our work and dialogue with our own clients. Accordingly, it is important for you to include your clients in the process, letting them know how you want to jointly enhance the relationship. As you and your clients apply these ideas in your work together, we are sure you will conclude, as we have, that developing relationship intelligence is key to meeting the needs of our clients and achieving success both for them and for ourselves.

We wish you great success as you embark on a new approach to working with leaders who depend on your advice and guidance. We trust you will see quick results in the level of gratification you and your clients experience, the level of responsiveness your clients show, and ultimately, the degree of change your clients achieve when you hone the elements of rQ for yourself.

rQ Self-Assessment Questionnaire

Instructions. The following questionnaire is designed to determine where your strengths and areas for development are on the Change Relationship Competency Model presented in this book. Our objective in creating this questionnaire was to offer a variety of items to measure each dimension of the CRCM. When using this questionnaire, you may decide to select a smaller subset of items instead of the full battery of items. Please read each statement and, using the scale on the next page, indicate the extent to which each statement is descriptive of your consulting practice. Add up your ratings for each subdimension and divide by the number of items you've answered within that category to compute your score for any given subdimension.

	1 = To a Very Little Extent	2 = To a Little Extent	3 = To Some Extent	4 = To a Great Extent	5 = To a Very Great Extent

	To a Very Little Extent	To a Little Extent	To Some Extent	To a Great Extent	To a Very Great Extent

GETTING CLOSE TO BUILD TRUST

Self-Awareness

1. I can detect in others the signs of emotional discomfort.	1	2	3	4	5
2. I have confidence in my own work capabilities.	1	2	3	4	5
3. I verbalize my emotions to my clients.	1	2	3	4	5

Subtotal: _____ /3 (or number of items answered) = _____

Modeling

4. I am able to model the behaviors I expect my clients to demonstrate.	1	2	3	4	5
5. I keep my emotions and behavior in check.	1	2	3	4	5
6. I take responsibility for shortcomings in my performance.	1	2	3	4	5
7. I demonstrate flexibility in handling change.	1	2	3	4	5
8. I welcome new ideas and methods that can move the work forward.	1	2	3	4	5

Subtotal: _____ /5 = _____

	To a Very Little Extent	To a Little Extent	To Some Extent	To a Great Extent	To a Very Great Extent
Emotional Intelligence					
9. My inner feelings help me sense what my clients are experiencing.	1	2	3	4	5
10. I read my clients' emotions through their verbal and nonverbal cues.	1	2	3	4	5
11. I am able to detect discrepancies between my clients' felt and expressed emotions.	1	2	3	4	5
12. I look for the causes of my clients' anxieties.	1	2	3	4	5

Subtotal: _____ /4 = _____

	To a Very Little Extent	To a Little Extent	To Some Extent	To a Great Extent	To a Very Great Extent
Ability to Set and Keep Boundaries					
13. I remind my clients of their responsibilities when they make out-of-role requests of me.	1	2	3	4	5

Subtotal: _____ /1 = _____

PERSONAL INVESTMENT

Put Skin in the Game

	To a Very Little Extent	To a Little Extent	To Some Extent	To a Great Extent	To a Very Great Extent
14. I let my client know that I am committed to our work together.	1	2	3	4	5
15. I create opportunities to meet more informally with my clients to just catch up.	1	2	3	4	5

	To a Very Little Extent	To a Little Extent	To Some Extent	To a Great Extent	To a Very Great Extent
16. I volunteer help on miscellaneous tasks such as writing communications or preparing for speeches.	1	2	3	4	5
17. My clients and I have conversations about non-work-related topics.	1	2	3	4	5
18. I find common areas of interest with all my clients.	1	2	3	4	5
19. Interactions with my client are energizing and fun.	1	2	3	4	5
20. I find ways to lighten up the situation when my clients feel overwhelmed.	1	2	3	4	5

Subtotal: _____ /7 = _____

Connect Personal Aspirations to the Work

	To a Very Little Extent	To a Little Extent	To Some Extent	To a Great Extent	To a Very Great Extent
21. I reflect on how the work helps me reach my personal goals.	1	2	3	4	5
22. In the midst of a project, I do not lose track of my personal objectives.	1	2	3	4	5
23. I tell my clients about my aspirations in working with them.	1	2	3	4	5
24. I tell my clients how I would typically behave in certain situations.	1	2	3	4	5

	To a Very Little Extent	To a Little Extent	To Some Extent	To a Great Extent	To a Very Great Extent
25. I personally feel excited when I notice that the work we are doing is moving in the intended direction.	1	2	3	4	5
26. I bring positive signs of change to my clients' attention.	1	2	3	4	5

Subtotal: _____ /6 = _____

Create Capable Clients by Avoiding Dependency

27. I work with my clients to identify and prioritize their developmental needs.	1	2	3	4	5
28. I use my client work as an opportunity to improve or acquire skills and capabilities.	1	2	3	4	5
29. I encourage my clients to apply new skills or knowledge that I think will lead to greater progress.	1	2	3	4	5
30. On most projects, I schedule time with my clients to pause and reflect on ongoing work.	1	2	3	4	5
31. I meet with my client at the end of a project to review and assess the work that was done.	1	2	3	4	5

	To a Very Little Extent	To a Little Extent	To Some Extent	To a Great Extent	To a Very Great Extent
32. Unsolicited, I provide my clients with resources, such as books and contacts, that can help them.	1	2	3	4	5
33. I update my clients on their progress in developing new competencies.	1	2	3	4	5

Subtotal: _____ /7 = _____

COURAGE

Have Confidence to Call the Tough Questions

	To a Very Little Extent	To a Little Extent	To Some Extent	To a Great Extent	To a Very Great Extent
34. I am willing to address conflict with my clients/internal collaborators.	1	2	3	4	5
35. I confront my clients on issues that are critical to the success of the change effort.	1	2	3	4	5
36. When delivering key messages, I spend time preparing what I will say and how I will phrase my questions.	1	2	3	4	5
37. I gather enough data before I attribute causes or assign blame.	1	2	3	4	5

Subtotal: _____ /4 = _____

Hold the Client Accountable

	To a Very Little Extent	To a Little Extent	To Some Extent	To a Great Extent	To a Very Great Extent
38. I work with my clients to define clear expectations about our projects.	1	2	3	4	5

	To a Very Little Extent	To a Little Extent	To Some Extent	To a Great Extent	To a Very Great Extent
39. I collaborate with my clients to create project plans.	1	2	3	4	5
40. I work with my clients to identify the measures of success of our projects.	1	2	3	4	5
41. I let my clients know when they aren't contributing enough to the project.	1	2	3	4	5
42. I ask my clients to show visible signs of commitment to the work we are doing.	1	2	3	4	5

Subtotal: _____ /5 = _____

Provide Nonjudgmental Feedback

	To a Very Little Extent	To a Little Extent	To Some Extent	To a Great Extent	To a Very Great Extent
43. At the beginning of the relationship, I set expectations on providing feedback to my clients.	1	2	3	4	5
44. I put myself in my client's shoes before disclosing negative feedback.	1	2	3	4	5
45. I am aware of the power of feedback and how it helps my clients.	1	2	3	4	5
46. I prepare my clients to receive feedback from me on an ongoing basis.	1	2	3	4	5

	To a Very Little Extent	To a Little Extent	To Some Extent	To a Great Extent	To a Very Great Extent
47. I carefully select opportunities to give feedback to my clients.	1	2	3	4	5

Subtotal: _____ /5 = _____

ADVOCACY

Help Leaders Acknowledge and Explore Their Apprehension

48. I spend time talking with my clients about the pros and cons of their options.	1	2	3	4	5
49. I recognize times when my clients lose momentum or are getting worn out.	1	2	3	4	5
50. I help my clients keep their focus on the vision they have set for their organizations.	1	2	3	4	5
51. I review with my clients where they have support for their decisions.	1	2	3	4	5
52. I talk with my clients about how to leverage key stakeholders who recognize the complexity of the situation.	1	2	3	4	5

Subtotal: _____ /5 = _____

	To a Very Little Extent	To a Little Extent	To Some Extent	To a Great Extent	To a Very Great Extent
Provide Genuine Encouragement at Critical Crossroads					
53. I remind my clients of how they reached their decision to follow the courses of action they are now on.	1	2	3	4	5
54. I offer to benchmark other organizations that have been through similar changes.	1	2	3	4	5
55. I share examples from my own experience with other clients I have helped through similar situations.	1	2	3	4	5
56. I help my clients come to grips with shortcomings that may arise on their executive teams.	1	2	3	4	5
57. I provide objective feedback to my clients about their strengths and weaknesses.	1	2	3	4	5
58. I help my clients identify which of their strengths can help compensate for their weaknesses.	1	2	3	4	5
59. I advise my clients to surround themselves with others who can balance their weaknesses.	1	2	3	4	5

	To a Very Little Extent	To a Little Extent	To Some Extent	To a Great Extent	To a Very Great Extent
60. I point out times when my clients demonstrate needed skills and help them "connect the dots."	1	2	3	4	5
61. I encourage my clients to think about how they have gotten over hurdles in the past.	1	2	3	4	5
62. I help my clients think about how they would want their employees to respond to making a genuine mistake.	1	2	3	4	5
63. I provide advice on what to do next immediately rather than in the long term.	1	2	3	4	5

Subtotal: _____ /11 = _____

Help Leaders Stay the Course During Implementation

	To a Very Little Extent	To a Little Extent	To Some Extent	To a Great Extent	To a Very Great Extent
64. I help my clients anticipate where change efforts are likely to meet resistance.	1	2	3	4	5
65. My clients and I find ways to leverage our respective roles as leaders and change expert to facilitate change.	1	2	3	4	5
66. I encourage my clients to engage organization members in remote offices or foreign-based subsidiaries.	1	2	3	4	5

	To a Very Little Extent	To a Little Extent	To Some Extent	To a Great Extent	To a Very Great Extent
67. I help my clients prepare for dealing with resistance from critical organization stakeholders.	1	2	3	4	5
68. My relationships with internal collaborators help me develop a perspective on what's going on that my clients don't see.	1	2	3	4	5

Subtotal: _____ /5 = _____

Help Clients Recognize When They Have Exhibited Highly Effective Behavior

69. I let my clients know when I think they have demonstrated the right kind of behavior or made the right decision.	1	2	3	4	5
70. I use processes such as AAR or Appreciative Inquiry to help my clients recognize what they have done well.	1	2	3	4	5

Subtotal: _____ /2 = _____

COMBINING CAPABILITIES THROUGH COLLABORATION

Understand Client Requirements

71. Early in a project, I spend time getting to know the members of the client system and their personal aspirations.	1	2	3	4	5

	To a Very Little Extent	To a Little Extent	To Some Extent	To a Great Extent	To a Very Great Extent
72. I encourage my clients to share their perceptions of how my work is contributing to reaching their objectives.	1	2	3	4	5
73. I tell my clients how I feel about their commitment to the work we do together.	1	2	3	4	5

Subtotal: _____ /3 = _____

Create a Shared View of Desired Outcomes

	To a Very Little Extent	To a Little Extent	To Some Extent	To a Great Extent	To a Very Great Extent
74. I keep my clients informed about the direction and progress of the work I am doing.	1	2	3	4	5
75. I stay closely connected with my client throughout a project, even after we have agreed on the work to be done.	1	2	3	4	5
76. I make a list for myself during each project of what interests me about the work I am doing.	1	2	3	4	5
77. I look for common ground between my personal aspirations and my client's.	1	2	3	4	5

Subtotal: _____ /4 = _____

	To a Very Little Extent	To a Little Extent	To Some Extent	To a Great Extent	To a Very Great Extent
Build Client Ownership Throughout the Engagement					
78. I do not get so caught up in the work and the progress made that I neglect to update my client.	1	2	3	4	5
79. I like to involve the client in all phases of the project.	1	2	3	4	5
80. I remind my clients of the decisions they need to make.	1	2	3	4	5
81. I help my clients recognize the potential ramifications of their decisions.	1	2	3	4	5

Subtotal: _____ /4 = _____

	To a Very Little Extent	To a Little Extent	To Some Extent	To a Great Extent	To a Very Great Extent
Build Client Capability Through Learning					
82. I encourage my clients to define their objectives beyond the current project.	1	2	3	4	5
83. I encourage my clients to find ways to reaffirm for others their leadership roles in our work.	1	2	3	4	5
84. I encourage my clients to explore areas for development revealed through our work together.	1	2	3	4	5
85. I help my clients assess and decide where change efforts are most needed.	1	2	3	4	5

Subtotal: _____ /4 = _____

	To a Very Little Extent	To a Little Extent	To Some Extent	To a Great Extent	To a Very Great Extent

Design Work to Guarantee Synergy

86. Before starting a project, I take time to explain my working and learning styles to my clients.

| | 1 | 2 | 3 | 4 | 5 |

87. When I start a new project, I don't just use the same small set of intervention formats I have used on previous projects.

| | 1 | 2 | 3 | 4 | 5 |

88. I recommend that my clients use interventions that fit their working styles.

| | 1 | 2 | 3 | 4 | 5 |

89. I adapt my consulting approach to fit my clients' cognitive styles.

| | 1 | 2 | 3 | 4 | 5 |

90. I ask my clients for their feedback on how our working relationship is meeting their needs.

| | 1 | 2 | 3 | 4 | 5 |

Subtotal: _____ /5 = _____

	To a Very Little Extent	To a Little Extent	To Some Extent	To a Great Extent	To a Very Great Extent

Discuss Expectations Regarding Working Relationships

91. When I find that my client is becoming "difficult," I do not just go ahead and do the work by myself.	1	2	3	4	5
92. I describe for my clients the pros and cons of alternative ways to do the work.	1	2	3	4	5
93. I spend a substantial amount of time early in the relationship with my clients to discuss our respective roles.	1	2	3	4	5
94. When the work changes, I make sure that my clients and I reassess our respective roles.	1	2	3	4	5

Subtotal: _____ / 4 = _____

INTERPERSONAL AGILITY

Exceptional Listening Ability

95. I don't fill in the gaps with what I assume my client would have said.	1	2	3	4	5

	To a Very Little Extent	To a Little Extent	To Some Extent	To a Great Extent	To a Very Great Extent
96. I actively listen for things that my clients say that may indicate their doubt or divergence from my point of view.	1	2	3	4	5
97. I let my clients finish what they have to say before I respond.	1	2	3	4	5
98. I avoid starting my responses with "Yes, but. . . ."	1	2	3	4	5

Subtotal: _____ /4 = _____

A Broad Range of Personal Styles

	To a Very Little Extent	To a Little Extent	To Some Extent	To a Great Extent	To a Very Great Extent
99. My observations of others help me decide how to work with them.	1	2	3	4	5
100. I can get along with all kinds of people.	1	2	3	4	5
101. I am open to working with all types of people.	1	2	3	4	5
102. I am aware of my developmental challenges as a consultant.	1	2	3	4	5
103. I try to identify my strengths and limitations in working with my clients.	1	2	3	4	5

	To a Very Little Extent	To a Little Extent	To Some Extent	To a Great Extent	To a Very Great Extent
104. I take advantage of opportunities to learn from individuals who have strengths I wish to develop.	1	2	3	4	5
105. I carefully observe actions of individuals who have the strengths I wish to emulate.	1	2	3	4	5
106. When speaking with my clients, I pay close attention to my communication style, such as my choice of words, tone, and verbal/nonverbal signals.	1	2	3	4	5
107. I strive to use attention-grabbing language when talking with my clients.	1	2	3	4	5

Subtotal: _____ /9 = _____

Signal Detection

	To a Very Little Extent	To a Little Extent	To Some Extent	To a Great Extent	To a Very Great Extent
108. I regularly make brief entries in my journal about things people have said and other incidental behaviors, as well as significant interactions and events.	1	2	3	4	5
109. I pay attention to how key members of the client organization exchange information.	1	2	3	4	5

	To a Very Little Extent	To a Little Extent	To Some Extent	To a Great Extent	To a Very Great Extent
110. Before acting in response to a negative situation, I reflect on how I am feeling about it.	1	2	3	4	5
111. I keep my emotions in check when working with clients.	1	2	3	4	5
112. I restrain myself from seeing my clients' negative moods as a sign of my failure.	1	2	3	4	5
113. When I detect negative moods from clients, I find ways to understand the reasons behind them.	1	2	3	4	5

Subtotal: _____ /6 = _____

A Light-Hearted Sense of Humor

114. I use humor in conjunction with more serious material.	1	2	3	4	5
115. I use humor as a way to help win over hostile audiences.	1	2	3	4	5
116. I encourage my clients to use humor with members of their organizations.	1	2	3	4	5
117. When using humor, I often use myself as a target.	1	2	3	4	5
118. I tend to make fun of myself if appropriate when working with clients.	1	2	3	4	5

	To a Very Little Extent	To a Little Extent	To Some Extent	To a Great Extent	To a Very Great Extent
119. Before using humor, I pay careful attention to its appropriateness to the client setting and circumstances.	1	2	3	4	5
120. I look for clues in my clients' environments to determine the suitability of using humor.	1	2	3	4	5
121. I laugh with my clients when encountering a humorous situation.	1	2	3	4	5
122. My clients and I share laughter in our working relationships.	1	2	3	4	5

Subtotal: _____ /9 = _____

Humility

123. I acknowledge to my clients when something is outside my area of expertise.	1	2	3	4	5
124. I test work assumptions by seeking the opinions of others.	1	2	3	4	5
125. I believe that my clients' questions do not undermine my professional credibility.	1	2	3	4	5
126. When working with my clients, I monitor the amount of time I spend talking about myself.	1	2	3	4	5

	To a Very Little Extent	To a Little Extent	To Some Extent	To a Great Extent	To a Very Great Extent
127. When talking about my personal experiences in my work, I make sure it is in response to my clients' needs.	1	2	3	4	5
128. I take on additional tasks to be helpful to my clients, even though that's not expected of me.	1	2	3	4	5
129. I volunteer to take on work that is on my clients' plates.	1	2	3	4	5

Subtotal: _____ /7 = _____

Dexterity with Different Methods of Communication

	To a Very Little Extent	To a Little Extent	To Some Extent	To a Great Extent	To a Very Great Extent
130. I feel comfortable using a variety of communication media.	1	2	3	4	5
131. I use different forms of communication for different types of messages.	1	2	3	4	5
132. I know my clients' preferred methods of communication, whether written documents or conversation.	1	2	3	4	5
133. When working with my clients, I tend to adapt to their preferred methods of communication.	1	2	3	4	5

	To a Very Little Extent	To a Little Extent	To Some Extent	To a Great Extent	To a Very Great Extent
134. I keep track of my thoughts and feelings during an ongoing conversation.	1	2	3	4	5
135. I routinely write down my thoughts and ideas as they come up while working with my clients.	1	2	3	4	5
136. I use an organized approach to capture important thoughts when working with clients.	1	2	3	4	5
137. I use a variety of modes of communication when presenting ideas to my clients.	1	2	3	4	5

Subtotal: _____ /8 = _____

Ability to Convert Experience to Relevant Wisdom

	To a Very Little Extent	To a Little Extent	To Some Extent	To a Great Extent	To a Very Great Extent
138. I look for clues in my client's environment that can help me envision future developments.	1	2	3	4	5
139. I make comparisons between my current engagement and past ones.	1	2	3	4	5
140. I maintain a dialogue with my clients during all stages of the work.	1	2	3	4	5
141. I don't prejudge the response to a problem too quickly.	1	2	3	4	5

	To a Very Little Extent	To a Little Extent	To Some Extent	To a Great Extent	To a Very Great Extent
142. I manage to transfer learning from one project to another, no matter how unique each may appear.	1	2	3	4	5

Subtotal: _____ /5 = _____

Knowledge of How Your Clients Learn and Accept Help

	To a Very Little Extent	To a Little Extent	To Some Extent	To a Great Extent	To a Very Great Extent
143. I tailor my approach to my clients' style and preferences.	1	2	3	4	5
144. I work with a variety of theoretical frameworks to analyze my interactions with my clients.	1	2	3	4	5

Subtotal: _____ /2 = _____

 **rQ Profile**

Instructions: Transfer your subdimension scores to the table below. On the right-hand side, use your average scores to plot your profile on the Relationship Competencies Questionnaire. To do this, make dots at the appropriate places on the scale and then connect the dots vertically in each category of rQ.

Competencies	Score	1	2	3	4	5
Getting Close to Build Trust						
Self-Awareness						
Modeling						
Emotional Intelligence						
Ability to Set and Keep Boundaries						
Personal Investment						
Put Skin in the Game						
Connect Personal Aspirations to the Work						
Create Capable Clients by Avoiding Dependency						
Courage						
Have Confidence to Call the Tough Questions						
Hold the Client Accountable						
Provide Nonjudgmental Feedback						

Competencies	Score	1	2	3	4	5
Advocacy						
Help Leaders Acknowledge and Explore Their Apprehension						
Provide Genuine Encouragement at Critical Crossroads						
Help Leaders Stay the Course During Implementation						
Help Clients Recognize When They Have Exhibited Highly Effective Behavior						
Combining Capabilities Through Collaboration						
Understand Client Requirements						
Create a Shared View of Desired Outcomes						
Build Client Ownership Throughout the Engagement						
Build Client Capability Through Learning						
Design Work to Guarantee Synergy						
Discuss Expectations Regarding Working Relationships						
Interpersonal Agility						
Exceptional Listening Ability						
A Broad Range of Personal Styles						

Competencies	Score	1	2	3	4	5
Signal Detection						
A Light-Hearted Sense of Humor						
Humility						
Dexterity with Different Methods of Communication						
Ability to Convert Experience to Relevant Wisdom						
Knowledge of How Clients Learn and Accept Help						

Interpreting Your Scores

Your profile of scores indicates the repertoire of relationship-building skills that you use in the context of your work as a consultant to organization leaders. The score profile you created above enables you to quickly identify your strengths and your areas for development. The six competencies of the rQ model are represented, along with the more detailed best practices described in the book.

The highest average score possible for each competency is 5 and the lowest score is 1. In general, the following are true:

- The higher your score, the more proficient you are in demonstrating that particular competency.

- The lower your score, the more you need to focus on developing that competency.

- Competencies for which you obtain your highest score are most descriptive of how you work with your clients.

- The greater the differences among scores, the greater your current reliance on those competencies with highest scores.

Finally, in addition to scoring yourself on this questionnaire, we encourage you to invite your clients or colleagues to fill out the questionnaire about you and indicate the extent to which they think you demonstrate these competencies. You then can compare your self-scoring with that of others and, through this multi-rater assessment application of the rQ questionnaire, identify the following:

- *Recognized Strengths*—Those competencies where your self-scoring and that of others converge on the higher end of the scale. This most desirable outcome indicates that you cannot only demonstrate these competencies but that you do so in a way that is visible to your clients and colleagues.

- *Unknown Strengths*—Those competencies for which you scored yourself low but that others scored high. This may indicate that you are setting high standards for yourself and need to recalibrate your expectations and communicate with your clients and colleagues more effectively.

- *Recognized Areas for Development*—Those competencies on which your scores and those of others converge on the lower end of the scale. These are your acknowledged weaknesses, and you need to find opportunities to develop in these competencies.

- *Unrecognized Weaknesses or "Blind Spots"*—Those competencies for which you scored yourself as high and that others saw as low. The least desirable of the four score patterns, this indicates you are not sufficiently attuned to your own competencies and risk being surprised by negative turns of events.

References

Adler, N. (1997). *International dimensions of organizational behavior* (3rd ed.). Cincinnati, OH: Southwestern.

Argyris, C. (1970). *Intervention theory and method: A behavioral science view.* Reading, MA: Addison-Wesley.

Argyris, C. (1990). *Overcoming organizational defenses.* Needham Heights, MA: Allyn & Bacon.

Ashkenas, R., Ulrich, D., & Jick, T. (1998). *The boundaryless organization: Breaking the chains of organizational structure.* San Francisco, CA: Jossey-Bass.

Baird, L., Deacon, S., & Holland, P. (1998) *From action learning to learning from action: Implementing the after action review.* Boston, MA: Systems Research Center, Boston University.

Barnard, C. (1968). *The function of the executive.* Cambridge, MA: Harvard University Press.

Bass, B.M. (1990). *Bass and Stogdill's handbook of leadership: Theory, research, and managerial applications* (3rd ed.). New York: The Free Press.

Beckhard, R. (1969). *Organization development: Strategies and models.* Reading, MA: Addison-Wesley.

Bennis, W. (1992). *Leaders on leadership: Interviews with top executives.* Boston, MA: Harvard Business School.

Block, P. (2000). *Flawless consulting* (2nd ed.). San Francisco, CA: Jossey-Bass/Pfeiffer.

Bourgeois, L.J., & Boltvinik, M. (1981). OD in cross-cultural settings: Latin America. *California Management Review, 23*(3), 75–81.

Bourgeois, L.J., III, & Eisenhardt, K.M. (1988). Strategic decision processes in high velocity environments. *Management Science, 34*(7), 816–835.

Boyatzis, R.E., Goleman, D., & Rhee, K. (2000). Clustering competence in emotional intelligence: Insights from the emotional competence inventory (ECI). In R. Bar-On & J.D.A. Parker (Eds.), *Handbook of emotional intelligence* (pp. 343–362). San Francisco, CA: Jossey-Bass.

Bridges, W. (1991). *Managing transitions: Making the most of change.* Cambridge, MA: Perseus.

Bryant, S. E. (1995). Behavior modeling training and generalization: Interaction of learning point type and number of modeling scenarios. *The Psychological Record, 45,* 495.

Buchen, I.H. (2001). The trusted advisor revealed. *Consulting to Management, 12*(2), 35–37.

Burke, W.W. (1993). *Organization development: A process of learning and changing* (2nd ed.). Reading, MA: Addison-Wesley.

Carucci, R.A., & Tetenbaum, T.J. (1999). *The value-creating consultant: How to build and sustain lasting client relationships.* New York: AMACOM.

Clark, H.H., & Brennan, S.E. (1991). Grounding in communication. In L.B. Resnick, J. Levine, & S.D. Teasley (Eds.), *Perspectives on socially shared cognition* (pp. 127–149). Washington, DC: American Psychological Association.

Cole, D. (1991). The future of international organizational development. In P.F. Sorensen, T.C. Head, N. Mathys, & K.R. Johnson (Eds.), *International organization development.* Champaign, IL: Stipes.

Cooperrider, D., Sorensen, P., Whitney, D., & Yeager, T. (2000). *Appreciative inquiry: Rethinking human organization toward a positive theory of change.* Champaign, IL: Stipes.

Daft, R.L., & Lengel, R.H. (1986). Organizational information requirements, media richness, and structural design. *Management Science, 32*(5), 554–571.

Dymond, R.F. (1949). A scale for the measurement of empathic ability. *Journal of Consulting Psychology, 13,* 127–133.

Dymond, R.F. (1950). Personality and empathy. *Journal of Consulting Psychology, 14,* 343–350.

Falk, D., & Johnson, D.W. (1977). The effects of perspective-taking and egocentrism on problem-solving in heterogeneous and homogeneous groups. *Journal of Social Psychology, 102,* 63–72.

Flavell, J.H. (1974). The development of inferences about others. In T. Mischel (Ed.), *Understanding other persons.* Lotowa, NJ: Rowman.

Fox, W.M. (1988, Summer). Getting the most from behavior modeling training. *National Productivity Review, 7*(3), 238–246.

Fracaro, K. (2001). Empathy: A potent management tool. *Supervision, 62*(3), 10–12.

Friday, R. (1997). Contrasts in discussion behaviors of German and American managers. In L.A. Samovar & R.E. Porter (Eds.), *Intercultural communication* (8th ed.) (pp. 297–307). Belmont, CA: Wadsworth.

Funder, D.C. (1995). On the accuracy of personality judgement: A realistic approach. *Psychological Review, 102,* 652–670.

Gates, W. (1999). *Business at the speed of thought.* New York: Warner.

Gibson, M.K. (1998). Avoiding intervention pitfalls in international consulting. *Journal of Management Consulting, 10*(2), 1–7.

Goldblatt, H. (1999, November 8). Cisco's secrets. *Fortune,* pp. 177-184.

Goleman, D. (1995). *Emotional intelligence.* New York: Bantam.

Goleman, D. (1997). *Emotional intelligence: Why it can matter more than IQ.* New York: Bantam.

Goleman, D. (1998a, November/December). What makes a leader? *Harvard Business Review,* pp. 93–102.

Goleman, D. (1998b). *Working with emotional intelligence.* New York: Bantam.

Grove, A. (1999). *Only the paranoid survive: How to exploit the crisis points that challenge every company.* New York: Bantam.

Gundling, E. (1999). How to communicate globally. *Training & Development, 53*(6), 28–31.

Hass, G.H. (1984). Perspective taking and self-awareness: Drawing an E on your forehead. *Journal of Personality and Social Psychology, 46,* 788–798.

Head, T.C., & Sorensen, P.F. (1993). Cultural values and organizational development: A seven country study. *Leadership & Organization Development, 14*(2), 3–7.

Hofstede, G. (1980). *Culture's consequences: International differences in work-related values.* Thousand Oaks, CA: Sage.

Hultman, K.E. (1986, December). Behavior modeling for results. *Training & Development, 40*(12), 60–64.

Ickes, W. (1993). Empathic accuracy. *Journal of Personality, 61,* 587–610.

Ickes, W. (1997). *Empathic accuracy.* New York: Gilford.

Jaeger, A. (1989). Organization methods in practice: A five country examination. In *Advances in international comparative management, vol. 4* (pp. 113–130). Greenwich, CT: JAI.

Janas, M. (2001). Getting a clear view. *Journal of Staff Development, 22*(2), 32.

Johnson, D.W. (1975a). Affective perspective taking and cooperative predisposition. *Developmental Psychology, 44,* 869–870.

Johnson, D.W. (1975b). Cooperativeness and social perspective taking. *Journal of Personality and Social Psychology, 31,* 241–244.

Johnson, K.R. (1991). Estimating national culture and OD values. In P. Sorensen, T.C. Head, N. Mathys, & K.R. Johnson (Eds.), *International organization development.* Champaign, IL: Stipes.

Katz, D., & Kahn, R.L. (1978). *The social psychology of organizations* (2nd ed.). New York: John Wiley & Sons.

Kearns, D., & Nadler, D. (1992). *Prophets in the dark: How Xerox reinvented itself and beat back the Japanese.* New York: Harper Business.

Kenny, D.A. (1994). *Interpersonal perception: A social relations analysis.* New York: Guilford.

Kets de Vries, M.F.R. (1990). The organizational fool: Balancing a leader's hubris. *Human Relations, 43*(8), 751–770.

Kim, W.C., & Mauborgne, R.A. (1993, Spring). Making global strategies work. *Sloan Management Review,* pp. 11–27.

Kolb, D.A. (1976). *Learning style inventory technical manual.* Boston, MA: McBer.

Kotter, J.P. (1999). *What leaders really do.* Boston, MA: Harvard Business School.

Kouzes, J.M., & Posner, B.Z. (1997). *The leadership challenge.* San Francisco, CA: Jossey-Bass.

Krebs Hirsh, S. (1985). *Using the Myers-Briggs Type Indicator in organizations.* Palo Alto, CA: Consulting Psychologists Press.

Laurent, A. (1983). The cultural diversity of Western conceptions of management. *International Studies of Management and Organization, 13,* 75–96.

Lewin, K. (1948). *Resolving social conflicts: Field theory in social science.* Washington, DC: APA Books.

Lorey, W. (1979). Improve communications with the Johari Window. *Training, 16*(6), 60.

Lubatkin, M., & Floyd, S. (1997). In search of a European model of strategic management. *European Journal of Management, 15*(6), 612–624.

Luft, J., & Ingham, H. (1955). *The Johari Window: A graphic model of interpersonal awareness.* Proceedings of Western Training Laboratory in Group Development, Los Angeles, UCLA Extension Office.

Martin, J. (2001, March). Wanted: CEO confidante. *Chief Executive,* p. 28.

Matsui, F. (2000). *Understanding acquaintance and empathy as predictors and performance as an outcome of self-assessment accuracy in professional firms: Test of a model.* Unpublished doctoral dissertation. New York: Columbia University.

Mayer, S.J. (1987, Spring). Behavior modeling training in organizations: Concerns and conclusions. *Journal of Management, 13*(1), 21–41.

McCarthy, J.C., & Monk, A. (1994). Channels, conversation, cooperation and relevance: All you wanted to know about communication but were afraid to ask. *Collaborative Computing, 1,* 35–60.

Messier, J.M. (2001). *J6M.com.* Paris: Livre de poche.

Morgan, G. (1986). *Images of organisation.* London: Sage.

Morrow, A. (Ed.). (1972). *The failure of success.* New York: AMACOM

Nadler, D.A. (1997a). *Champions of change: How CEOs and their companies are mastering the skills of radical change.* San Francisco, CA: Jossey-Bass.

Nadler, D.A. (1997b). *Feedback and organization development: Using data-based methods.* Reading, MA: Addison-Wesley.

Nadler, D.A., Gerstein, M.S., Shaw, R.B., & Associates. (1992). *Organizational architecture.* San Francisco, CA: Jossey-Bass.

Nadler, D.A., & Spencer, J.L. (1997). *Executive teams.* San Francisco, CA: Jossey-Bass.

Nadler, D.A., & Tushman, M.L. (1977). A diagnostic model for organization behavior. In J.R. Hackman, E.E. Lawler, & L.W. Porter (Eds.), *Perspectives on behavior in organizations.* New York: McGraw-Hill.

Nadler, D.A., & Tushman, M.L. (1997). *Competing by design.* New York: Oxford University Press.

Navis, E.S. (1990). Listen to what they don't tell you. *Journal of Management Consulting, 6*(2), 13–15.

Papows, J. (1998). *Enterprise.com: Market leadership in the information age.* Cambridge, MA: Perseus.

Perkins, D.N.T. (1988). *Ghosts in the executive suite: Every business is a family business.* Branford, CT: Suncretics Group.

Pescuric, A. (1996, July). The new look of behavior modeling. *Training & Development, 50*(7), 24.

Ratiu, I. (1985). Multicultural tides in European consulting. *Journal of Management Consulting, 2*(4), 30–37.

Rivero, J.C., & Spencer, J.L. (1997) Designing CEO and COO roles. In D.A. Nadler & J.L. Spencer, *Executive teams.* San Francisco, CA: Jossey-Bass.

Sabath, R.E. (1990). The serious use of humor. *Journal of Management Consulting, 6*(3), 40–42

Schein, E. (1987). *Process consultation, vol. II.* Reading, MA: Addison-Wesley.

Schwenk, C.R. (1984). Cognitive simplification processes in strategic decision-making. *Strategic Management Journal, 5,* 111–128.

Shepard, H.A. (1975, December). Rules of thumb for change agents. *Organization Development Practitioner,* pp. 1–5.

Shimokawa, K. (1994). *The Japanese automobile industry: A business history.* Atlantic Highlands, NJ: Athlone.

Slywotzky, A. (1996). *Value migration: How to think several moves ahead of the competition.* Cambridge, MA: Harvard Business School.

Smither, S. (1977). A reconsideration of the developmental study of empathy. *Human Development, 20,* 253–276.

Spears, L.C. (Ed.). (1995). *Reflections on leadership: How Robert K. Greenleaf's theory of servant-leadership influenced today's top management thinkers*. New York: John Wiley & Sons.

Stinson, L., & Ickes, W. (1992). Empathic accuracy in the interactions of male friends versus male strangers. *Journal of Personality and Social Psychology, 62,* 787–797.

Tichy, N.M. (1990). *The transformational leader*. New York: John Wiley & Sons.

Tichy, N.M., & Stratford, S. (1999). *Control your destiny or someone else will*. New York: Harper Business.

Tjosvold, D., & Johnson, D.W. (1977). Effects of controversy on cognitive perspective taking. *Journal of Educational Psychology, 69*(6), 679–685.

Trompenaars, F. (1998). *Riding the waves of culture* (2nd ed.). London: Nicholas Brealey.

Vetlesen, A.J. (1994). *Perception, empathy, and judgment: An inquiry into the preconditions of moral performance*. University Park, PA: Pennsylvania State University Press.

Watkins, J., & Mohr, B. (2001). *Appreciative inquiry: Change at the speed of imagination*. San Francisco, CA: Jossey-Bass/Pfeiffer.

Welch, J., with Byrn, J.A., & Barnicle, M. (2001). *Jack: Straight from the gut*. New York: Warner Books..

Werner, J. M. (1994, Summer). Augmenting behavior-modeling training: Testing the effects of pre- and post-training interventions. *Human Resource Development Quarterly, 5*(2), 169–184.

When to pull the trigger: Individual performance on the executive team. (1998). New York: Mercer Delta Insights.

Wispé, L. (1986). The distinction between sympathy and empathy: To call forth a concept, a word is needed. *Journal of Personality and Social Psychology, 50,* 314–321.

About the Authors

Ron **A. Carucci** is a partner with Mercer Delta Organizational Consulting, a management consulting firm that provides services related to the management of strategic level organization change to major corporations and other institutions. He works in the areas of executive leadership, building executive teams, strategy formulation and implementation, and large-scale organization and culture change.

Prior to working at Mercer Delta, Mr. Carucci managed his own consulting practice specializing in aligning and implementing organization change initiatives in the financial services, consumer products, and information technology industries. He worked on several large-scale merger integrations and subsequent culture change initiatives in the pharmaceutical industry. He has also held executive positions in several Fortune 100 organizations, leading internal human resource consulting and change management functions.

Most recently, he has been working with CEOs of large enterprises as well as start-up organizations on the challenges of managing rapid growth in consolidating industries. He has helped organizations to re-architect themselves for global scale-up and to build appropriate talent pipeline strategies to ensure the effective selection, development, retention, and reward of key leaders of major growth businesses. Mr. Carucci is a faculty member at Fordham University Graduate School, serving as an associate professor of organizational behavior in the Human Resource Education program.

He is co-author of the book, *The Value Creating Consultant: How to Build and Sustain Lasting Client Relationships* (AMACOM, 1999).

He holds a B.A. in communication and human relations and an M.A. in human resource management and organizational behavior.

William A. Pasmore is a partner with Mercer Delta Organizational Consulting. He advises CEOs in the areas of organization design, senior team effectiveness, acquisition integration, strategy implementation, and managing large-scale change.

Dr. Pasmore has published more than fifteen books and fifty articles on the topics of managing change and designing effective organizations. His work is recognized internationally. He has been a professor of organizational behavior at Case Western Reserve University and has taught executive courses at universities in the United States, France, and Belgium. He has been a consultant to organizations for more than twenty-five years.

He holds a B.S. in aeronautical engineering/industrial management and a Ph.D. in administrative sciences, both from Purdue University.

About the Editors

William J. Rothwell, Ph.D.,** is president of Rothwell and Associates, a private consulting firm, as well as professor of human resource development on the University Park Campus of The Pennsylvania State University. Before arriving at Penn State in 1993, he was an assistant vice president and management development director for a major insurance company and a training director in a state government agency. He has worked full-time in human resource management and employee training and development from 1979 to the present. He thus combines real-world experience with academic and consulting experience. As a consultant, Dr. Rothwell's client list includes over thirty-five companies from the *Fortune 500.*

Dr. Rothwell received his Ph.D. with a specialization in employee training from the University of Illinois at Urbana-Champaign, his M.B.A. with a specialization in human resource management from Sangamon State University (now called the University of Illinois at Springfield), his M.A. from the University of Illinois at Urbana-Champaign, and his B.A. from Illinois State University. He holds lifetime accreditation as a Senior Professional in Human Resources (SPHR), has been accredited as a Registered Organization Development Consultant (RODC), and holds the industry designation as Fellow of the Life Management Institute (FLMI).

Dr. Rothwell's latest publications include *The Manager and Change Leader* (ASTD, 2001); *The Role of Intervention Selector, Designer and Developer, and Implementor* (ASTD, 2000); *ASTD Models for Human Performance* (2nd ed.) (ASTD, 2000); *The Analyst* (ASTD, 2000); *The Evaluator* (ASTD, 2000); *The ASTD Reference Guide to Workplace Learning and Performance* (3rd ed.), with H. Sredl (HRD Press, 2000); *The Complete Guide to Training Delivery: A Competency-Based Approach,* with S. King and M. King (Amacom, 2000); *Human Performance Improvement: Building Practitioner Competence,* with C. Hohne and S. King (Butterworth-Heinemann, 2000); *Effective Succession Planning: Ensuring Leadership Continuity and Building Talent from Within* (2nd ed.) (Amacom, 2000); and *The Competency Toolkit,* with D. Dubois (HRD Press, 2000).

Roland Sullivan, RODC, has worked as an organization development (OD) pioneer with nearly eight hundred systems in eleven countries and virtually every major industry. Richard Beckhard has recognized him as one of the world's first one hundred change agents.

Mr. Sullivan specializes in the science and art of systematic and systemic change, executive team building, and facilitating Whole System Transformation Conferences—large interactive meetings with 300 to 1,500 people. Over 25,000 people have participated in his conferences worldwide; one co-facilitated with Kristine Quade held for the Amalgamated Bank of South Africa was named runner-up for the title of outstanding change project of the world by the OD Institute.

With William Rothwell and Gary McLean, he is revising one of the field's seminal books, *Practicing OD: A Consultant's Guide* (Jossey-Bass/Pfeiffer, 1995). The first edition is now translated into Chinese.

He did his graduate work in organization development at Pepperdine University and Loyola University.

Mr. Sullivan's current interests include the following: Whole system transformation, balancing economic and human realities; discovering and collaborating with cutting-edge change focused authors who are documenting the perpetual renewal of the OD profession; and applied phenomenology: developing higher states of consciousness and self-awareness in the consulting of interdependent organizations.

Mr. Sullivan's current professional learning is available at www.rolandsullivan.com.

Kristine Quade is an independent consultant who combines her background as an attorney with a master's degree in organization development from Pepperdine University, and years of experience as both an internal and external OD consultant.

Ms. Quade draws from experiences in guiding teams from divergent areas within corporations and across many levels of executives and employees. She has facilitated leadership alignment, culture change, support system alignment, quality process improvements, organizational redesign, and the creation of clear strategic intent that results in significant bottom-line results. A believer in whole systems change, she has developed the expertise to facilitate groups ranging in size from eight to two thousand in the same room for a three-day change process.

Recognized as the 1996 Minnesota Organization Development Practitioner of the Year, Ms. Quade teaches in the master's programs at Pepperdine University and the University of Minnesota at Mankato and the master's and doctoral programs at the University of St. Thomas in Minneapolis. She is a frequent presenter at the Organization Development National Conference and also at the International OD Congress and the International Association of Facilitators.

Index

Printed in the United States
30311LVS00007B/111-150

9 780787 960803

NIGHTHAWK

HATE MAKES HATE

DAVID F. WALKER
WRITER

RAMON VILLALOBOS (#1-2, #4 & #6)
& MARTIN MORAZZO (#3 & #5)
ARTISTS

TAMRA BONVILLAIN
COLOR ARTIST

VC's JOE CARAMAGNA (#1-5)
& TRAVIS LANHAM (#6)
LETTERERS

DENYS COWAN, BILL SIENKIEWICZ & CHRIS SOTOMAYOR
COVER ART

CHRISTINA HARRINGTON
ASSISTANT EDITOR

KATIE KUBERT
EDITOR

MARK PANICCIA
SENIOR EDITOR

COLLECTION EDITOR: **JENNIFER GRÜNWALD**
ASSOCIATE MANAGING EDITOR: **KATERI WOODY**
ASSOCIATE EDITOR: **SARAH BRUNSTAD**
EDITOR, SPECIAL PROJECTS: **MARK D. BEAZLEY**
VP PRODUCTION & SPECIAL PROJECTS: **JEFF YOUNGQUIST**
SVP PRINT, SALES & MARKETING: **DAVID GABRIEL**
BOOK DESIGNER: **JAY BOWEN**

EDITOR IN CHIEF: **AXEL ALONSO**
CHIEF CREATIVE OFFICER: **JOE QUESADA**
PUBLISHER: **DAN BUCKLEY**
EXECUTIVE PRODUCER: **ALAN FINE**

NIGHTHAWK: HATE MAKES HATE. Contains material originally published in magazine form as NIGHTHAWK #1-6. First printing 2016. ISBN# 978-1-302-90162-2. Published by MARVEL WORLDWIDE, INC., a subsidiary of MARVEL ENTERTAINMENT, LLC. OFFICE OF PUBLICATION: 135 West 50th Street, New York, NY 10020. Copyright © 2016 MARVEL No similarity between any of the names, characters, persons, and/or institutions in this magazine with those of any living or dead person or institution is intended, and any such similarity which may exist is purely coincidental. **Printed in the U.S.A.** ALAN FINE, President, Marvel Entertainment; DAN BUCKLEY, President, TV, Publishing & Brand Management; JOE QUESADA, Chief Creative Officer; TOM BREVOORT, SVP of Publishing; DAVID BOGART, SVP of Business Affairs & Operations, Publishing & Partnership; C.B. CEBULSKI, VP of Brand Management & Development, Asia; DAVID GABRIEL, SVP of Sales & Marketing, Publishing; JEFF YOUNGQUIST, VP of Production & Special Projects; DAN CARR, Executive Director of Publishing Technology; ALEX MORALES, Director of Publishing Operations; SUSAN CRESPI, Production Manager; STAN LEE, Chairman Emeritus. For information regarding advertising in Marvel Comics or on Marvel.com, please contact Vit DeBellis, Integrated Sales Manager, at vdebellis@marvel.com. For Marvel subscription inquiries, please call 888-511-5480. **Manufactured between 11/4/2016 and 12/12/2016 by QUAD/GRAPHICS WASECA, WASECA, MN, USA.**

10 9 8 7 6 5 4 3 2 1

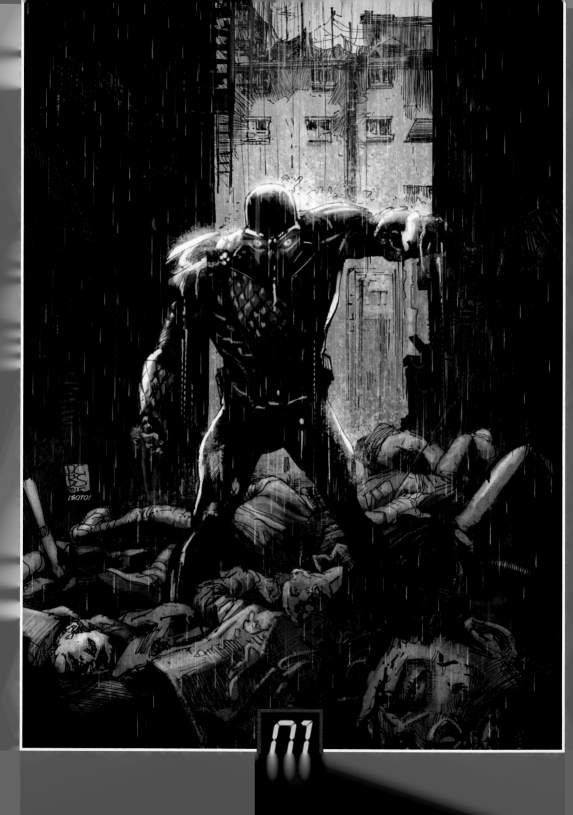

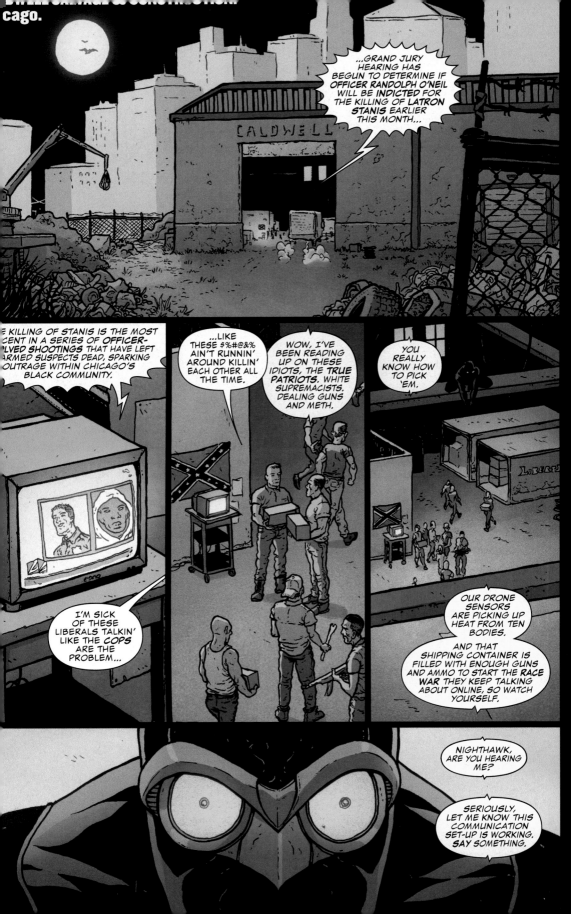

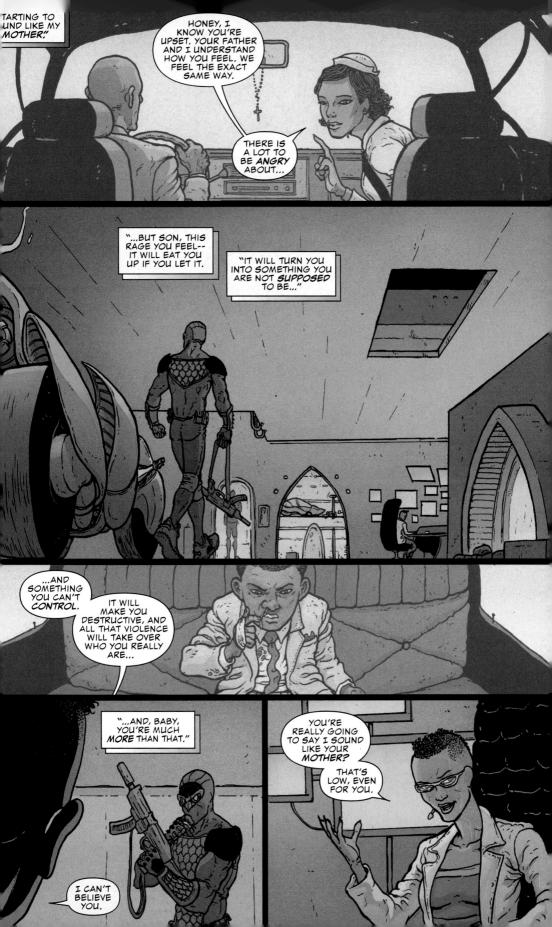

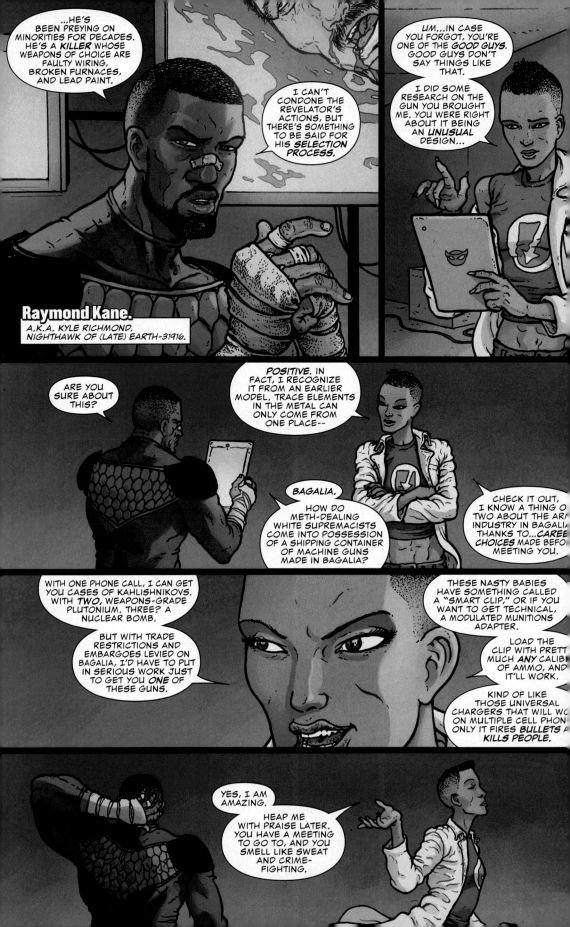

THE OFFICE OF DAN HANRAHAN, REAL ESTATE DEVELOPER. Downtown Chicago.

...TENSIONS CONTINUE TO RISE, AS THE GRAND JURY HEARING OF OFFICER RANDOLPH O'NEIL ENTERS DAY TWO.

I'VE BEEN WATCHING THE NEWS ALL MORNING...

CIVIC LEADERS ARE DEMANDING THAT O'NEIL BE CHARGED WITH FIRST-DEGREE MURDER IN THE SHOOTING DEATH OF LATRON STANIS--

AND SO FAR, THERE'S NOTHING ABOUT LAST NIGHT'S INCIDENT AT CALDWELL SALVAGE.

WHICH TELLS ME YOU'VE GOT SOME SEMBLANCE OF CONTROL OVER THE SITUATION, DETECTIVE DIXON.

IT WASN'T EASY, MR. HANRAHAN...

...SOMETHING LIKE THIS MAKES FOR GOOD HEADLINES.

HEADLINES AREN'T MY CONCERN. INCRIMINATING EVIDENCE IS.

THE LAST THING I NEED IS SOMEONE CONNECTING THE DOTS I'VE WORKED TO KEEP DISCONNECTED.

HOW COME I GET STUCK INSIDE WATCHING MONITORS WHILE *YOU* GET TO RUN AROUND CHASING CLUES, LOOKING FOR A SERIAL KILLER AND BREAKING BONES?

I CAN BREAK BONES WITH THE *BEST* OF 'EM.

HOW'S THE NETWORK SIGNAL?

I LIKE HOW YOU IGNORED EVERYTHING I JUST SAID.

THAT WAS *SARCASM*, BY THE WAY. I POINT THAT OUT, BECAUSE SOMETIMES I WORRY ABOUT YOUR ABILITY TO GRASP THE *NUANCE* OF HUMAN COMMUNICATION.

THAT *WASN'T* SARCASM. THAT WAS *SINCERE* CONCERN.

THE NETWORK SIGNAL IS LOUD AND CLEAR, AND ALL THE BIRDS ARE SINGING.

DISPATCHING ALL OF 'EM NOW TO THEIR PROGRAMMED PATROL COORDINATES.

KEEP ME UPDATED.

WILL DO. TRY NOT TO HAVE *TOO MUCH FUN* WITHOUT ME, AS I SIT HERE, MAKING SURE YOUR CRIMEFIGHTING CRUSADE OPERATES SMOOTHLY...

TILDA, THANK YOU.

SEE, THAT'S ALL I WANTED. YOU'RE WELCOME.

...ESPECIALLY NOW THAT THE FEDS ARE TAKING OVER THE CASE.

I ALREADY TOLD YOU, NINA, I GOT AN IMPORTANT LEAD--SOMETHING THAT MIGHT TIE INTO ALL OF THIS *REVEALER* STUFF.

IT'S *REVELATOR.* AND IT WOULD BE NICE IF YOU *SHARED* THIS LEAD, OR THIS HUNCH, OR THIS WHATEVER IT IS THAT YOU THINK IS SO IMPORTANT, BURRELL.

THE REVELATOR HAS TAKEN THINGS TO AN ALL-NEW LEVEL. *FIVE MORE DEAD COPS.* ANOTHER DOZEN INJURED. HALF A CITY BLOCK BLOWN TO HELL.

AND ON TOP OF THAT, THIS ISN'T OUR CASE ANYMORE. NOW THAT THE REVELATOR HAS BLOWN UP HALF A CITY BLOCK, HE'S BEEN UPGRADED FROM SERIAL KILLER TO *TERRORIST.*

WE GET TO SIT BACK AND WATCH WHILE FBI, ATF, AND S.H.I.E.L.D. DO *OUR* JOB.

I NEED YOU TO GET IT TOGETHER.

I KNOW.

TRUST ME ON THIS, NINA...

...I KNOW HOW MUCH IS AT STAKE HERE.

...RESULTING IN THE DEATHS OF SEVERAL HEAVILY ARMED MEMBERS OF THE RIGHT-WING MILITIA GROUP CALLING THEMSELVES THE *TRUE PATRIOTS.*

WHAT THE TRUE PATRIOTS WERE DOING IN CHICAGO'S PREDOMINANTLY AFRICAN AMERICAN NEIGHBORHOOD OF ENGLEWOOD REMAINS UNKNOWN...

...AS DOES THEIR CONNECTION TO UNPRECEDENTED VIOLENCE THAT GRIPS NUMEROUS PARTS OF THE CITY.

SONOVA--

THOSE REDNECKS YOU GOT TO GO RAISE SOME HELL...WELL...I'M PRETTY SURE NIGHTHAWK *SENT* THEM STRAIGHT THERE.

%&$#.

YOU CAN SAY THAT AGAIN.

DO YOU THINK HE'S MADE THE CONNECTION BETWEEN THEM AND ME? I CAN'T HAVE ANY OF THOSE METH-DEALING NAZIS LEADING BACK TO ME.

HOW SHOULD I KNOW? BESIDES...

...I'VE GOT MORE IMPORTANT THINGS TO WORRY ABOUT. I THINK SOMEONE IS ONTO ME.

ANOTHER COP--A SELF-RIGHTEOUS BALL-BUSTER NAMED BURRELL. I SPOTTED HIM *FOLLOWING* ME.

...TAKE CARE OF THIS OTHER COP.

TAKE CARE OF HIM *HOW?*

IF YOU THINK MAKING HIM PANCAKES WILL WORK, TRY THAT.

YOU DON'T *PAY* ME ENOUGH TO KILL A COP.

NO, BUT I PAY YOU ENOUGH TO MAKE SURE NEITHER OF US GOES TO PRISON. I DON'T WANT TO GO TO PRISON. DO YOU?

FINE, I'M LISTENING.

CORONER

CHICAGO POLICE DEPARTMENT, HOMICIDE DIVISION.

...YOU DON'T, UNDERSTAND, TILDA. I *HAD* HIM...

AND HE GOT AWAY, I UNDERSTAND. WE'VE ALL HAD THE ONE THAT GOT AWAY.

DID I EVER TELL YOU ABOUT THE TIME I ALMOST GOT *CAPTAIN AMERICA?*

THAT'S ONE OF MY FAVORITE STORIES.

YOU CAN TELL IT TO ME AGAIN--*AFTER* WE'VE DEALT WITH THE SITUATION AT HAND...

...WE'VE GOT OUR WORK CUT OUT FOR US.

WHAT'S THE *PLAN?*

I TOOK PICTURES OF EVERYTHING IN THE REVELATOR'S HIDEOUT. WE CAN USE THIS TO FIGURE OUT HIS NEXT MOVE.

I'LL UPLOAD EVERYTHING NOW--START SORTING THROUGH IT.

I GOT A LOOK AT HIS FACE. I'M GOING TO SEE IF I CAN PUT TOGETHER A COMPOSITE TO IDENTIFY HIM.

TO BE CLEAR...WE'RE DOING *GOOD GUY* WORK, RIGHT?

YES.

INTERESTING. NOT NEARLY AS STRESSFUL AS WAITING FOR THE AVENGERS TO THWART YOUR PLANS.

YOU DON'T SAY.

NOT NEARLY AS *EXCITING,* EITHER.

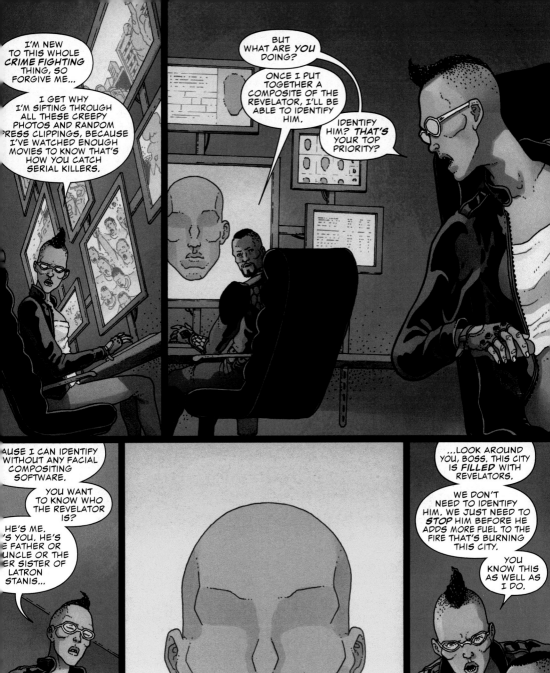

I'M NEW TO THIS WHOLE *CRIME FIGHTING* THING, SO FORGIVE ME...

I GET WHY I'M SIFTING THROUGH ALL THESE CREEPY PHOTOS AND RANDOM PRESS CLIPPINGS, BECAUSE I'VE WATCHED ENOUGH MOVIES TO KNOW THAT'S HOW YOU CATCH SERIAL KILLERS.

BUT WHAT ARE *YOU* DOING?

ONCE I PUT TOGETHER A COMPOSITE OF THE REVELATOR, I'LL BE ABLE TO IDENTIFY HIM.

IDENTIFY HIM? *THAT'S* YOUR TOP PRIORITY?

...CAUSE I CAN IDENTIFY HIM WITHOUT ANY FACIAL COMPOSITING SOFTWARE.

YOU WANT TO KNOW WHO THE REVELATOR IS?

HE'S ME. HE'S YOU. HE'S THE FATHER OR UNCLE OR THE OLDER SISTER OF LATRON STANIS...

...OR MAYBE THE BROTHER OF SOMEONE THE COPS DISAPPEARED AT *HOMAN SQUARE*.

HE'S THE GUY WHOSE WIFE WAS FOUND DEAD IN A JAIL CELL AFTER SHE WAS ARRESTED FOR A TRAFFIC VIOLATION.

...AND YOU WANT TO *IDENTIFY* HIM?

HE'S ANYONE WHO'S FELT THE STING OF THE WHIP, OR THE BOOT ON THEIR THROAT...

...LOOK AROUND YOU, BOSS, THIS CITY IS *FILLED* WITH REVELATORS.

WE DON'T NEED TO IDENTIFY HIM, WE JUST NEED TO *STOP* HIM BEFORE HE ADDS MORE FUEL TO THE FIRE THAT'S BURNING THIS CITY.

YOU KNOW THIS AS WELL AS I DO.

COWAN
SIENKIEWICZ
SOTO

06

YOU SICK FREAK!

DO YOU KNOW WHO I AM?!

OF COURSE I KNOW.

THWIK THWIK THWIK

OWWWWW!

WHY [...] YOU T[...] I PICK[...] YOU[...]

THE R[...] QUEST[...] IS TH[...]

...DO YOU KNOW WHO I AM?

YOU KILLED THAT JUDGE, AND THE COP, AND ALL THOSE OTHERS...BUT I'M NOT LIKE THEM. PLEASE--

NO, THAT'S WHO I AM NOW.

BUT BEFORE...

I WAS THAT VOICE CRYING OUT FOR HELP, SCREAMING FOR HIS LIFE, BEGGING FOR JUSTICE-- FOR MERCY.

AND NO ONE LISTENED. NO ONE HEARD ME...

...JUST LIKE NO ONE CAN HEAR YOU.

THWIK THWIK THWIK

AIIIEEEE!

"HE'S GOING TO LIVE..."

THWIK
THWIK
THWIK

I CAN SEE THAT.

PRIMARY GYROSCOPIC STABILIZER IS DAMAGED-- LOSING POWER FAST.

DITCH THE RIDE, BEFORE IT DITCHES YOU.

AND BE CAREFUL-- IT'S A LONG DROP.

THWAPT

I KNOW.

...HE'S A GENTRIFIER.

YOU REALLY WANT TO SAVE SOMEONE LIKE HIM?

#1 HIP-HOP VARIANT BY **BILL SIENKIEWICZ**

#1 VARIANT BY **SKOTTIE YOUNG**

#2 VARIANT BY **DECLAN SHALVEY & JORDIE BELLAIRE**